christian
life coaching
CALLING AND DESTINY DISCOVERY TOOLS FOR CHRISTIAN LIFE COACHING
HANDBOOK
TONY STOLTZFUS

Published by Coach22
3101 Barberry Lane, Virginia Beach, VA 23453.
www.Coach22.com

ISBN-10: 0-9794163-9-6
ISBN-13: 978-0-9794163-9-2

Cover Design by Mark Neubauer
Back Cover Portrait by Jasmine Stoltzfus

Some of the anecdotal illustrations in this book are true to life, and are included with the permission of the persons involved. All other illustrations are composites where names and details have been changed. Any resemblance to persons living or dead is coincidental.

To order copies of this book and other coaching materials, visit www.Coach22.com or phone 757-427-1645.

Table of Contents

Self-Study Schedule and Exercise List

This schedule is also included in *A Leader's Life Purpose Workbook* as a self study guide. The Core Exercises in the left column plus chapter reading are the suggested starting point for each area. The "Optional Exercises" column on the right provides additional options if the client gets stuck, plus ways to go deeper and increase self-understanding in that area. Or start with the Baseline Assessments (1.1) to determine which areas need work, and then go through core and optional exercises as needed.

Note that while the four baseline exercises are associated with the corresponding sections in this *Handbook*, all four are found in chapter one of the *Workbook*. The *Handbook* also includes additional exercises (such as 6.4) designed for the coach.

Lesson	Core Exercises	Optional Exercises	Pg.
Chapter 1-2	2.1: Jesus' Teaching on Eternal Rewards		36
	2.2: Structuring for Eternal Rewards		37
		3.1 Coaching Bible Studies (on-line)	
Chapter 3-4	4.1: Allegiance Checkup		70
		4.2: Needs, Losses and Bonds	71
		4.3: Clarifying Your Allegiance	72
Chapter 5		*1.1a: Design Baseline Assessment*	77
	5.1: Strengths Inventory		89
	5.2: Strengths Examples (Worksheet)		90
		5.3: Strengths Behind Successes	91
		5.4: Strengths Validation	92
	5.5: Identifying Weaknesses		93
		5.6: Strengths, Type and Energy	94
Chapter 6	DiSC™ Personality Assessment (on-line)		
	6.1: Peer Validation		104
		6.2: Type Night	105
		6.3: My Ideal Team	106
		6.4: Coaching Ex: Typing a Team	107
		1.1b Passion Baseline Assessment	114
Chapter 7	7.1: Passion Bull's eye		121
	7.2: Energy Activities		122
Chapter 8	8.1: Big Dreams/Fun Dreams Inventory		136
	8.2: Life Wheel Categories		138
		8.3: Dream Lifestyle	139
		8.4: Envisioning Your Dream	140
	8.5: Dream Themes		141
Chapter 9	9.1: Identifying Obstacles		158
		9.2: Regrets	159

Introduction

"When you start out on the journey you think it is all about taking in experiences to fulfill yourself. But it's not. The greatest experience is changing someone else's experience of life. And once you come to that realization, it becomes your foundation, the ace in your pocket, who you are... When you see the world through the lens of others, that's when you find yourself."

Andre Agassi, tennis champion, in *Sports Illustrated*

A committed young missionary wanted help figuring out his life purpose. Over the weeks we'd been together he'd poured out his heart to me. We talked about his dreams for starting a ministry center as well as the disappointment of losing his support, his relational challenges with other missionaries, the passion he had for reaching youth and the times he'd chafed under controlling leaders. "So," I finally offered, "Let me sum up our conversation. I'm hearing that you really feel called to ministry; you just don't want to get hurt anymore."

"Yeah, that's about it," he replied.

After a moment's reflection, I asked, "Think about Jesus' life for a second. He was betrayed by one of His inner circle, abandoned by His best friends and tortured to death in the process of living out His life purpose. How will you become like Him if you never get hurt? And how will you ever really know Him if your life is nothing like His?" That rocked him back a bit.

For the few remaining moments we had together, we reflected on the story of Jesus' life, pondering how the fellowship of His sufferings is inextricably linked with the power of His resurrection. That conversation transformed this young man's expectations about his vocation.

That coaching encounter started me thinking down the road that led to this book. Most of the life purpose tools I'd used were geared toward helping people look inside, discover their design, passion and abilities, and then pursue them. But it didn't seem like that kind of process would have ever led Jesus to His agonizing choice in the Garden, where He groaned, "If there is any way to get out of this awful death, that's what I want. But this isn't about me: I'm going to do what *you* want no matter what." The life purpose tools I was familiar with simply couldn't stretch far enough to discover a destiny like Jesus'. And if the way we do destiny discovery doesn't work with Jesus' life, then something is missing.

I believe that missing piece is "calling": *an external commission **from** God **for** the sake of others.* Since it is an external commission, it's found by revelation, not by looking inside. Since it is for others, it can lead us to do things that don't result in fulfillment or happiness for ourselves, at least in this life. And it rests on the foundation of Allegiance: you answer a call from God because you have pledged your life to His service. The concepts of Calling and Allegiance give us a way to integrate biblical ideas like suffering and sacrifice into life purpose—ideas that are missing from most popular approaches.

Calling is an External Commission from God for the sake of others.

There are several reasons why coaches seem to shy away from talking about calling. One is that calling has gotten a bad rap: for many Christians, the image they have of calling is God ordering them out of the blue to do something they don't want. "*Commit yourself to celibacy, take up your Cross, and become a missionary to Outer Berzerkistan.*" In high school, I remember wondering if God wanted me to kneel down in the halls of the high school and pray (about the most embarrassing thing I could think of) or marry a girl I wasn't attracted to. When you don't know God deeply, you still think He uses you like a tool instead of loving you as a son or daughter. In that mind set, calling is a life sentence of indentured servitude instead of a partnership with your first love that brings you into who you were created to be. No wonder we don't want to look for it!

The second reason calling isn't a big part of our vocabulary is that most destiny discovery tools coaches use originated in the secular arena. In American culture, the idea that living your destiny involves obeying an external commission isn't part of the plan! Instead, the focus is on finding what our own internal compass says we can do with fulfillment and excellence. When these life purpose tools migrated into the ministry world, the underlying view of destiny discovery as an individual, internal process came with them. When we fail to root out this unbiblical approach, Christian life purpose becomes about the King's kids walking in all the blessings of health, wealth and fulfillment God wants to give them in this life. Paul would be appalled.

That's why it is vital that we rediscover calling as part of life purpose. As Christians, our purpose is woven into the fabric of the purposes of God for all of creation. Purpose is implanted in us as well as revealed to us—we were made for what God calls us to be. So a balanced, biblical approach to destiny discovery looks in four directions:

- **Outward** at what God reveals *to* us (the external *Call*)

- **Inward** at what our *Design* reveals within us
- **Backward** at how he has purposefully *Prepared* us through our life experiences
- **Forward** at the dreams and *Passions* that draw us to our future destiny

Objectives

My overarching purpose in writing this suite of books is to help us as a Christian coaching movement develop a balanced, biblically-grounded approach to discovering a Christian's life purpose. As such, I'm going to focus on what's unique about being a *Christian* life coach who is coaching other believers toward their destiny. Certainly, almost everything here can be used in coaching non-Christians also. But instead of starting with secular coaching principles and adapting them for ministry, we'll begin with what Scripture says about a Christian's life purpose and develop a coaching structure that fits around that.

My second objective is to put in one place a complete suite of destiny discovery tools designed for Christian life coaching. These tools can be used with clients, to run life purpose discovery classes or to train others in life coaching skills. I've also included the specialized set of tools I use to coach mature leaders toward entering their convergent destiny roles. Organizational leaders have unique questions to answer when it comes to purpose—like influence style, team or sphere of influence—and since I work mostly with leaders, these are tools I utilize frequently.

These two objectives define the two sections of this *Handbook*. Section one covers the underlying philosophy of Christian life coaching, what on-purpose living looks like, and how suffering, success and significance fit in with purpose. Section two offers a comprehensive suite of life purpose discovery tools, structured around a five-part life purpose model that integrates *Calling* and *Allegiance* with *Passion, Preparation* and *Design* to create a fully rounded picture of a Christian's life purpose.

I've presented the most-used discovery tools in an exercise format. Much of the time I coach these informally, but it is handy to have a tool or worksheet you can just hand to clients so they can keep working between appointments. The exercises reside at the end of each chapter, numbered *chapter.x*. So exercise 5.1 is located at the end of chapter five.

Objectives

1. Present a biblical framework for Christian life coaching
2. Offer a set of life purpose discovery tools
3. Add a set of discovery tools for organizational leaders

Companion Volumes

These same exercises also appear in *A Leader's Life Purpose Workbook*, a companion volume designed to be used by life coaching clients or in destiny discovery classes and workshops. It includes all the tools in the *Handbook*, a chapter on Christian life purpose and descriptions of each of the main discovery areas. When clients purchase the *Workbook*, they'll be able to do any of the exercises while you'll have an additional layer of examples, tips and techniques for how to coach those tools. The two books have an identical exercise numbering system, so you can easily go back and forth between them without worrying about page numbers.

The third book in this suite, *The Calling Journey,* describes how leaders grow in their calling over a lifetime. Based on in-depth studies of biblical and contemporary leaders, *The Calling Journey* presents a five-stage model of calling development. The book shows how to create personal calling time lines, how to recognize each stage and how to coach people through the stages. Each stage has unique tasks and challenges, so the coaching techniques and objectives you'll use vary dramatically from stage to stage.

You can never cover everything, so I have chosen to focus on the first half of the life purpose coaching process (destiny discovery) and leave out how you help clients walk out what they have discovered. I am assuming that you already know the basic coaching tools and conversational disciplines used in this process, such as listening, asking questions, generating options and goal-setting. If not, these tools are covered in depth in my prior book, *Leadership Coaching: The Disciplines, Skills and Heart of a Christian Coach.*

Offering Life Purpose Classes

Would you like to offer a life purpose discovery class or workshop based on *A Leader's Life Purpose Workbook* in your church or organization? A complete Presenter's Package with everything you need to do so is available through Coach22.com. You'll walk participants through discovering and clarifying their unique life purpose in a fun, interactive process using the exercises in the *Workbook.*

Or, if you want to train your leaders to coach using the destiny discovery skills in this *Handbook*, several turn-key coach training courses (part of a complete system of royalty-free coach training modules) are available on the Open Source Training page at www.Coach22.com.

Discover Your Destiny

God has uniquely *Designed* every individual to display facets of His character in their being, and to enact His love in their doing. He has gifted us with unique *Passions* to motivate us in His service, provided a lifetime of *Preparation* experiences, and *Called* us to a life mission that provides real joy as a by-product of giving our lives to His larger purposes.

God has great purpose for all His people. Let's help them discover and live their unique destinies so they can better serve the Kingdom and love the King in the process. That's *our* purpose as Christian coaches.

Chapter 1: What is Life Coaching?

"Our chief want is someone who will inspire us to be what we know we could be."

Ralph Waldo Emerson

The first appointment of the day was a complimentary session with a Christian businessman. After chatting for a few minutes and making a personal connection, we started exploring what Roger wanted to accomplish by working with a life coach.

"Thanks for giving me some background—that's really helpful. Let's talk a bit about the coaching agenda. What would you like to work on with a coach?"

"Well, here's the thing. I'm 49 years old. Since I was a kid my goal has been to own several businesses and be an entrepreneur. Over the last 30 years my wife and I have developed five franchise stores, a supply business and a development company. It keeps me busy, but lately I've been getting restless—trying to find excuses to get out of the office, watching the clock, that kind of thing. I've never done that before. I've started to wonder: 'Is this all there is?' I mean, I've accomplished most of what I've set out to do in life, but it feels like there ought to be something more."

"Do you have any idea what that 'more' might be?"

"I get these wild ideas. Like starting orphanages in Ethiopia, or selling everything off and starting over, or writing a book and joining the speaking circuit—or even becoming a

missionary. My wife just rolls her eyes at that one."

"How come?"

"Not sure. Sometimes she'll say, 'after all these years you want to start over!?!' Change has always been harder for her than for me."

"OK. So what captures you in all those different ideas—the orphanage, the mission or the book?"

"I guess… now that I've met my business goals, they don't seem so important any more. I want to do something with my time and talent that makes me feel like my life counts instead of just going through the motions."

"That makes sense. Tell me—what do you feel called to in life? What has God put you on earth for?"

*"Up until this year I would have said, 'To own a business and be a witness in my community, give people jobs, do unto others, give money to the church'—that kind of thing. But now, I don't know. I have this little voice in me—maybe it's God—that's urging me to do more. To take on something wild, radical, impossible. I've been a good solid citizen, but if I died tomorrow, I'm not sure the world would be that much different." Roger suddenly swiveled toward me and looked me in the eye. "I want to change **that**."*

"So what do you need from a coach to live a life that makes a difference?"

*"I need to figure out what I'm supposed to do. And do to that, I need to figure out what I **can** do. It might surprise you, but I'm not sure what I'm good at. I've been so focused on the business-owner thing that I've never tried anything else. And since what I believed I was called to do doesn't seem to be it—well, a lot of what I thought I knew just went out the window. Is that something you can help me sort out?"*

"Definitely. In fact, I have a whole set of tools for that very thing. Just to name a few, we could nail down your strengths, do an assessment of your personality type, find out what type of roles suit you best, create a personal value set to capture your core, or look at the messages God has planted in your life for others. Does that sound like the kind of help you are looking for?"

"Yes—exactly! I have done some work on strengths, and we have a corporate value set, but I've never figured out my personal values or personality type or the messages thing. I feel like God is saying to do something different, but I just haven't known how to get a handle on it."

"So that's what you want to work toward?"

"Yes—let's do it!"

The search for meaning and purpose in life is as old as humanity itself. In some of His first words to mankind, God gave Adam and Eve a life mission: "Be fruitful and multiply, and fill the earth, and subdue it…" (Gen. 1:22). Our sense of purpose about life is rooted in the way we were made. We all have an instinctive yearning to do and be something, to make our lives count, to stand before our Creator and hear the words, "Well done" pronounced over our lives. Even before the fall, we were made to work, to steward and to shape our world.

When our basic life needs are met, at some point we all (like Roger) turn toward the bigger questions: Who am I? Where can I find joy and fulfillment in life? What is my purpose? What does God want me to do with what He's given me?

Young people embarking on careers and relationships frequently ask those questions. At mid-life, many like Roger find that the old answers no longer work, so they begin anew the search for answers. This reflex to search for meaning in life reveals an important truth: purpose is something that must be *discovered.* And when we find it, we have to come to the place of conviction that *this* is the thing to give our life to. The stakes are high, and that means the choices aren't easy. That's why people who are asking the big questions often look to a life coach for the tools, perspective and process to help them find that clarity of purpose.

Life Coaching is...
Life coaching helps people *discover* their purpose and align their lives with it.

Once discovered, purpose is something we *align* our lives with. Knowing what we are supposed to do with our lives isn't worth a whole lot unless we actually do it. That's hard work. Realignment means changing habits, taking risks and sacrificing the good to get the best. That's why people look for a friend and supporter on the journey. A life coach can help us take our dreams, convert them into goals and strategies, and cheers us on until we reach them.

Life coaches also help us align the little things in our lives to maximize our contribution. When our environment is draining our energy or spending habits undermine our calling, a life coach can help us realign the way we live with our core values, so our lifestyle supports our purpose instead of undercutting it.

Coaching Defined

To start clarifying what life coaching is we first need to define coaching in general. Coaching is the art of helping people grow without telling them what to do. Coaches are change experts who help us take responsibility and act to maximize our potential.

Coaches aren't about telling and directing. Instead, the genius of a coach is simply to believe in people. That's why coaches ask instead of tell—they believe that we can do what we dream, and their faith inspires us to reach higher than we can on our own. Coaches employ superb listening and asking skills to draw the answers out of us, so our buy-in is maximized and we assume full responsibility for our lives.

Life Coaching is a special coaching niche that focuses on discovering our values and purpose and aligning our life with them. Life coaching is about destiny discovery and alignment. A life coach works toward two things: creating a better future and a better life today. Roger's desire was for someone to help him discover a sense of purpose in life and move toward it. He needed a life coach.

Coaches in general are change experts. Life coaches are also self-discovery experts. A life coach's toolkit contains a plethora of assessments and exercises for figuring out who an individual is. Life coaches use their understanding of personality types, developmental stages, strengths, values discovery and more to help clients like Roger identify and fill any gaps in their self-knowledge. Knowing ourselves more fully allows us to move forward with confidence in what we were born to do.

So to be a life coach, you have to study people—how different personalities think, how skills develop, what drives us or makes us passionate, and what makes for a great

life. You must also study the ways of God—how He calls people, uses life experience to develop character, and the different ways He speaks to us. The more you know about people and how God interacts with them, the more valuable a self-discovery expert you will be.

Not long ago I had a coaching session where the client's goal was to become more assertive in the workplace. One of the action steps this manager chose was to ask God for opportunities to practice standing strong in stressful situations.

> **Definitions of Coaching**
>
> *"Coaches are change experts who help leaders take responsibility and act to maximize their own potential."*
>
> *"Coaching is practicing the disciplines of believing in people in order to empower them to change."* Tony Stoltzfus
>
> *"Coaching is unlocking a person's potential to maximize their growth."* John Whitmore
>
> *"Coaching is the art and practice of guiding a person or group from where they are toward the greater competence and fulfillment that they desire."* Gary Collins
>
> *"Mentoring is imparting to you what God has given me; coaching is drawing out of you what God has put in you."* Dale Stoll

I had already figured out that she was an "S" on the DiSC™ personality profile. For that personality type, harmonious relationships and going along to get along is the modus operandi. "S" types tend to be conflict avoiders who become passive when things get tense. So we talked about her type, how others experience conflict differently than she does, and how to recalibrate her internal "conflict meter" to account for the fact that conflict is more uncomfortable for her than most others. We explored some situations at work where strong personalities would play brinkmanship games with conflict to try to get her to blink first and give in.

Her answer to prayer that week was getting rear-ended by another driver—a high "D," strong personality at that! Although the accident was clearly his fault, he tried to bully and bluster her into paying for the damage. Although she felt quite uncomfortable, her new view of herself in conflict enabled her to stand firm.

I enjoyed celebrating that victory together with her! Having a coach that encouraged her to understand her own experience of conflict and that of others made the difference for her.

Types of Coaching

Comparing life coaching with other types of coaching can also be helpful. *Performance coaching* is used in the workplace to help people get more done, be more efficient or improve productivity. Where life coaching says, "What is your purpose, and how can we align with it?" performance coaching tends to look at the assignment you already have (whatever it is) and say, "How can we do that better?" Performance coaching seeks to make you more effective at what you do; whereas life coaching examines whether those are the things you are made to be doing in the first place.

Executive coaching often focuses on organizational issues, like where your business is going, or your growth, succession or marketing strategy. Business coaches start with the business (and then often get into the leader's personal life from there). Life coaches start with the personal life and expand into other areas of life where that purpose needs to be translated into action.

The Impact of Life Coaching

So what difference does it make to work with a life coach? Here are some practical benefits life coaching clients receive:

- **Understand your life purpose**
  Produces a sense of meaning and significance, provides a foundation for making great decisions, and offers direction for how to live a purposeful life.
- **Align with core values**
  Increases life satisfaction, reduces stress and frustration as you do what's important instead of what's expected or what life thrusts upon you.
- **Eliminate tolerations**
  Frees energy to pursue important goals in life, while increasing your joy on the journey.
- **Identify and overcome internal obstacles**
  Gets you unstuck and moving forward, and provides the freedom you've always wanted from nagging fears and self-doubt.
- **Create life purpose action plans**
  Creates real movement toward your life purpose, with the sense that your life is going somewhere.
- **Clarity on God's call**
  Greater obedience to your Lord, intimacy in your relationship with Him, and impact for the Kingdom of God.
- **God's guiding hand in your life revealed**
  Produces wonder, love and worship for your Creator.

Sometimes the best answer to "Why should I have a life coach?" is your personal story. What has coaching done for you? Here's an example of a coach sharing how he was impacted by being coached through a major life transition:

> *"In the end, I pulled the trigger on coaching because I have never faced such a critical decision-making time in life, and I didn't want to miss any opportunity to hear from God and tune into what He was doing in me and through me... Coaching costs time, money and effort, but the results have been priceless. Not only do I have someone in my corner who believes in who I am, but one who is empowered to challenge me to think outside the box in order to walk in step with God in the destiny*

for which He has created me.

Coaching is a bargain for all I get from you. Any one nugget—a powerful question or a challenge to clarify my focus and take action to fulfill my goals—is worth way more than all the costs. I leave our sessions feeling like I should be paying more, but that's the last and greatest thing about you. You charge a fair fee, but you pay so much more forward as a truly generous servant who seeds into the Kingdom through me. What price could ever be set on that?"

Defining Terms

There are a lot of similar terms floating around in life coaching, and we aren't always clear on what each one means. Here they are defined in a way that works when coaching Christians and non-Christians alike:

- **Design:** My innate traits or my nature: strengths, personality type, talents, and natural abilities.
- **Experience:** The learned skills, credentials and other assets I acquire in life that I leverage for my life purpose. The nurture counterpoint to Design's nature.
- **Passion:** The internal energy and motivation I have to pursue something I care deeply about.
- **Calling**: An external commission I accept in order to serve a greater good. (For Christians, calling is "an external commission from God for others.")
- **Destiny:** A synonym for life purpose.
- **Life Mission:** The ultimate task that channels your life message. The doing part of call.

Why Hire a Life Coach?

Here are some ways to respond if a potential client is wondering if life coaching will be worthwhile:

- *"What would it be worth to you to know your calling and have a plan to reach it?"*
- *"What outcome would make working together a great success in your eyes?"*
- *"What would it be like if five years from now you weren't any further along in knowing what you want to do in life than you are now?"*
- *"Dream for a minute—how would your life be different if you reached this goal?"*
- *"What kind of success have you had pursuing this goal without outside help?"*
- *"Here's what some of my client's have gotten out of being coached…"*
- Share about the impact of coaching in your own life.

This leads us to an overall definition of life purpose:

> ***Life Purpose*** *is the energy of* ***Passion****, channeled through* ***Experience*** *and* ***Design*** *in the service of a greater* ***Calling****.*

These four elements (Passion, Experience, Design, and Calling) form the basic framework for the overall life purpose discovery model covered in section II. It may be helpful to define a few more related terms:

- **Fulfillment:** A lasting sense of joy, significance and satisfaction from living within my life purpose.
- **Dream:** Something I'd love to do someday but haven't committed to.
- **Vision**: A picture of an ideal future I am mobilizing resources toward. (A kingdom vision is a God-given picture of an ideal future that captures my allegiance. It is not mine: I serve it and it serves others.)

Adding calling to our life purpose definition moves purpose from getting what I want to finding fulfillment through serving others. People who serve and love something bigger than themselves have a greater sense of purpose in life, and that's true of Christians and non-Christians alike. For instance, some people find a sense of purpose in serving an external commission from their country, culture or tribe that isn't a calling from God. Since God designed life to work best when we are blessing others (and worst when we become self-absorbed takers), the simple fact that these folks are serving moves them into closer alignment with the way they are designed by God to live. That doesn't mean they are Christians—it just means that they are likely to find more real joy in life than those who spend their lives in the pursuit of self.

Uniquely Christian Life Coaching

To create a uniquely Christian definition of life purpose, we need to make one change:

> A Christian's Life Purpose is the energy of Passion, channeled through Experience and Design *in Allegiance to a God-given* Calling.

For Christians, calling comes from God. Allegiance means that I have signed ownership of my life over to the lordship of Christ, and my fulfillment lies in a Kingdom that is not of this world. The idea of letting go of what we can gain in life and living to serve God is one of the distinctives of Christian coaching.

Another distinction is that Christian life purpose is founded on the idea of the eternal. We believe that there is a real, ultimate reward and ultimate judgment in the next life. This leads us to coach what I call "living toward heaven"—aligning our lives to maximize the eternal payoff instead of the temporal one.

> *A Christian's Life Purpose is the energy of* Passion, *channeled through* Experience *and* Design *in* Allegiance *to a God-given* Calling.

One of the most serious errors among those who coach Christians on life purpose is concentrating exclusively on creating temporal blessings and improving this life. Making the focus aligning with our passions and design to create a significant, satisfying life in the here and now falls far short of God's plan for us. Jesus did **not** spend His life seeking a better existence on earth—*He was seeking to do on earth what created a better future for many others in heaven.* And in that way, every Christian's life purpose resembles Jesus'—it is about doing what creates a better future for many in heaven, not about making a better life for me on earth.

There are many situations where we will coach people in practical ways toward a great life. But for our coaching to be distinctively Christian, that ideal of the "great life" must be grounded in the reality and primacy of the eternal as the ultimate objective.

A final distinctive for Christian life coaching is the idea of purpose as being. Our primary calling in life is not to do a certain task, but to incarnate the person of Christ through that task. In other words, we are first called to *be* something, then to *do* something that communicates that being to others.

Defining calling in being terms is a huge win for the client. While the stars may never align for us to *do* all we dream, nothing and no one can ever stop us from *becoming* the unique embodiment of Christ we are called to be.

Distinctives

So let's summarize five crucial distinctives of uniquely Christian life purpose coaching:

- **Allegiance**
  We foster alignment with the Kingdom through allegiance to Jesus, viewing believers as stewards who have chosen to order their lives for His purposes.
- **Calling**
  We help people discover God's call on their life and learn how to steward their life for the Kingdom instead of spending it on self.
- **Giving**
  We understand that it is more blessed to give than to receive, and that the giving, serving life is not only the best life, but the greatest life.
- **Eternal Rewards**
  We seek to help coachees to find practical ways to live for lasting, eternal rewards instead of only creating temporary benefits in this life.
- **Being-Centered**
  We help people find the heart of their call. Their primary purpose is not to *do* something for the world, but to *be* Christ to the world through what they do.

Chapter 2: The On-Purpose Life

"When I'm focused, there is not one single thing, person, anything that can stand in the way of my doing something. There is not. If I want something bad enough, I feel I'm gonna get there."

Michael Phelps, Olympic Swimmer, in *Sports Illustrated*

Michael Phelps, the winner of eight gold medals at the 2008 Olympics, was in a pool before his first birthday. His older sisters swam competitively (one came heartbreakingly close to making the Olympic team), and as he followed in their footsteps he developed both a love for swimming and a fierce competitive desire. At only 11, Coach Bob Bowman recognized him as a rare talent. Besides his swimmer's physique (large hands and feet, abnormally large wingspan, double-jointed ankles, and an eventual height of 6'4"), the youngster had a capacity for hard work and preternatural calm under pressure that gave him tremendous potential.

Phelps identified something he was made to do early in life, and gave himself completely to it (at one point practicing five hours a day every day for five years straight). By pursuing his Olympic dream he raked in millions in endorsements, attained worldwide recognition and became the most decorated swimmer in Olympic history.

The other day I saw an interview of him talking about his new book, No Limits. *The host acknowledged Phelps' incredible practice regimen and discipline, then asked a question that cuts to the heart of the idea of destiny: was what he had done possible for others? Or was it something he was uniquely gifted for; that not everyone, even if they gave a maximum effort, could do?*

Phelps responded in keeping with his book's title. "I think it's possible... If anyone puts their mind to it and they want it that bad, anything is possible."

In this generation, the concept of life purpose has become a powerful theme in the American psyche. We've adopted the belief that every person has a life purpose, that our purpose is within our reach, and that finding and following this purpose leads to a satisfying, significant life. It's an extension of the original American dream—that this is a land of opportunity where anyone who works hard can "make it," regardless of their social or economic background. Life purpose expands this ideal of the Good Life beyond financial and social success to offer significance and personal fulfillment as well. It is life and liberty with an extra helping of the pursuit of happiness.

There is much for believers to celebrate in this new theme. The idea that we are one-of-a-kind and have a unique contribution to make endows value to the individual human life. Believing that destiny is for everyone and not just a chosen few great leaders is a vital bulwark against controlling or authoritarian leadership. That one's destiny can be found and followed inspires us to leave a legacy for others instead of devoting all our energy to getting what we want.

The idea of destiny also leads inexorably towards a Creator—otherwise, where does this destiny we have built into us come from? Destiny means we are made for something; that life is unfolding according to a plan. There can only be a plan if there is a Planner. Having the freedom to dream up your own destiny sounds fun, but it ultimately leaves you empty. If there is no God and no afterlife, your destiny dies with you. A destiny that doesn't make us part of some lasting, larger purpose loses much of its significance.

Society's new focus on life purpose signals a change in our definition of success as well. In the past money, power and reputation were the measuring sticks. But now success is also about doing what gives you satisfaction, joy and significance. Many still live as if wealth and fame are the path to the good life, but more and more people are leaving behind these old idols. Some search for significance in causes like saving the planet or working for good government, while others focus on relationships instead of accomplishments, and still others abandon both social and career ambition to live simpler lives. This is a great opportunity for Christianity—pursuing significance in life seems much more likely to lead to God than running after money or power.

Testing Our Picture of Purpose

However, the new life purpose ideal also makes assertions believers need to test. For instance, Michael Phelps repeats the oft-stated view that we can do anything we dream of. There are no limits to human accomplishment. But I beg to differ with Phelps—I'm five-foot-nine, with short arms and small hands, and no amount of extraordinary effort could *ever* have made me into an Olympic-caliber swimmer.

How do we separate truth from fiction in the area of life purpose? One simple test is whether our ideals actually work in real life. The "no limits" idea doesn't. (It's funny how these old ideas come back around—the "no limits" concept is found in one of the oldest stories in the Bible: the Tower of Babel.) God never says that we can be and do anything. But when we fully embrace His design for us and grow into exactly what He created us to be, we'll really be living.

Another life purpose tenet we should examine closely is the view that living this healthy, wealthy Good Life is something God promises we'll have. In ministry circles this ideal is often expressed as "the believer's birthright"—that Christians who learn to operate in the realm of faith can appropriate all the promises of God who has designed us to live a wonderful, wealthy, trouble-free Good Life.

But is this really true? Another good check of a purpose principle is to see if it works in the real lives recorded in the Bible. Does the believer's birthright theology match with what we know actually took place in the life of, say, Paul? If the writer of half the New Testament was afflicted with things like shipwreck, beatings, hunger, and sleepless nights, then maybe we need to rethink that idea.

A third concept that bears reexamination is that completing your life mission (the doing part of call) is always within reach. Laying hold of what God has and living obediently is all you have to do to gain this inheritance. We might test this by asking, "Does this idea hold true in every culture and at every time in history, or is it unique to 21st century North America?" Think about the believers under persecution in first century Rome, or those killed in the ethnic cleansing in Rwanda, or the pastors in China who have been imprisoned for their faith. In what sense are or aren't they fulfilling their life mission?

This idea brings to mind a committed, lifetime missionary friend who died suddenly of a heart attack in his forties. He left two kids and a wife behind—I doubt if on the day of his death he was celebrating the completion of his life's work.

We live in a dangerous world, and no one knows how many days each of us has left. Wars, persecution, disease, financial turmoil and a myriad of other circumstances can interfere with the best laid plans. You may live a life of great obedience to God, and never even have the chance to live your dreams. What you can do is fully live *toward* what you were made for each moment, and maximize each day. Will you live to complete your life mission? That's in the hands of God. There are no guarantees.

Even the idea that you should be in a role that fits your life purpose right now needs another look. As coaches, we tend to approach life purpose as something that is independent of age, character or maturity. But after coaching hundreds of leaders, I've seen few move into a convergent destiny role before their late forties. Just because you know your calling doesn't mean you can make it happen (just look at the lives of Joseph or David!) So the age and maturity of your clients makes a big difference in how you coach them. For clients under 50, it is most helpful to coach toward the destiny development *process* instead of trying to move them into their destiny *role.*

Your Purpose within God's Purposes

Since being made for something means there is a Maker, the starting point for understanding life purpose is grasping God's overall purposes for humanity. Paul states that his purpose is "to show the immeasurable riches of his grace in kindness toward us in Christ Jesus" (Eph. 2:7; RSV). God's fundamental intention for the universe is simply to love us. We are at the center of His purpose because we are at the center of His love.

Love is not about you: it is about the object of your love. God is not focused on what He can get out of His relationship with you. He isn't trying to win your loyalty, He doesn't need your worship, and He's not angling to get something back. He is already full. He does not need. But rather than making him aloof and disinterested, His already-full-ness is what allows Him to love us with unconditional, immeasurable, overwhelming abandon. It is precisely because God does not need anything from us that He can love us unconditionally.

When Scripture says love "does not seek its own" (I Cor. 13:5) it is describing God Himself. God is love, and God is about love, not about getting what He wants. God is not about Himself.

And that is why Jesus is so clear about not living for self: to focus on your own needs and live life for self is completely un-Godlike. How could you understand a God who gives Himself totally for us when you are the complete opposite? The only way to have any kind of a mutual relationship with an all-giving God is to learn to give and love freely like he does. Otherwise, you have nothing in common. Living for personal gratification so twists the human heart that it becomes literally impossible to comprehend the heart of God.

Living for personal gratification so twists the human heart that it becomes literally impossible to comprehend the heart of God.

What you focus on and make priority in life is what you love. The first love of our society is things. But you cannot love God and things (mammon)—because giving your heart to one will make loving the other incomprehensible.

Here's an analogy. At several points in her childhood, our daughter desperately wanted to go to public school (we were home schooling) to be with her friends. Friends were the most important thing in her life. She prodded us, played off mom and dad, sulked occasionally, but no go. We hung tough and stuck to our plan. She got lonely, got left out of her neighborhood friends' circle, and life was tough.

At the time, it was hard for her to perceive us anything but capricious and controlling. She was so locked into what she thought would make her happy that she couldn't see the bigger picture. Because she was focused on herself, the instinct was to see us as selfish as well.

Of course, there is a back story to all this. A few years before, she'd come home from school one day and said, "If you don't have any friends, what's the use of living?" She'd actually been miserable in the catty, third-grade-girls world at school. That comment was a wake-up call for us as parents, and after a lot of prayer and discussion we decided to make some major sacrifices in our own lives for her sake. So the thing that seemed to her to be taking away her happiness really was designed to give it to her. And what looked to her like a selfish decision on our part was actually a huge sacrifice from my wife on her behalf. (By the way, she's very happy now that we did what we did.)

We tend to see others through the lens of our own character. If we're honest, we just assume others are. If we lie and manipulate to get our way, we're constantly on the lookout to keep from being taken. The only way to really get to know God is to become more like Him, because if we don't, His goodness is obscured by our fallenness.

Purpose as Becoming

That's why at the most fundamental level, our life purpose is to become like Christ, so that we can enter fully into our love relationship with Him. We are first called to *be*, to incarnate Christ, and then to *do* out of that being. Our life mission (what we do) is simply the channel for the Christ in our being to come out.

And since God is love, letting Him come out in what we do means loving others. That's our life mission. Only a life focused on loving and serving others meets the standard of looking like Jesus. The amazing thing is that as we focus on giving instead of taking, the temporal blessings of joy, fulfillment and significance come to us even though we are not pursuing them.

> *At the most fundamental level, our life purpose is to become like Christ.*

Seeing the heart of life purpose as an incarnation you become, instead of a mission you do, can make an enormous difference in the trajectory of your life. For example, my father's dream was to teach at one of our denomination's colleges. He actually had a position there, but couldn't get tenure because he only had a master's degree. So he left to get his PhD, with the hope that he'd have a long-term job when he came back.

But once he graduated, he had a tough time finding any position at all, let alone one within the denomination. The good jobs in his field often had hundreds of applicants, and he ended up taking something that wasn't really what he wanted.

Years later, he again got the chance to land his dream job, this time at his alma mater. He was one of the final two candidates for the position—and then the college decided they needed more gender balance in the department and only offered a one-year contract. He was hurt and frustrated. When the position came up again in a year, despite our encouragement he didn't even apply. My dad felt his life dream was thwarted because he couldn't do what he wanted in the place where he envisioned himself. If he had thought of his purpose in *being* terms, he would have realized that he *had* fulfilled it.

The role my dad sought was only a container for his purpose. The true desire of his heart was to communicate his wonder and love of learning about nature to others. The teaching role he thought was his call was merely a vehicle. But because he mistook the vehicle for the heart of his call, he missed a part of the joy of his destiny that was right there for the taking.

The Blessing

That painful story unlocks one of the mysteries of life purpose: focusing on the outward roles, mission and rewards of purpose is a dead end. Only staying focused on what we are supposed to *be* yields the blessings of living on-purpose.

It also shows us how temporal blessings fit in with life purpose: as *by-products* of putting first things first. When you focus on money, success or fame as the objective, you may gain those things—but the fulfillment you seek *through* those things will slip through your fingers. As Jesus put it, "Whoever seeks to keep his life will lose it, and whoever loses his life will preserve it" (Luke 17:33). And God becomes hazy and distant, because your capacity to know Him is diminished—you've become about yourself. If you focus on the mission or task as the main thing, even if it is a worthy cause, your doing eventually becomes hollow and devoid of impact, because you've missed the whole reason for doing the task in the first place: to channel the Christ embodied in your being.

On the other hand, if you put first things first, you may never have money, success or fame—or even health or freedom—but the joy and fulfillment we all try to find through those things will be yours, in spades. Paul, worshipping in chains in prison, was at a place of deeper peace and purpose than the powerful jailer who held the keys to his cell.

To put it in practical terms, the core life purpose of a God-centered individual is never about being financially independent, or being able to do what I enjoy in my retirement years, or traveling the world, or being successful in my career.[1] Those objectives are small and self-centered—they look inward, toward my wants and needs, while love looks outward, to the wants and needs of others. Obviously, we will never be free of basic needs, or the need to attend to them. But even in things like food, clothing and shelter, Jesus urges us to fully trust Him, and "seek first his kingdom and his righteousness, and all these things will be added to you" (Mt. 6:30-33).

Three Levels of Purpose

It can help us understand this to go back to Scripture and break down God's purposes for humanity into some categories. In Ephesians 1 Paul discusses our destiny: we were chosen "before the foundation of the world, that we would be holy and blameless before him" and that we are predestined for adoption as sons. The passage concludes with God's overriding purpose: "to unite all things in Christ; things in heaven and things on earth" (Eph. 1:10; RSV). Paul saw our ultimate aim as *being together* with God in Christ, in the Kingdom of Heaven. The Holy Spirit is given to us now as the pledge of this inheritance: He lives in us now, so that we can be sure we will be together with Jesus in heaven. All God's other objectives for humanity flow from this purpose.

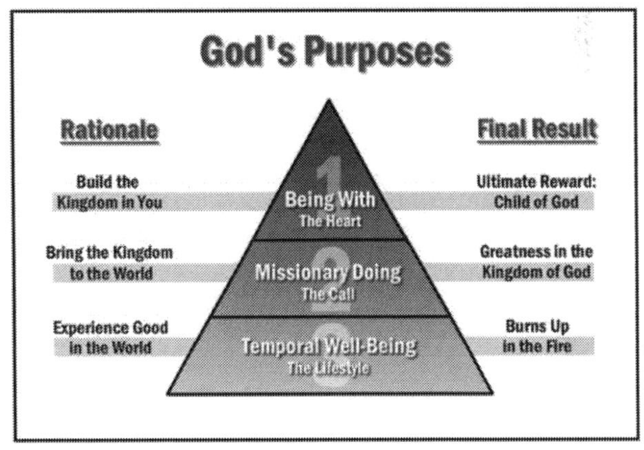

Paul also talks about purpose in terms of a life mission he had to do: "To me,

1 And if you got into coaching because you feel born for it; and you want to work at home, invest in high-achievers who are going somewhere, be your own boss, and do something that is fulfilling instead of just punching a clock, you've also chosen something less than the best.

the very least of all the saints, this grace was given: to preach to the Gentiles the unfathomable riches of Christ" (Eph. 3:8). This is to be done "in accordance with the eternal purpose which he carried out through Christ Jesus our Lord" (3:11). This connection is crucial. The eternal purpose Paul speaks of is the primary, *being together* purpose from Ephesians 1 mentioned above. The *doing* purpose of our lives—our life mission—needs to come under and be done in alignment with the *being together*

Fulfillment

What makes an experience (or a life!) truly fulfilling and satisfying? Here are nine ingredients of fulfillment, stated in terms of eternal rewards:

- **Approval**
  We will hear "Well done!" pronounced over our lives by our Creator, the one who has the last word. We will know our lives have been worthwhile.
- **Recognition**
  Those you've helped in life will welcome you to the eternal habitations with full honor and thanks. God's reward system includes recognition from peers.
- **Accomplishment**
  The great task is truly over, the victory is complete. You've fought the fight and finished the race, and know beyond doubt that it's all been worth it.
- **Significance**
  We are an important part of a much larger story—God's purposes in history—that is of ultimate value.
- **Celebration**
  We're going to have the biggest, longest party ever, and celebrate both what we've already done and the arrival of a future that is better than we could ever have dreamed.
- **Sacrifice Rewarded**
  We have invested everything in this Kingdom, and we'll see the fruit of our sufferings and be satisfied. Suffering for something makes the reward sweeter.
- **Legacy**
  What we have built with our lives will last, and be known and celebrated forever. Time will never dim it—we'll have an eternal share in God's glory.
- **Intimacy**
  Our marriage into the family of God is consummated. We will enjoy being fully known, fully intimate, fully loved and able to love in the greatest relationship ever.
- **Contentment**
  We will be full and complete, lacking in nothing. There will be no more mourning, crying or pain, but only perfect contentment.

purpose that is God's ultimate aim.

Here's what that signifies in practical terms. God's first priority is *you*: to be in a loving relationship with you and to bring you into oneness with Him.[2] Being comes first, and doing second. So *God will sometimes put your life mission on hold to have your heart.* If your life (or your client's life) is out of balance because you are doing too much ministry, God will eventually call you back to a balanced life, even if the ministry suffers. Even when you are doing well, living on-purpose and making a difference, God will prune your life back and lead you into outwardly-unproductive wilderness seasons to gain a greater grip on your heart.

One of my clients is a great example of this principle. Steve owned a 40-million-dollar company and was fully absorbed in running it, to the glory of God as best he understood it at the time. In the process of capturing his heart, God pruned Steve's life way back to prepare for greater growth. His company went bankrupt, he endured a string of legal battles, and finally his home burned down.

These challenges reformed him into a man of prayer, a friend of solitude, and someone with a heart for the nations. He now travels overseas regularly to train leaders and bring businesspeople to Christ. He's expressed to me several times how grateful he is for God's intervention in his life, because he has come to a level of intimacy with God that he never knew before.

Steve learned that when God runs your life, growth in being together takes precedence over growth in productive doing. Relationship with God grows as becoming more like Christ enables us to understand Him and enter into Him more fully.

There is a third level of purpose as well. God is concerned not just with our *being together* with Him (the Heavenly Kingdom) and our *missionary doing* to bring His Kingdom to others, but with our *temporal well-being*, too. "If God so clothes the grass of the field... will he not much more clothe you? ... your heavenly Father knows that you need all these things" (Mt. 6:30-32).

God wants you to see good in this life. He wants you to succeed, to experience love and intimacy in relationships. As the Westminster Catechism teaches, man's chief end is to glorify God and enjoy Him forever.[3]

However, this isn't God's only (or even primary) purpose for you. Your union with Him and growth in being conformed to Christ is much more important. So *God will put your happiness on the back burner to gain more of your heart.* That's right: success in your career, financial security, satisfying relationships, good health, you name it—all these things God may supply or withhold to gain your heart, because they are of

---

2 Becoming like Christ is what brings more of our being into union with Him—it is what increases His Kingdom in our hearts. See Rom. 8:28-29, where being called according to His purpose means being conformed to His image.

3 When we are parsing out these human categories, we need to keep sight of the fact that God loves us completely, with a totality and unity of purpose we cannot understand in this life. I think that for God these categories are meaningless: he fully wills our good in every area, all the time. But when God's love is put in terms we can understand through Jesus' teaching, he consistently prioritizes God's eternal purpose for our growth in being and union with Him over our temporal well-being.

incomparably less value than what He has for you in heaven.

Take success, for example. A common Preparation experience of biblical leaders is demotion. God regularly moves leaders (like David, Joseph and Moses) out of a large, successful role and into a much smaller sphere of influence at certain stages of life in order to shape them inwardly. Moses' case is particularly poignant—from being a big shot in the palace in Egypt, he went to being a shepherd (remember that herdsman were despised by the Egyptians) and a husband. His sphere of influence shrank down to his sheep and his wife, whose name aptly means "little sparrow." That's one of those little details that hints at God's sense of humor—Moses the great deliverer reduced to serving one little sparrow.

Living the On-Purpose Life
Living on purpose means aligning with the three levels of God's purposes for us:

- **First, Deep Intimacy** with God and others; becoming a person who is full, with a overflowing capacity to love
- **Second, a Significant Mission** in life; total commitment to be a unique part of God's eternal purposes and leave a legacy behind
- **Third, Joy in the Journey**. The ability to find contentment in your lot in life based on being rooted in the deeper reality of Christ's love.

In his subsequent ministry, Moses' defining characteristic was humility. He immediately turned to God in every difficulty and asked for help and direction. Moses became that man in the desert. God put his success on hold to gain his heart, and in the process Moses became the man who could successfully fulfill his true call. Without the humility he learned from serving a little sparrow, Moses would have been a deliverer in the style of Egyptian power politics he knew—totally unsuitable for creating a nation out of God's chosen people.

Purposes in Balance

However, life is not about focusing on being to the exclusion of all else. I coach lots of ministry leaders who view the level III purpose (temporal blessing) as unspiritual and not worthy of their time. So they don't have anything in life they do just for the sheer joy of it—no dreams of interesting vacations, no hobbies, no time to just savor God's creation without a ministry agenda. The problem is, *when you don't meet God at all three levels, you don't have a complete picture of who God is.* If the level II mission dominates your life, it reflects a skewed view that God is mostly about getting us to do something for Him. And since ministry is a function of being, that reflection is picked up and imitated by those you lead.

The gut-wrenching reframing question I like to ask pastors is, "Let's say that the people you lead follow your example instead of what you say—that they imitate the way you live. Say that everyone in your congregation worked your hours, had your stress level, spent the amount of time you do with your wife and kids, and had your exercise and eating habits. If the legacy of your ministry was that your people took on your lifestyle, what would you think of that?" When you are unable to live in one of the levels, deleting that part of God's identity from your life gets replicated onto all your followers. Ouch!

The three levels have profound applications to some of the basic questions about ministry. For instance, some churches focus their outreach almost totally around bringing people to Christ, while others put all their energies into on practical service to society (like running a day care or homeless shelter). Which is best?

The three levels provide an interesting answer. God's highest purpose is to bring us into union with him, so evangelism is vital. However, to focus exclusively on the individual's personal relationship with Jesus without serving his or her practical needs creates disciples with a warped picture of God and a limited ability to relate to his goodness. On the other hand, service without evangelism is giving people the good without adding the best.

Coaching and the Abundant Life

One of the beauties of Christianity is that the important things are pretty simple. The on-purpose Christian life simply reflects God's purposes: to love God with all your heart, soul, mind and strength (purpose level I), and to love your neighbor (level II) as yourself (level III)—exactly what Jesus said when asked what was most important in life.

Think about it: wouldn't the best possible life be one with the freedom, power and goodness to offer the gifts of love, right relationship, justice, compassion, and service to everyone you meet, without needing to get something back? Imagine living that way: full instead of needy; free from any craving for security, significance or acceptance; unencumbered by anger and inner wrestlings, with the internal resources to always offer the best to those around you. That would be an overflowing, abundant life!

In general, the leading figures in the coaching movement agree with Jesus on this picture of life lived out of an overflow as the good life. They urge creating a superabundance that lets you live free from worry and stress, enjoy security, give to others, and pursue the opportunities that life gives. We all agree that having more than enough and not being needy are key ingredients for a great life.

> **Mis-Understanding the Scriptures**
>
> - *"Seek ye first to get the financial inheritance that is your birthright as a child of God, because you deserve for all these things to be added to you."*
> - *"For the love of money is the root of all fulfillment; those who never get rich have... pierced their hearts with many pangs."*
> - *"Have this mind amongst yourselves, as Christ did, who, though he was in the form of God, did not think that that was enough, so he built a ministry empire, and sought many others to serve his vision, so that every tongue would confess what a great leader he was."*
> - *"For none who seek to live godly in Christ will be persecuted or meet any kind of struggle or suffering."*

Mainstream coaching has taught a concept called "extreme self-care" as the road to a maximized, abundant life. It starts with you. Take responsibility for your life.

Find your energy drains and plug them. Learn to say, "No." Align with your values. Get rid of unhealthy relationships that drag you down. Don't tolerate things—change them. Find what matters most to you, and pursue it. Give yourself what you'd want the person you love most to have. Take superb care of yourself.

Taken individually, these can all be appropriate steps. The problem comes when we try to align this way of thinking with the three levels of God's purposes. Mainstream life coaching has said, if you treat yourself really well, like you'd treat your best friend, you'll have a great life, and others around you will feel well-treated, too. In other words, level III comes first: *take care of yourself first to live a great life.* And this is where mainstream coaching and Christianity diverge. Jesus says exactly the opposite: *die to yourself first to have a great life.*

For Jesus, the way to a life of overflow is not to get more, but to give up everything for Him, and live to serve. "Give and it will be given to you, pressed down, shaken together and running over" (Luke 6:38; RSV). Instead of getting in order to give, you give and find that somehow it comes back to you. A surplus in the Kingdom of God is not something you acquire—it simply flows through the hands of stewards that God gives to precisely because they have shown they won't keep it all for themselves. Learning to love like Jesus is the path to a life of overflow that fills others—and in the process produces fulfillment within us as well.

There is nothing wrong with coaching people to remove energy drains, learn to say "No" or align with their values. The things that bring health and satisfaction to us in life are an integral part of God's purposes. *The problem comes when we make level III ends our primary pursuit, and* fail to hold them in proper balance with God's higher purposes.

When the primary focus is on Level III objectives like provision, happiness and success, Christian life purpose becomes simply a new version of the Prosperity Doctrine. The fundamental error of the success and prosperity stream is not in saying that God wants to bless us in the here and now (level III), but in elevating the pursuit of that blessing above being with and becoming like Christ (level I). God *does* want us to enjoy health, happiness and success in life. Any Father loves to see their child do well, and is grieved when that child is hungry, sick or hurting. But God's ultimate purpose is to unite all things in Him, and He will accept less of these good things in order to give us the best. When living your destiny becomes mainly about the here-and-now, you've lost sight of what is most important.

Here's the coaching application. Coaches help people grow and move toward great futures. For *Christian* coaches, the picture of that great future is drawn in terms of nothing less than God's eternal purposes. And to God, being united with Him in Christ forever is such a big priority that everything on earth is a distant second. Therefore, *I've got to coach as if heaven is real and it is the only future that matters.*

If I coach an unbeliever to a success so big that the world is her oyster, and in the process miss the opportunity to help her grapple with how she is losing her soul in the process, what have I accomplished? And if I coach a fellow Christian toward happiness, health, career success and financial security, but that individual is not growing in Christ, am I truly helping? Or has our coaching relationship actually become a hindrance to living out the on-purpose Christian life?

The greatest challenge Christian life coaches face is learning how to coach people toward heaven, not just a great life on earth. This is the coach's level II vocation—to have such a profound understanding of the purposes of God, and to so dynamically live those purposes out, that everyone you work with finds themselves coming into fuller alignment with God's purposes than they ever thought possible.

Values, Agendas and Influence

One thing that may stop us from aggressively coaching toward heaven is figuring out how to mate that idea with the coaching methodology. The question would go something like this: "If we coach people toward heaven, isn't that our agenda? Aren't we just putting our own values on the client?"

> *The greatest challenge we face in the Christian life coaching movement is learning how to coach people toward heaven.*

That's an excellent question, and it deserves a solid answer. The place to start is to think about what we already would and wouldn't coach. For instance, would you coach someone to pursue career failure? To break the law? Toward becoming poorer, or sicker or more frightened?

Probably not. If a prospective client said, "I want to find a codependent romantic relationship where I get used—I'm just not comfortable in mutual relationships," I don't think we'd accept that as a goal! We would want to explore why being used is attractive to this person, and move the conversation toward emotional health instead. I for one could not say, "Yes! Codependence is an excellent goal—let's go for it!"

Clients rarely come with such blatantly unhealthy goals, so we don't often bump into situations we won't coach. But the fact that we wouldn't see some things as appropriate coaching goals means *we already have a value system we coach toward.* It's one that says that accomplishment, health, freedom and fulfillment are good; and self-destructive behaviors, neediness, failure and wasted potential are undesirable.

This value system that we effortlessly coach in without even realizing it is the American cultural ethos. We coach people toward life, liberty and the pursuit of happiness with no values clash because we share those cultural values. But if the client moves outside that value system, we question the agenda and feel perfectly justified in doing so. We are so at home in our culture that we don't even notice how it pervades the coaching process.

Behind the values question is a deeper philosophical issue: is it possible to be in a position of influence and yet operate neutrally, not allowing our values to influence others?

Back in my college years, my denomination was recoiling from years of overly controlling, authoritarian denominational leadership. My college professors were at the forefront of that realignment. Because they grew up being told what to believe right down to the petty details, they were determined not to put their views on us—to the point where they wouldn't tell you *anything* about their own faith. They so valued freedom of choice in faith issues (what they didn't have when they were young) that they hid their own beliefs for fear of influencing us.

Of course, they failed. In the very act of trying not to exert influence, they modeled an anti-authoritarian value system—and modeling is a form of influence! The result was that a whole generation of students swung to the opposite pole and eschewed authority and leadership altogether. The denomination is still recovering.

It is impossible for leaders in influence roles not to exert influence. Your clients have come to you for help—therefore you are in an influence role in their lives. Your values will shape the coaching process no matter how hard you try to be neutral.

Let's be honest: we do exert influence on the people we coach. I'm not trying to say that we should cast off restraint and push our clients into whatever we want for them. We are coaches, not mentors or consultants. But to back off completely and operate as if whatever the client desires is appropriate is still functioning within a value system—just not a biblical one. There is no "off" button that magically allows you to be values-neutral with your clients.

How to Take Their Choice Away
Here are five techniques that take the client's choice away and violate the principle of personal responsibility:

1. **Give Only One Good Option**
   "Well, you could apologize."
2. **Force Disagreement with the Coach**
   "I think you should apologize."
3. **Play the God Card**
   "God would want you to apologize."
4. **Shame**
   "I'm disappointed that you didn't respond better to the challenge."
5. **Religious Guilt**
   "The Christian thing to do would be to take up your cross, humble yourself and ask for forgiveness."

Liberty Versus Responsibility

There is a way to use the coaching approach biblically. Here's the key: *the biblical coaching value is personal responsibility, not complete individual liberty*. We don't coach people to achieve complete freedom to do whatever they want, but to take responsibility for their own lives and their actions. We make room for our clients to choose, not because all choices are equally good or worthy, but because they alone bear the eternal right and responsibility to make choices for their own lives.

So I will influence my clients toward the best, while at the same time allowing them real freedom to make their own choices. I will introduce them to the idea of living toward heaven; push them to grapple with whether it is more blessed to give than to receive and challenge them to be all they were made to be in Christ. I want to give them every opportunity to find the best. But it is also my responsibility to stop short of applying pressuring and to allow them full responsibility to choose, whatever their decision is. The dance is to tell the truth, but do it in a way that leaves them in charge.

And isn't that how God deals with us? He allows us to be fully responsible for our choices, and He has set up the world so that his presence isn't so overwhelming that we are forced to choose Him. But at the same time He is actively wooing and drawing us to leave the good (and the bad!) to get the best. There is a significant difference between the cultural idea of coaching a person to their own values, whatever they are, and the biblical idea of coaching the person to take responsibility for their lives. As Christian coaches, we model our approach on how God works with us.

Coaching the Levels of Purpose

The levels of purpose aren't just a theory: they can also be utilized as a practical coaching tool. Here's an example of how to coach a client up through the levels of purpose to help them align with God's purposes.

"So what I'm hearing, Tom, is that there isn't much fun in your life."

"I guess so. I just feel like life is gray and I am going through the motions without any joy in it."

The client begins by engaging life at Level III: I want more joy in my life.

"OK. So what are some simple, practical steps you could take to enjoy life more? What do you like to do?"

"Well, I like to be able to get up in the morning, have a cup of coffee and read the paper instead of jumping right from the shower into work."

The coach helps Tom develop practical options at Level III.

"That's good. What else?"

"I used to like walking the dog. It got me outside and gave me time to think. But lately I've just been flipping on my cell phone while I walk and it isn't the same."

"What can you do about that?"

"I guess could just leave the phone at home. It'd be a lot more peaceful."

"Sounds good. What else would bring joy?"

"I'm not sure."

"OK. Here's another way to think about it. Say that it's more blessed to give than to receive—that you could actually bring joy into your life through helping others. What options would that give you?"

Once Tom starts running out of options, the coach invites him to brainstorm on Level II. Asking for multiple options sends the message that the coach isn't just looking for one good religious answer.

"Good question. One thing I think of right off the bat is doing little projects around the house for my wife. That's fun. Taking a few minutes to hang a picture or fix a door is always good for a smile and a hug—and sometimes a lot more!" Tom added mischievously. "It's most fun to do something when she's gone and then let her discover it."

"What happens then?"

"She has this little happy dance that she does. Speaking of which, she has always loved dancing. We stopped going to ballroom classes years ago, but maybe we could put on some music and dance around the living room. Since we got rid of the sectional there is a lot more room."

Here the coach

"It sounds like you are really clicking now! Let's take this one step further. I know your relationship with God is important to you. What brings life and enjoyment to that?"

"Hmmm. I'd have to admit, that's gotten sort of stale lately, too."

"So what have you done in the past that has been life-giving?"

"One thing was reading novels about Bible characters—it made the Scriptures come alive. When we lived in Ohio I'd spend Sunday afternoons in a hammock under a big oak tree just reading and sipping lemonade. It felt like God and I were reading those books together," Tom sighed wistfully. "Those were sweet times."

"Could you do that? Would something like that still hit the spot?"

"Right now I tend to just flop down on the couch and watch sports on Sundays. It's nice to look forward to some down time, but I can't say I feel very satisfied afterward."

"So if it isn't satisfying, what makes you do it?"

"Maybe because I'm so tired. Maybe just because I haven't taken the time to find a good book, and TV is the default."

"So if you had a stack of three of those novels on your night stand right now that you know you'd really like, would that make a difference?"

"You know, that sounds really good! It's like I'd forgotten that spending some time with God can be fun and not just something to check off my list. Time to make some lemonade!"

invites level I ideas around the client's relationship with God.

The coach expresses belief that Tom can recall things he enjoys doing with God—taking care to stay out of religious guilt feelings and stay real.

Interesting: the client's level I solution isn't bringing the joy he seeks!

The "What if?" question helps Tom envision himself reading again—and he gets inspired.

When you are aware of what level the client is thinking on, you can introduce the possibilities of thinking on other levels. And this doesn't just work for coaching upward: some ministry leaders get so locked into doing the level II mission that they need to relearn how to experience God and enjoy life on levels I and III.

Structuring Life for Eternal Rewards

Another practical way to work at allegiance to Christ is inviting clients to structure their lives for eternal rewards. In other words, figure out what God rewards, and treat it as a value system you can align your life with. The idea is to start acting like heaven is real, the promises of eternal rewards are true, and it is worth selling everything to pursue this pearl of great price.

Jesus mandated structuring life for eternal rewards an integral part of being a follower. The book of Matthew alone records over 40 ways (see exercise 2.1 on page 36) to choose treasures in heaven over rewards on earth. These examples involve letting go of temporal things for the eternal, going beyond what the world does to act like God toward others, and forgoing temporal acclaim to gain honor from God.

For instance, one familiar maxim is not letting your left hand know what your right hand is doing when you give. If you draw attention to your good deeds for the sake of your reputation, that's all the reward you'll get. But if you are willing to keep them a secret between you and God, for the other person's sake,[4] God will take special pains to honor you Himself. When you align the way you give with this principle you are structuring your life for eternal rewards.

Years ago I coached an assistant pastor named Ed in the midst of a difficult conflict. Pete, a former elder in the church, had been wounded by something Ed said. Instead of talking about what was largely a misunderstanding, he set out to get Ed fired by pulling strings in the background and spreading a skewed version of what had happened. Ed in turn felt hurt and betrayed when he found out what was going on, then vindicated when his senior pastor backed him and relieved when Pete finally left church.

When Ed brought up what had been going on in a coaching conversation, I asked if he had taken the step of forgiving Pete and asking for forgiveness. The idea of forgiving was fine, but asking forgiveness went over like a lead balloon. Ed's position was essentially, "He attacked me—why should I apologize for something that was basically all his fault?" Ed was dealing with the situation on level I—wanting God to vindicate him and change his circumstances.

To get Ed thinking on a different level, I offered this challenge: "You can deal with this situation in terms of who is right, or in terms of your relationship with God. Let's say for the sake of argument that this is 95% Pete's fault—why not meet God and get everything He has to teach you on your five percent no matter what Pete does? And which course of action best lives out who you really are: to take initiative to restore what you can of your relationship or leave the ball in his court?"

Ask we talked, Ed began to realize that there was more at stake than just his honor. Pete had been a friend for years and he was grieved about the broken relationship. He also realized that he had the opportunity to move from a defensive posture to a healing one if he chose to engage God's purposes at a higher level than simply what was best for him.

In this situation, there wasn't much temporal gain in going and apologizing—in fact, it took effort and placed Ed in a position of humility and vulnerability with someone who had attacked him. If all we were coaching for was happiness in this life, we might say, "Leave Pete behind, and spend your time with people who build you up and value who you are instead of tearing you down." Some mainstream life coaching literature advises that very approach. But we are coaching for eternity, so we can say, "Laying down your life for a friend is greatness in the eyes of God. This is your moment to be the fullness of who you are in Christ in this world—and that's

---

4 I think one reason God instituted this principle so that those who receive our gift receive it as from God Himself, not from us. Giving anonymously provides a wonderful opportunity for those who receive to meet God as their personal provider, instead of meeting Him indirectly through the agency of others. And because we've been willing to forego what's coming to us so that another person can meet God, God specially favors us. We aren't giving secretly so we can get something back. We are giving secretly because it maximizes the level I impact (people being draw into fellowship with God) of our level II act of service.

something worth living for!"

Embodying a Quality of Christ

Another practical way to live toward heaven is to choose a quality of God's heart you are drawn to model. Then rearrange your life and work to display that facet of the heart of God in a way so other-worldly that it has the scent of the eternal. This is a great way to move up from level II to level III thinking—instead of doing something for Christ, the focus is on being like Him. In fact, the heart of your call to embody one unique aspect of Christ's heart and reflect it to the world. These questions help move the dialog in that direction:

- *"What if you went beyond just the physical service? If you could model just one particular facet of Jesus' personality to others through your service, in a way that gave people an encounter with Christ through you, what would that facet be?"*
- *"How could you structure your business or work life to demonstrate a particular facet of Christ's character?"*
- *"If people could see one quality of Jesus' heart through you, what would you be most excited to show them?"*
- *"Give me some options for how you could put that into action."*
- *"How could you structure that into the way you live your daily life?"*

Exercise: Modeling God's Heart

Pick a quality of God's heart for people that you find particularly compelling and want to demonstrate to others. It could be mercy, generosity, grace, faithfulness, being true to your word, sacrificial love, patience, gentleness, you name it.

Now, do some brainstorming. What are 10 options for how you could demonstrate that through your lifestyle, work habits or business? Remember, we are trying to produce the fragrance of heaven here. What would go beyond what the world does and make people really take notice of God in what you do?

What does this look like put into practice? Here's an example. I've chosen to model the quality of generosity in my business structures and in the way I engage people. My objective is for those around me to experience God's generous heart for their success and their good through the way I do business.

The challenge is to do it in a way that's radical enough to be God-like, but without giving away the store and impoverishing my family. One way I practice this is simply setting aside time to help whoever calls me. If someone has a question or needs a resource or a networking connection, I've got time to help whether I get anything out of it or not.

Another way I work this out is in how I treat my vendors. The other day I purchased 200 custom CDs. When they arrived they had the right audio but were all labeled incorrectly. It was clearly the vendor's fault, and I could have just called him up and asked for a do-over. Instead, I took 10 minutes to pray and think: how could this turn out for the best for both of us, instead of them having to take a loss?

I ended up proposing that I hang onto the 200 cases (which had simply been printed for the wrong product) instead of pitching them, and the next time I reordered that product, they could send me the discs only but bill me for *both* the cases and the discs. That wouldn't cost me anything, but it would cut their loss on the misprint in half.

It cost me a little of my time to think of a solution and repackage the new discs. But look what we got in return! The vendor saved hundreds of dollars and got an otherworldly experience of working with a customer who actually cared about *his* success. My kids will repackage the CDs for me and make a little money for their summer mission trips, so they're happy. I get 200 misprinted discs that I can give away to another ministry to bless them without losing money on the deal. And I'll get to tell the vendor about the gift, making him a participant in blessing someone else. What a return on my two-hour investment!

If you make the commitment to pursue eternal rewards, you won't lack opportunities to do so. In this example, it turned out to be beneficial all around. Sometimes doing the right thing is costly. There is no guarantee that you will be financially compensated or receive honor in this life for serving Christ. But once you've made the lordship decision, that's no longer the issue. Lordship gives you an unerring compass that fixes your attention on the eternal. As Paul says, "… keep seeking the things above, where Christ is, seated at the right hand of God. Set your mind on the things above, not on the things that are on earth. For you have died and your life is hidden with Christ in God" (Col. 3:1-3).

2.1 Jesus' Teaching on External Rewards

Below are 30 examples from the book of Matthew on how to live toward heaven.

1. The sermon on the mount (Mt. 5:1-14) is about pursuing eternal rewards:
   - The poor are blessed in the spirit realm—they get the kingdom of heaven
   - Those who mourn will be comforted
   - The gentle will inherit the earth
   - Those who hunger for righteousness and justice will be satisfied
   - Those who give mercy will get it back
   - The pure in heart will see God as the reward for their purity
   - The peacemakers will be recognized as sons of God
   - The persecuted will get the kingdom of heaven as their reward
   - Those falsely accused because of Christ will get a great reward in heaven

2. Whoever is godly and teaches others to be will be great in heaven. (5:19)
3. If *anything* in your life is keeping you from heaven, rip it out! (5:29)
4. If you only love people who love you back, what's different about that? (5:46)
5. If you befriend only your friends, even the world does that. (5:47)
6. If you act religious to get recognition, don't expect any more reward. (6:1)
7. Give gifts secretly instead of publicly, and God will reward you in heaven. (6:2-4)
8. When you practice self-denial, don't flaunt it—or that's all the reward you'll get. Do it secretly for a heavenly reward. (6:16-18)
9. Don't accumulate stuff on earth—add to your bank account in heaven. (6:20)
10. Don't worry about your basic needs (food, clothing and shelter)—God is aware you need them. Seek the Kingdom and that stuff will fall into place. (6:30-32)
11. Grasp onto life and lose it; but let go of it for Jesus' sake and find it. (10:39)
12. Serve the person on the platform and you'll get the same reward. (10:41)
13. Even acts of service as small as giving a child a drink will be rewarded. (10:42)
14. Stand up for Christ before people and He'll stand up for you before God. (10:32)
15. To follow Christ, you must die to self and walk the road of suffering... Don't gain everything the world offers but lose your soul in the process. (16:25-26)
16. If you want treasure in heaven, give away your possessions and follow me. (19:21)
17. If you've left home, family or business to follow Jesus, you'll get back much more in the life to come. (19:29)
18. The greatest in heaven will be everyone's servant on earth. (23:5-11)
19. If you try to look great, you'll be humbled; greatness comes to the humble. (23:12)
20. If you faithfully steward what you've been given, the master will put you in charge of all His possessions in heaven. (24:45-51)
21. Work hard, take risks and make the most of your life for God, and you'll have a high position in heaven. (25:14-30)
22. How you treat the nobodies in your life is how you're treating Jesus. (25:31-46)

In the book of Matthew, Jesus gives many examples of what it can look like to structure your life for eternal rewards. Some involve letting go of temporal things for the eternal; some push us to go beyond what the world does to be like God, and some challenge us to forgo acclaim in the here and now to gain honor from God. Thirty of these principles are listed on the previous pages. Use the three reflection questions below to help you think about how to apply them in your life.

1. Which of these examples most challenge me today? What one could I implement in a circumstance or decision I face right now?
2. Which of these messages have I been drawn to throughout my life, and most desire that people see in me? What one step could I take to more compellingly convey this message through my life?
3. Which of these do I feel God calling me to begin doing in secret, just for Him?

Coaching Tip
Use the Five Options Technique[5] *to help the coachee identify at least five creative possibilities for living for eternal rewards in this area.*

5 See *Coaching Questions* pg. 41 for a description of the Five Options technique.

Chapter 3: Suffering, Success and Significance

"Achieving what you want and realizing that no favorable psychological changes have automatically ensued is far worse than failing to meet a goal. With failure, you can always go back to the drawing board, or 'try, try again'—these are actually energizing conditions. With success, that forces you to ask, 'Is that all there is?' No such second chances exist. The disappointment of exposing the myths that surround success is devastating because we are obsessed with success."

Peter Berglas, *Reclaiming the Fire*

Take a few minutes and visualize fulfilling your destiny in this life. As much as you can, picture what that moment of ultimate accomplishment would be like. You might be sitting with a group of students you taught years ago, and hearing the difference you made in their lives. Or it could be attaining a certain position, seeing your children mature and successful, planting a thriving church, or graduating with a certain degree. You are there, in that instant. Who is with you? What is the setting? What is the impact you are having on others? Close your eyes and immerse yourself in the details for a bit.

Now, what are you feeling? What emotions surface when you visualize reaching your destiny?

When I ask groups this question, I hear words like happiness, fulfillment, satisfaction, peace, thankfulness, accomplishment, thrilling, or contentment. We tend to see destiny fulfillment as something joyful and satisfying. And those are common emotions in destiny experiences.

But let's look at another example. What do you think Jesus was feeling at the moment when *He* was fulfilling His destiny in this life? Jesus' life call was to take on the sins of the world and die on the cross to offer us life. What did Jesus feel at His penultimate moment?

The Bible records His agony, despair, loneliness—"My God, My God, why have you forsaken me?"—scorn, thirst and pain. Isaiah captures it well:

> *"He was despised and rejected by men;*
> *a man of sorrows and acquainted with grief;*
> *And as one from whom men hide their faces*
> *he was despised, and we esteemed him not.*
>
> *Surely he has borne our griefs*
> *and carried our sorrows;*
> *Yet we esteemed him stricken,*
> *smitten by God and afflicted...*
>
> *Yet it was the will of the Lord to bruise him;*
> *He has put him to grief;*
> *When he makes himself an offering for sin,*
> *He shall see his offspring, he shall prolong his days;*
> *The will of the Lord shall prosper in his hand;*
> *He shall see the fruit of the travail of his soul and be satisfied."*
>
> Is 53:1-11; RSV

Juxtaposing our idea of how destiny works with Jesus' life story helps us evaluate our understanding of life purpose. Although our calling may not be the same as His (we aren't all dying for the world!), a guiding principle is that *our concept of destiny fulfillment must also be able to fit Jesus' life.*

Purpose and Suffering

So what can we learn from Jesus' life purpose story? The most obvious insight is that *suffering is a part of purpose.* This is a facet of destiny that coaching has consistently overlooked. I've always been sort of intrigued by the list of lives of the faithful in Hebrews 11. Paul talks about those who through faith conquered Kingdoms, stopped the mouth of lions, escaped the sword, or won their dead back by having them resurrected. Sounds really good so far! And then, without even pausing for breath, Paul goes on to talk about those who were tortured, stoned, sawn in two, destitute, afflicted, poorly treated, who never got the honor they deserved—and he attributes to all of them the same faith! These are all people who lived their destiny.

Paul is saying that a Christian's life purpose may as easily lead to great temporal suffering and loss as to great deeds and great gain. This isn't very attractive at first glance! But viewing suffering as a part of life is actually a very powerful tool for the coach. If suffering is included in God's plan, then God works through it, and the Planner still has things in hand. He may even bring us gifts in suffering that lead us to our purpose and empower us to fulfill it. If, on the other hand, we aren't supposed to suffer, or the goal of coaching is to eliminate suffering, then anything bad that happens to us is either an obstacle or an indicator that we are off course.

But Jesus' life powerfully affirms that suffering has great purpose. Therefore, all of life, good and bad, has purpose. God is at work in *everything* that is going on in your client's life. One of the most powerful coaching tools you can deploy is knowing that God will take *anything* that happens to your coachees and work it to build them into the image of Christ, if they engage it with a sense of purpose (Rm. 8:28). The objective of coaching is not to eliminate adversity (which is impossible anyway), but to help the client meet God in it. True Kingdom greatness for your client is always only a moment away—the time it takes to say, "OK God: how do you want to meet me in this?" At any moment, in any circumstance, your client can move from, "My life isn't working; something is wrong!" to, "My life isn't working, but I'm meeting God in it, and that makes it all worthwhile!" Remove every difficulty and hardship from life, and you also remove the opportunity to meet God in it.

> *"Indeed, I count everything as loss because of the surpassing worth of knowing Christ Jesus my Lord. For His sake I have suffered the loss of all things, and count them as refuse, in order that I may gain Christ and be found in him... that I may know him and the power of his resurrection, and share in his sufferings, becoming like him in his death, that if possible I may attain the resurrection of the dead."*
>
> Paul, speaking about his own life purpose (Phil. 3:7-11; RSV)

I'm coaching a leader who just resigned under pressure from a church he helped to plant. It's one of those classic, dysfunctional church horror stories—a senior pastor with control issues, poor communication, private issues being dealt with in public, players with hidden agendas pulling strings behind the scenes but unwilling to address things out in the open. When my friend finally stood his ground and resigned, the leaders of his church called everyone he knew to make sure they got the church's side of the story first.

Naturally, he's pretty wounded. Not only is he losing his job and his life's work to this point, he's also being cut off from his friends and his normal support systems, unable to talk honestly about what's going on so as not to cause more damage.

It's been helpful to him to get perspective from someone outside the situation who has been through that kind of thing and understands the leadership dynamics of church conflicts. But as we get beyond the immediate pain, we're talking more and more about the gifts this situation can give him. The key is moving the dialog from the circumstances (which are crappy) to *who he is becoming in the situation,* which holds the key to fulfilling his life purpose. As this man meets God in his pain, God is moving him to places he never would have gone without it.

One great gift is the revealing of his points of vulnerability, that cause him to just take the blows in conflict instead of responding in strength and love as an equal. Another gift is that it pushes him out to engage his call. He admits that he stayed too long in that place of security, instead of following the risky path God was calling him to. Many leaders are stuck in frustrating situations because they fear the financial risks their dreams entail. God has given this leader the gift of pushing him beyond the small dream of security and into the big dream of his life purpose. The most transformational, important things we learn in life we usually learn the hard way. Without difficulty, we tend to settle for a comfortable, secure existence. Pain pushes us out of the nest.

This leads to an important coaching truth: *calling is often discovered within a person's own sufferings or the sufferings of others.* For example, everyone who goes on a short term mission trip and feels drawn to serve those living in darkness and squalor has found a call within the sufferings of others. Anyone who grew up as a social misfit and determines to reach those on the fringes of society, or was a child of divorce and finds a call in fostering healthy marriages, or who grieved her own miscarriage and ends up working with mothers who miscarry, has found destiny within their personal suffering. Since experiences of suffering are such a common foundation of calling, coaches need tools to mine the difficult experiences in life for destiny clues. Chapter 15 provides practical techniques for doing this.

Purpose Beyond this Life

A second key insight we get from studying Jesus' life purpose is that the story doesn't end with this life. Jesus' ultimate destiny is for God to put all things under His authority, and to finally "unite all things in him, things in heaven and things on earth" (Eph. 1:10; RSV). Death is not an end, but a milestone on a larger journey. Jesus lived for the day He'd be joined to a beautiful, spotless bride for an eternity of celebration, with nothing to mar that perfect relationship. It was "who for the joy set before Him endured the cross, despising the shame, and has sat down at the right hand of the throne of God" (Heb. 12:2).

I believe Jesus truly enjoyed life on earth. I think He loved the people He was with, the message He brought and skin He lived in. He certainly wasn't serious and religious all the time. Remember, this is the guy who was widely criticized for going to wild parties with prostitutes, criminals and embezzlers. Jesus loved life, but He trusted God enough to let go of everything He had here for the promise of something infinitely better. *To Jesus, the important thing was living toward heaven.* All his hopes and dreams and rewards were fixed there.

The Isaiah 53 passage about "the man of sorrows" at the start of the chapter ends with,

> *"He shall see the fruit of the travail of his soul and be satisfied."*

I love that line. Jesus' suffering (like ours) accomplishes a purpose, and He will see the fantastic results of His purposeful suffering (so will we) and experience the satisfaction of seeing with His own eyes (as we will) that it was all truly worthwhile. Jesus refused to live for cheap substitutes in the here and now, and held out for the real prize in heaven.

In the same way, a Christian's destiny story only makes sense when it extends beyond the grave. It's easy to lose sight of eternal ends in the press of daily life. So one of the things coaches do for their clients is reframing their circumstances in the light of eternity:

- *"You and Jesus have something new in common—now you've both been through something like this. There's a fellowship of His sufferings you can have with Him when you share His place of pain. How can you meet Him and know Him more deeply here?"*
- *"Let's refocus on the ultimate outcome here. What's the payoff for handling this well instead of giving in to your anger?"*
- *"Let's take a bigger view: instead of looking at how this affects your day, how does it fit in with God's ultimate purpose for your life?"*
- *"Let's say you've walked through this really well. Visualize standing before God and talking about this. What would He say to you? How would that impact you?"*
- *"If you completely, radically abandoned yourself to the idea that heaven is really real and God rewards, what would you do?"*

This life is full of unpredictable suffering and deep loss, and sometimes nothing seems to make sense. Christian coaches bring an extraordinary gift to the table in those moments—that we know a purpose that reaches beyond this life to another.

Measuring Success

There is one more important life purpose principle I want to highlight in Jesus' destiny story. By almost any familiar measure, Jesus' temporal life was a failure. He died young. The last of His clothes were raffled off by the Roman guards. He was unable to support His widowed mother. His teaching was rejected by the religious authorities, He received a death sentence from His own people, and His small band of followers had scattered to the four winds. He left no writings or organizational structure behind. He never traveled farther than 70 miles from His hometown, and was unknown outside of that small corner of the world. From all appearances the new Kingdom Jesus talked about was going to die with Him. By temporal leadership standards, Jesus was a failure.

However, from the perspective of 2000 years later, He's the most influential man who ever lived. Which raises an important coaching question: how do you measure success?

Figuring out what success means is one of those issues that is constantly tripping clients up. Here's a coaching example:

"So—it's three weeks into your sabbatical! How's that going?"

"Pretty good. I enjoyed getting away for a week with my wife, just the two of us. We spent a few days extra at her mother's house, then just been hanging around since we got back."

"And how are you experiencing being home?"

"Well… good and bad. I know sabbatical is about rest, but I find myself getting antsy."

"Describe that."

"OK. In the morning I spend some time with the Lord, read the paper, have a cup of

coffee—kind of ease into the day. I check in with my wife before she's off to work, clean up the dishes, and then… what do I do for the rest of the day? I have time to just sit and smell the flowers like I've been dreaming of, but when it comes right down to it it's hard to relax and do nothing. I keep thinking I could be reroofing the garage, or doing a research project, or finishing up the classes for my Master's, or something productive. Or I want to schedule the sabbatical—you know, one hour of reading, an hour of yard work, and so on. At the end of the day I feel better about myself—it keeps me from feeling guilty and negative—but I wonder if I am missing out on what this time is for."

"What do you feel guilty about?"

"I guess… that I'm not accomplishing anything worthwhile."

"That's a common feeling for people in the first part of a sabbatical."

"It is? OK—that helps."

"Let me ask you this. Let's go back to your objectives. What led you to take your sabbatical in the first place?"

"Well, I wanted to get some time away and refocus. I felt like I was becoming a doing machine, just grinding away from one thing to the next all day long. Life was just a series tasks, not a life."

"And what did you expect that your sabbatical time would be like?"

"Well, that I rest up a little, get away from the rat race at work and then do the things I haven't had time to do for years."

"So you were going to stop doing some things and start doing others in their place?"

"Right."

"So how would that help you stop being a 'doing machine?'"

"I'm not sure what you mean."

"Let me try again. If doing so much was turning you into a machine, and during your sabbatical you are still doing, just with different things, how will that help you break the cycle of just going from one task to the next?"

"Well, um… Good point. I guess I just visualized myself doing different things, instead of really doing things differently. OK—so doing different things won't get me to where I want to go. So now what?"

"One way to clarify is to define what success means. What would be the outcome if you succeeded at your sabbatical?"

"That's easy. I would be a person who could stop measuring myself by accomplishment, work at a slower pace, and live while I do instead of having my doing squeeze out the living. Success would be slowing down and feeling good about it."

"Excellent. So if that's what success is, let's think about what to expect when you are walking that path. If a person had lived his whole life measuring his worth by accomplishments, and suddenly decided to stop doing that, how do you think he would feel?"

"Probably a lot like me—aimless, antsy, and maybe sort of guilty. That's interesting. It always feels a little awkward when you start doing something new. So if I'm on-course right now, I'm going to struggle with being in an unfamiliar place; but if I get off-course and go back to the old way, I'll feel better about myself but I'll be missing my objective. Does that make any sense?"

"Sure. Change is always uncomfortable at first until you get used to it. Sounds normal to me."

"That's really helpful—thanks. I guess I just didn't know what to expect since I've never done this before."

The tension this client experienced came from his unconscious definition of success. He took a sabbatical in order to redefine what was meaningful in life, but without realizing it was still judging how he was doing on sabbatical by how much he was accomplishing! The goal involved slowing down, but his internal compass (his conscience) was still saying that doing more was better. As he learned to align his expectations with his goal, the inner discomfort gradually eased and he developed the ability to enjoy being at rest.

Greatness by God's Standards

Many clients unknowingly define success in counterproductive or unbiblical ways. Measuring yourself against others is a common trap—success becomes relative, a moving target instead of something attainable. Other clients expect to feel certain feelings if they succeed, or that all problems in life will magically disappear if they are really faithful Christians. And still others measure success in terms of outward religious behavior instead of the heart—I'm a success if I do everything right, or pray enough, or practice the right disciplines. An unbiblical picture of success can cause a lot of heartache. That's why it's useful for the coach to have a solid grasp of success from God's perspective.

God has a simple success standard, and it's one that fits right in with the coaching methodology. In the Kingdom of God, success is about stewardship: making the most of what you have been given. The parable of the talents, for instance (Mt. 25:14-30), teaches us that we are stewards of our lives, and taking good care of God's gift means taking risks and stretching ourselves to use our abilities, rather than letting them lie dormant. The master rewarded the servants who fully used whatever they had been given, and criticized the one who wasted the opportunity. He never compared them with each other; instead comparing their results to the resources they'd been given. (This also provides a real imperative for life purpose discovery: how can you effectively steward what you've been given when you don't know what you've been given?)

Defining success in terms of stewardship also means we don't need to strive to be something we're not. Life is not a competition: it has nothing to do with being as good as or better than someone else. Jesus was a success because He completed the unique task He was sent to do. Our success comes the same way.

It is often a great relief when we grasp that God does not judge us in comparison to the accomplishments of others. In my younger days I remember reading about John Wesley, who preached an average of three sermons a day and is estimated to have traveled over 100,000 miles (on horseback!) in his lifetime to preach the gospel. What a great hero of the faith! So I chose Wesley as my internal standard for what it meant to be a radical Christian. If I was really sold out to God, I should pray as much as Wesley, serve with as much energy, and have the same kind of impact.

After several years of condemnation, it finally dawned on me that God never created me to be John Wesley. I didn't have his energy, his personality or his famously-devout upbringing—and I didn't have to. What a relief! I only have the abilities I was born with and the background I was born into, and my assignment is to make the most of that. The only way to surpass Wesley is to become more of what I was uniquely created to be than Wesley did—and only God can really measure that.

Coaching for Real Success

Success is not what most people think it is. There are caring mothers, diligent factory workers and guys who coach little league on Saturdays who will be more greatly acclaimed in the Kingdom of Heaven than some of our most famous authors, preachers, and missionaries, because *they were more faithful to steward everything they'd been given for Christ than those who had been given much more.*

That may seem implausible given our western star system, but it was very real to Jesus. When He saw a poor widow drop two little pennies into the offering (Mt. 21:1-4), He remarked that she had contributed more than all of the big donors put together. The reason? They had so much they could give a flashy gift out of their surplus and never miss it, but she gave everything she had to live on. In other words, God isn't looking at who can give the largest *quantity*, but the largest *percentage*. Judging by quantity is about competition; judging by proportion is about stewardship. Some Christian workers who are first in talent and recognition now are going to be last in the Kingdom, because they've squandered much of their enormous talent, or they wasted what they'd been given on creating their own empires. Others who seem at the bottom of the totem pole now may end up the most celebrated in heaven. It wouldn't surprise me if a little old grandma who'd taught Sunday school for 40 years or even some child with Down Syndrome is among the greatest in the Kingdom.

> *Greatness in the Kingdom isn't about doing more than someone else—it's about making the most of what you've been given.*

What that means for the coach is that no matter who you are working with, *your client has the potential for ultimate greatness in the Kingdom of God.* Today, in your next appointment, you could be coaching one of the standouts in heaven. What a God-sized perspective we can take on as Christian coaches, and what an advantage we have in radically believing in people! It doesn't matter if you are coaching top executives or assembly-line workers, mega-church pastors or lay people, senior leaders or teenagers from the youth ministry: your client can live today as one of the great ones in the Kingdom of Heaven. And *that's* worth coaching your heart out for!

Success and Becoming

The other side of God's success definition has to do with who you are. To God, *success is more about becoming the right kind of person than doing all the right things.* Fulfilling your inward potential as someone created in the image of God is what enables you to do what you were created to do. Because doing flows out of being, real success is about who you are.

The beauty of defining success in being terms is that you can experience success even in the midst of outward failure. One client I coached came to me because of a negative performance review: his boss had turned him down for a promotion because his co-workers evaluated him as distant, aloof, demanding and hard to work with. He came to me somewhat bewildered—he'd always seen himself as good with people. He was at a loss for how to respond.

At first, he saw that review as a very negative event. It jolted his self-confidence and threatened his career. But as he began to grasp why people saw him as distant and how he could change, his perspective changed. That seeming-failure taught him to slow down, pay more attention to emotions and feelings, and enjoy his life and work more. At his next review, things turned out much differently.

Success in God's eyes is more about becoming the right kind of person than about doing all the right things.

Most people would see that first review is as a failure or defeat—he wasn't "doing it right," and so he suffered the consequences. This is a golden opportunity for the coach to reframe the situation in terms of becoming. Adverse circumstances are like a plow that breaks up the compacted ground of our hearts so that the seed of real change can take root. So seeing those who face adversity as beneficiaries of a great opportunity for inward growth is a powerful approach. When this man discovered he was not who he thought he was, he hired a coach, did the heart work of taking an honest look at himself, and changed. By laying hold of the opportunity for heart change, his negative review became a life-changing success.

Another client came to me because he felt like a failure. He had left a job and a home he really enjoyed to pursue a different career; but once he was in it, he realized it didn't fit him at all. Now, with three years of preparation and tens of thousands of dollars worth of education down the drain, he wondered if he had totally missed God's will for his life.

Once we got down to that feeling, it provided a wonderful chance to coach from an alternate perspective. "Here's how things look from where I sit. Your marriage has been in trouble for years, but this year you finally asked for help, and you are making great progress. For the first time, you hired a coach to help you discover God's will for your life, instead of making those decisions on your own. And you are working intentionally at your devotional life and spending more time with God than ever. This doesn't look like a failure to me! I'd say you are more in the center of God's will for your life than you have ever been."

Success in this situation was not based on being in the right place at the right time doing the right thing, like many clients believe. It was becoming the man God called him to be. Sometimes when we are moving forward, outwardly it looks like we are sliding back!

Think of it this way: if you are coaching someone in decision-making skills, is it most important that the person makes a good decision or becomes a good decision-maker? If I help you make a good decision, you've done one thing well. But if I help you become a great decision maker, I've affected every decision you make for the rest of your life. Becoming a different person bears more fruit than doing something right.

Significance and the Abundant Life

Because many individuals come to coaching in search of significance (the sense that my life is worthwhile and what I am doing is meaningful), understanding how significance fits into a biblical worldview is also important. Jesus had keen insight into what is significant in life. His idea of the meaning of life is so profound it can be expressed in a single word: Agape. The center of life is to love God with all your heart, soul, mind and strength, and to love your neighbor as yourself. That's what makes life work. The best possible life is a life with the freedom and power to offer the gifts of love, justice, compassion, service, peace, and kindness to everyone you meet, without needing to get something back. Imagine yourself living out of that kind of overflow: full instead of needy, free from any craving for security, significance or acceptance, un-entangled by anger and inner wrestlings, with the internal resources to always offer the best to those around you. That would be a great life!

In general, the leading figures in the life coaching movement agree with Jesus on this picture of life lived out of an overflow as the good life. They urge you to create a superabundance that lets you live free from worry and stress, under-promise and over-deliver, give to others, and pursue the opportunities that life gives. We all agree that having more than enough and not being needy are key ingredients for a great life!

Life coaching in the secular arena has taught extreme self-care as the road to the life of overflow. It starts with you. Take responsibility for your life. Find your energy drains and plug them. Learn to say, "No." Align with your values. Get rid of unhealthy relationships that drag you down. Don't tolerate things—change them. Give yourself what you'd want the person you love most to have. Find what matters most to you, and pursue it. Don't let other's expectations define you. Take superb care of yourself.

Taken individually, these can all be appropriate steps. What needs to be challenged is the underlying philosophy. In essence, mainstream life coaching says if you treat yourself well, you'll have a great life, and others around you will feel well-treated, too. *Take care of yourself first to have a great life.* And this is where the paths diverge. Jesus says exactly the opposite: d*ie to yourself first to have a*

Examples of the Divergence

Here are three published mainstream examples of how to practice extreme self-care. I've chosen cases where the divergence from biblical values is fairly obvious (try applying these statements to Jesus, Paul or Abraham!). The underlying philosophy we coach from does make a big difference!

- *"If your job, business or profession is harming you and you can't seem to make it completely stress-free, quit, sell it, or change professions."*
- *"Make a list of ten promises you have made to others that are causing you stress, even if it's stress you can handle. Revoke all ten of these promises and work out alternatives with the promisees."*
- *"Identify the three sources (people, roles, expectations) of your current stress. Completely eliminate these three items."*

great life.

According to Jesus, the way to a life of overflow is giving up everything to love and serve Him, not to focus on getting more. "Give and it will be given to you; pressed down, shaken together and running over" (Luke 6:38; RSV). Abundance is not a matter of accumulation, but of being in relationship with a best friend who has more than enough of everything, and loves to share it. A surplus in God's Kingdom is not something you must acquire—it simply flows through the hands of stewards that God gives to precisely because they don't keep it all for themselves. Agape love is Jesus' path to an overflow that fills others out of our fullness in Him—and in the process produces fulfillment within us as well.

There are many examples of Christian life purpose materials based on this "take care of self first" philosophy. Let's aim higher. A good place to start is to pull out the goals and values you created for your coaching practice, and look at them in light of these two competing philosophies:

- *"What are you coaching for?"*
- *"What caused you to get into coaching?"*
- *"How do your goals for your coaching practice align with the values of loving, serving and giving?"*
- *"How have you structured your practice around serving others, and where are you focused on getting your own needs met first? How could you align more closely with Jesus' way?"*
- *"If someone simply watched how you run your coaching practice, what would they say are your true values and priorities?"*
- *"Who benefits except you if you reach your goals for your practice? What does that say about you?"*

Coaching Significance

A good place to talk about significance is around the client's objectives. "What I'm hearing is you want to get more out of your work. So let's start by defining the target. What would a significant work life look like?" If the client is operating out of a cultural standard for success or significance, asking them to verbalize their philosophy can be a great help. We all have inconsistencies in the way we live our values—and cultural values are easy to overlook until we are forced to articulate how we live. Often when we're examining areas like significance or fulfillment, clients will choose actions steps around prayer or Bible study to help them find out what God is saying on the topic.

Since underlying values explain why we do what we do, another way to get at them with a client is to ask the "Why" question:

- *"Why are you pursuing this goal? What will it give you?"*
- *"Let's say that the most significant life is the one focused simply on loving. What would need to change if you were going to make love the center of your life?"*

- *"How does this make life better for you? For those around you? How do you want to prioritize those two ends?"*
- *"It seems like the belief that is behind this is that if you focus on taking care of things in your own life, you'll have something to give. Talk to me a bit about how that philosophy matches with your faith."*
- *"If you pursued significance the same way Jesus did, what would you do?"*
- *"What are you looking to for significance (or provision, or security) in this situation? How has that worked for you in the past?"*

Another fun way to explore significance is a character study. Who in Scripture do you admire who led a significant life? What made it significant? Discussing the life experience of biblical characters often draws people to want to study those passages as action steps. Or they may want to talk to a person they look up to about what gives life meaning.

Jesus showed us that aligning life with loving, giving and serving is the path to significance. Since the hunger for significance is often what drives people to seek a coach, I want to give them the opportunity to grapple with creating a life around love instead of one around recognition, accomplishment, or personal fulfillment. It really is better to give than to receive.

Part II: The Seven Questions Framework

"I don't know what your destiny will be, but one thing I do know: the ones among you who will be really happy are those who have sought and found how to serve."

Albert Schweitzer

Now that we've looked at the philosophical basis of Christian life coaching, let's dive into the practical exercises and techniques coaches use to help people find and follow their God-given destiny.

There are many different ways to structure discovering and pursuing one's life purpose. We're going to organize the search with a model called the *Seven Life Purpose Questions.* By focusing around these seven themes, we'll help coachees understand where the process is going and how the different pieces of the puzzle fit together.

The seven questions are:

1. **Whose** am I?
2. **Who** am I?
3. **What** has my whole life prepared me for?
4. **Why** do I desire *this*?
5. **Where** is the Master sending me?
6. **When** will this happen?
7. **How** will I get there?

The first five questions have to do with *discovering* life purpose, while the final two have to do with pursuing it (walking out what you've discovered). We'll first do a quick overview of each question, then dive into how to coach these areas in subsequent chapters.

The Meaning of the Seven Questions

The first question—"**Whose** am I?"—deals with our fundamental allegiance. Who are we living *for*? When we make life choices, our basic allegiance may be to ourselves, to another person (where we've subverted our identity to theirs), to our tribe or nation, or to Jesus as master of our lives. This question asks, "When the chips are down, whom have we chosen to serve? Is this life mine to order for my own pleasure and benefit, or do I owe allegiance to something bigger?" Obviously, this can make a huge difference in the trajectory of our lives. To shorten the question, we'll refer to this area as **Allegiance**.

"**Who** am I?" is the Design question. It covers your inborn nature: characteristics like personality type, gifts, strengths, and talents. At this level, people change slowly over time if at all, so understanding who you are is extremely valuable in relationships, career, decision-making and other areas. We'll also refer to this area as **Design**.

The other side of the nature/nurture dichotomy is the question, "**What** has my whole life prepared me for?" There are valuable things you pick up along the way in life that shape your destiny: learned skills, work and life experience, character and self-understanding. Taking stock of who you have become in life both completes and compliments the Design picture. We also call this area **Preparation**.

The next question asks, "Why?" It taps into our desire, passion and motivation. "**Why** do I desire this? Why is this important enough to give my life to?" Passion is a vital part of living an on-purpose life. To accomplish something extraordinary, you'll need exceptional desire to finish the race. This area covers dreams and desires, what energizes you, and your core values and beliefs. Coachees usually find important life purpose indicators within these **Passions**.

The fifth question is **Calling**: "**Where** is the Master sending me?" A calling is a commission that comes from outside of you to serve a larger end (it primarily serves others, not you). As a Christian life purpose model, the Seven Questions framework assumes that a call from God is an integral part of *every* believer's life purpose. In this area we explore what God has revealed to you about your life mission, the people and needs you are drawn to serve, the message of your life, and how experiences of suffering and sacrifice integrate with your life purpose.

"**When will this happen?**" is the question of timing. Most of us express this question as, "How long, O Lord?"! If part of your call is to own a business, it may be that now is the time to launch out, or you could have years of preparation ahead of you. This question of **Timing** is covered in the companion book, *The Calling Journey* by Tony Stoltzfus. This volume explores life stage models, patterns of calling development, and shows how to create calling time lines that explain how coachees are moving toward their destinies. We'll also learn how to coach a person through the calling development process and not just point them toward the end point: their life mission and convergent role.

The final question is, "**How** will I get there?" This question moves the coaching process toward goals and actions that make the person's life purpose a lived-out reality. The basic coaching tools for this **Implementation** process (like conversational models) are laid out in my previous books, *Leadership Coaching* and *Coaching Questions.*

Back in the introduction we talked about how a balanced, biblical approach to destiny discovery looks in four directions:

- **Outward** at what God reveals *to* us (the external *Call*)
- **Inward** at what our *Design* reveals within us
- **Backward** at how he has purposefully *Prepared* us through our life experiences
- **Forward** at the dreams and *Passions* that draw us to our destiny

These four directions are represented in questions two through five—the heart of the Seven Questions model.

The Purpose Diagram

So to sum up, we have seven potential areas to explore with our clients to help them discover and pursue their life purpose, each category with a fundamental question:

1. **Allegiance:** Whose am I?
2. **Design:** Who am I?
3. **Preparation:** What has my whole life prepared me for?
4. **Passion:** Why do I desire *this*?
5. **Calling:** Where is the Master sending me?
6. **Timing:** When will this all come together?
7. **Implementation:** How will I get there?

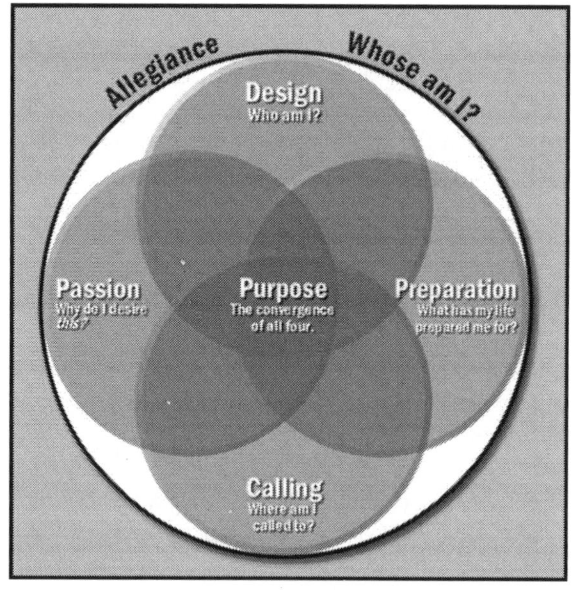

Discovering one's life purpose (the first five questions) is the focus of the remainder of this book. The purpose diagram (at right) shows how these questions fit together. The overall context is *Allegiance*: someone who is sold out to Christ is operating on an altogether different playing field than the person whose allegiance is to self. Within the circle of allegiance are four overlapping areas we mine for life purpose clues: *Design, Passion, Preparation* and *Calling*. Where these four circles converge is the sweet spot: our *Life Purpose*. In other words, we find our purpose at the intersection of who we are, what our life has prepared us to do, what we are passionate about and our external commission from God for others.

Where Do You Look for Destiny?

This model addresses a question unique to Christian coaching: how does God reveal our destiny to us? Most life purpose models have us look inside, at our passion, design and life experience, and say, "What am I passionate about doing? What fits me? What would give me a sense of purpose and fulfillment?" These questions begin to reveal our deepest desires, which is a valuable exercise. In many ways these desires align with our life purpose, since we are created by God for our destiny (the good works which He planned for us beforehand).

However, as fallen humans, our desires are also shot through with selfishness, fear, hurt, pride, and everything about us that still needs to come under the lordship of Christ. If our inner world contains both the glory of God and the cravenness of human nature, looking inward will offer the same mixture—a flawed picture of what we are made to be and do. Life purpose discovery models which only look inward will always leave us wanting, because we sense deep down that our corrupt side is always lurking beneath even our highest aspirations.

If our true destiny can't be accurately discerned by looking within, where do we find it? We have to go back to the original architect and take a look at the blueprints. It's when we see the designer's intention that the half-finished building in our heart begins to make sense. This is why a truly biblical life purpose model must include the additional component of *Calling*: an external commission *from* God *for* others. Using only one's inner dreams and desires as the road to life purpose works as easily for a Hitler as it does for a Mother Teresa.

People can get hung up on the other side of this issue as well. Why don't I just pray and wait for God to reveal my life purpose? Why all this navel-gazing and looking inside at my personality and passions? Isn't trying to find my destiny just being self-focused? No—because God in His foresight *has also created you for your role*. The way you are designed, your best dreams, and even your life history (which prepares you in God-directed ways) reveals the Creator's intention. Or, we might say that a portion of the revelation of your call lies within you, in how you are made. Joseph was a dreamer from a young age. Paul had a radical, all-in personality from the first day we meet him as Saul. Who these men were partially revealed God's purpose for their lives. So the call of God on a believer's life and the best desires in his or her heart are complementary[6].

And once you hear a call, following it still requires knowing yourself. Have you ever worked with someone who was following God's call but didn't seem able to

---

6 This is also a function of maturity and sanctification. As we take on the mind of Christ, our thoughts and desires become conformed to his. Then more and more we *want* to direct our natural passions and strengths toward God's purposes.

enjoy it? It is possible to work within your area of call but outside of your design. For instance, a person who is *Called* by God to lead a visionary organization but has never learned to delegate well (*Preparation* is lacking), ends up doing a lot of administrative details that she isn't good at (the role doesn't align with her *Design*) and starts wishing she was in another job (her *Passion* is quenched.) So even though she is pursuing her call, this lack of alignment with her identity means there is little joy or effectiveness in it.

The God who knit us together in our mother's womb in a fearful and wonderful way knew from the beginning what we would do well, and He assigns His calls accordingly. Design, Preparation and Passion must align with calling for us to maximize our impact, longevity and joy in our life mission. We must look *both* inward and outward to find our destiny.

If you'd like to do some biblical study of purpose on your own, several Bible studies on this topic are provided at www.ALeadersLifePurpose.com.

The Life Purpose Play

An excellent analogy for the purpose diagram is acting in a play. When you play a part, you have to get in character and *become* that role in order to complete the task (acting in the play). That's a much stronger analogy, because it incorporates both the being and doing aspects of destiny. Listed below are six guiding principles of our life purpose model, laid out using the play analogy. When these come together, you can put on the performance of your life.

1. **God has created you for a unique part in His purposes in history**
   Life has meaning as part of God's larger story of creation, redemption and uniting all things in Christ. You have a personal part to play in that story.
2. **You must follow the script**
   You can be part of God's grand production, or you can do a monologue by yourself on your own stage. In order to be part of God's larger story, you have to acknowledge ***Allegiance*** to the director's authority and stick to the script.
3. **You were *Designed* for that part from birth in God's foresight**
   You can look inward at your talents, strengths and personality type to find clues to the part that you are fit to play. You were made for this role.
4. **Your *Passion* for your part carries you through**
   There is a fire that burns inside of you to tell this story. Your passion for the part is what gives you the determination to learn your lines and give your all to the play.
5. **You are *Prepared* for your part through life experience**
   Your whole life to this point is the rehearsal for this ultimate performance. Until you've rehearsed, you aren't ready for the opening.
6. **The director casts your role**
   You must look *outward* to receive the casting ***Call*** assigned by the director. You won't fully know the director's purpose for the play until he tells you.

Coaching Christians and Non-Christians

If that's the model for coaching Christians, how do you use it with non-believers? The starting place is that everyone, Christian or non-Christian, has a destiny. God has created everyone for a part; we just get to choose whether we join God's play or not. Even when you have not yet given Allegiance to God, you have the design He placed in you from the beginning. And God is still at work in your life, sending you the experiences you need to prepare you, stir your passion and make you ready to accept His call.

Therefore, the same tools work for coaching Christians and non-Christians alike in the areas of Design, Preparation and Passion[7]. Only Allegiance to God and being Called as part of His larger story are missing.

The good news here is that for those who come to Christ later in life, *their life before faith is not wasted!* For instance, some of the greatest evangelists have come out of the deepest gutters. Why? Because their life experience has Prepared them to understand the lives of the unsaved. They have been through everything that the people they want to reach have, and knowing the pain of their journey and the joy of their redemption, they are Passionate about introducing others to the great God they've found. The most effective way for people to get beyond the fallacy that their life is wasted is to help them find their call, and then discover how their life experience has prepared them for it.

Coaching with Reflection Exercises

I'd like to touch briefly on the topic of reflection before we dive into the next section. This book includes a whole suite of life purpose reflection exercises for the coach. There are some important adaptations you can make to get the most out of them given the unique reflective style and personality type of each client.

One involves introvert and extrovert learning styles. Introverts discover by getting alone and reflecting—their primary drive is to engage something inwardly first, then use it outwardly once they've figured it out. Extroverts think out loud—they learn best by talking. So while introverted clients do fine with lots of individual reflection, the same approach can drive an extrovert crazy. One great way to adapt to extroversion is simply to turn personal reflection exercises into discussion exercises by asking clients to talk things through with a friend or spouse. Another option is for extroverts to speak their reflections into a portable tape recorder instead of writing them.

It is especially important for extroverts that reflection is acted upon. While an introvert can think about something for weeks without feeling a need to do, extroverts are driven to act on what they are thinking about, and then keep thinking about it in the process of acting. Tying life purpose discoveries to immediate implementation steps (or even just making sure reflective steps are discussed in your appointments) helps extroverted clients.

Journaling is another place where you'll run into obstacles unless you adapt to the client's style. Some people (like me) journal in complete sentences and paragraphs.

---

7 And to a certain degree, even in the area of calling. Remember, some people choose to give their lives to a calling from their nation, tribe, family or other external source.

Others prefer bullet lists, or scrawling in all directions over the page, or tape-recording their journal instead of writing it. And for some, the word journaling means a daily diary that you keep on your bedside table—not what you are probably after as a coach.

I make a practice of talking through with clients what their journaling options are, which reflective style works best for them and how they'd like to record their insights. Being pro-active eliminates many potential obstacles in the reflection process before they ever occur.

Question 1: Whose Am I? (Allegiance)

"Your life is not your own: it belongs to God. To 'be yourself' is to be and do what God wants you to be and do, knowing that God created you for a mission and knows you and your mission better than you do."

Leonard Sweet

Jackie showed up at our door bursting to tell us her news. "Look—I'm engaged!" she exclaimed, proudly holding out the ring on her finger. "We're getting married in June!"

It was one of those moments where it's hard not to let your feelings show. We'd spent several months discipling Jackie as she reoriented her life around the gospel. The big issues were marriage and romantic relationships. Jackie's dream was to get married, and she had fallen in love with the ideal of married life. However, her current boyfriend drank heavily, majored in Nintendo and wasn't a believer. It had been a real struggle for her to realize that this relationship was not compatible with her faith. Two weeks ago she'd finally made the decision to cut ties with him.

"So, come on in and tell us about it," my wife Kathy finally said, rescuing us from an awkward moment. In a few minutes we got the full story. She'd finally mustered up the courage to tell him it was over. The next night he had come over to her apartment, put a knife to his throat and threatened to kill himself if she didn't make up with him—so she did!

And now they were engaged.

Kathy asked what God had spoken to her about the decision. Jackie just brushed the question off. "He's the one I want to marry, and that's that."

We didn't see much of Jackie until about a month after the wedding when she came over again to talk. It was a much different conversation this time.

"I just made the biggest mistake of my life," she said soberly, "and now I'm stuck."

When it came to her love life, Jackie's answer to the question, "Whose are you?" was "Mine!" That choice brought her into a painful relationship and great loss. Now that she has come back to the place of choosing allegiance to God in relationships, her pain is being redeemed for His purposes, and God has even incorporated that redemptive work into her life purpose.

Jackie's story is one of grace and renewal, but it is also one of lost opportunity and rejecting God's purposes. The lesson is that it's impossible to fulfill your destiny as a believer without a fundamental allegiance to the lordship of Christ. Allegiance is the palette you paint your life purpose with. Change the colors, and everything else about the picture of your purpose changes. Unfortunately, Jackie found that out the hard way.

The Pledge of Allegiance

One of the mistakes I've made as a coach is just assuming that the believers I work with have made the lordship decision. In doing so, I missed an important area of transformation, and served my clients less well than I could have. So let's take a look at what allegiance is, and then we'll discuss how to coach it.

Making Jesus Lord goes beyond trusting Him as savior.[8] It is a one-time decision make that sets the fundamental direction of your life as one of allegiance to Christ. It is taking your hands off and putting God in charge of everything in your life. A "Pledge of Allegiance" to the Kingdom of God might go something like this:

> *"Jesus, I want you to be in charge of my life. You decide what you want me to do, and I'll do it. I'm inviting you now into every area of my heart and my actions. I choose to keep nothing hidden, under my control or off limits to*

8 The early church did not seem to recognize this distinction—you got the whole package at once or nothing at all. Putting the theological questions aside, I think in our day it seems to help people understand lordship to talk about the lordship decision and salvation separately.

you. You and I both know I can't even walk this out without your help, so I am asking for that, too. Whenever I hit a place where I can't let go, you have permission to change my heart and make me willing to go there with you."

Making Jesus Lord doesn't mean that from then on we always do the right thing, or never resist what God intends for us. Otherwise, we'd all be disqualified. The lordship decision means our answer to the question, "Whose am I?" is "Jesus'."

Here's an analogy with a more everyday goal. Let's say that at 16 Holly decides to pursue her dream of becoming a soccer player, and rising to the maximum level of her abilities. There is a one-time decision where she sets her heart on being a soccer player (her identity) and doing what it takes to become one. Her decision sets the overall trajectory of her life.

Each day contains decisions related to Holly's athletic aspirations. Am I going to run today? How far? Do I have the courage to try out for the varsity? Will I spend my vacation at a soccer camp or hanging out with my friends? Will I believe in my future enough to risk my savings on joining a summer travel team?

Before Holly made the decision to focus on soccer, every choice involved balancing soccer against other priorities in her life and trying to sort out what was most important at that moment. But once she made that one dream her life mission, those other choices became much easier. The one-time decision of what was supremely important guided all the lesser decisions about daily priorities.

It is impossible to fulfill your destiny as a believer without a fundamental allegiance to the lordship of Christ.

That kind of "pledge of allegiance" is a good picture of the lordship decision. It is powerful because once made, every other choice to follow God is easier. When believers with a life pattern of making Jesus Lord realize that God is asking for something, they are able to choose it and move on while others are still wrestling with competing voices.

The lordship decision frees up an incredible amount of energy for pursuing God's purpose for your life. Instead of struggling over each small decision, or spending half your time following God and half running away, your heart's inclination pushes you steadily in one direction. Over time, you reach the place where your heart is so set toward God that you have to put forth quite an effort to **not** obey.

Allegiance Case Study

In this coaching dialog, watch how the coach helps this Christian couple connect what they want in marriage with a deeper allegiance to Christ in their marital life.

Pete and Valerie met in their 50's, two years after Pete's first wife died. Neither was looking to remarry, but as they got to know one another they felt a strong attraction and said their vows to each other two years later. Valerie was closely linked with her extended family, still lived near them in the neighborhood she grew up in, and didn't want to move. Pete had come to Rochester to be with his wife during her treatment, but had never been able to find satisfying work in the city, and yearned for the wide open spaces of Montana. We'll pick up the coaching conversation part-way through:

"So what I'm hearing you say is that you really want this job."

"Yeah, it's a once-in-a-lifetime opportunity. A 5,000-acre property, I'm head of the team, great benefits, the whole nine yards."

"So what are you going to do?"

"I really want to go for it! I've been in this dead-end job for three years, and I get a paycheck, but this is my chance to do what I've always wanted."

"So how are you going to make that decision?"

"Well, they want me to go up there and work the job for three weeks to make sure I'm the right guy, and then we'll finalize it."

"Let me rephrase that: what's your process for hearing the Lord on this? Do you need to get any counsel, or talk to your wife, or spend time in prayer, or anything along those lines?"

"Oh, right. It all came up pretty quickly. Val and I have talked a bit and she says she is willing to follow me if this is what I think I'm supposed to do. I just feel like I should be a good steward of my gifts and really use them."

"So Val is saying she will follow you to Montana. Is that what she really wants to do?"

"Um… I'm not exactly sure."

"Just take your best shot. If Val were going to tell you right now where she really wanted to live, what do think she'd say?"

"She'd probably say she wants to stay here with her family."

"So what I'm hearing is that she's willing to go but she doesn't really want to. How does that feel to you when you say it out loud?"

"Not so hot…" [long pause]

"Can I make an observation here?"

"Sure."

"Several times I've noticed that when you two make a major decision, Val defers to you and tells you what you want to hear, even though she'd be disappointed. And you defer to what she wants and decide not to follow your dreams, even though you are disappointed. But what I don't see is the two of you coming together and reaching the place where you are both fully convinced you are doing what God is telling you, together. Chew on that a bit—is that accurate, or am I missing something?"

Pete has a strong desire for career fulfillment, but the coach is not hearing much of a decision-making process other than, "I want it so I'm going for it." So he asks about process.

Since Pete didn't get the question the first time, the coach provides several sample answers in the question.

That this couple has talked briefly about a major move and she is "willing to follow" is a red flag.

Instead of moralizing to about loving his wife, the coach helps him tune into her needs.

The coach shares an observation, then asks Pete to evaluate it. In coaching, the client gets to assign meaning to his own actions.

"Well... we both tend to be conflict avoiders. And you're probably right that I tend to just give in rather than have a conflict, and so does she. Maybe after losing Carol I'm just afraid of losing someone again. So when a conflict starts, I just back off."

"So play that out. What would the outcome be for your relationship if for the next 10 years every time there is tension you acted on that fear and backed off?"

"That wouldn't be good. I would probably end up pretty angry because I hadn't really been myself."

"And what would happen to Val if she didn't say what she really wanted and deferred to you for 10 years?"

"That's not good either. I'm thinking she wouldn't feel very loved. It seems like if I keep acting on that fear, that I'm going to get the very thing I'm afraid of."

"Good insight. So what do you want to do about that?"

"Well, I think we need to talk this through. I need to be honest about where I'm at, and ask her to tell me what she really wants, too."

"Do you want to make that an action step?"

"Yes, I do."

"Sounds great! Now let me challenge you to take one step further: I really believe that God will speak to you about what you should do, and that both of you hearing Him can bring you together as one on this. What would it look like if you as a couple set out to move beyond those fears to follow God together as 'one flesh?'"

"We'd be talking a lot more. And being open about what we felt instead of trying so hard to please the other person—and probably even praying together some. I like that idea of doing decisions together instead of dancing around each other like we are now."

"Now here's the challenge. For that to work, you're going to have to commit your marriage to Christ together—make a once and for all choice that in your marriage you'll do things God's way. Is that a step you'd consider taking?"

"It sounds scary, but it also sounds sort of exciting, to really shoot for the best. We'll talk about it!"

Observing in a non-judgmental way leads quickly into talking about root fears (these are the real lordship issues).

The coach allows the client to hypothetically play out the long term implications of a choice—this tends to increase motivation for change.

The coach affirms Pete's relationship with God, while challenging him to go deeper. The coaching approach to confrontation is to challenge people forward, to what they can become, instead of backward toward what they did wrong.

When to Go Deeper

The key to this conversation hitting pay dirt was that it engaged a clear teachable moment: a place where current circumstances motivated Pete to reexamine his core beliefs. Teachable moments are the clearest sign that lordship issues can be broached, because they are evidence of the Holy Spirit's activity, convicting and readying the person for change. When this preparatory work is done, you won't need to break down the door to a person's heart, because that person is already feeling a deep need for change.

Here are some additional clues that can indicate a readiness to deal with fundamental allegiance questions:

1. **Connections between current circumstances and ultimate destiny**
God often leverages what we care about most deeply to gain access to our hearts. So when God is messing with the coachee's life purpose, that's a signal. One client was sharing how frustrated he was to always be working in organizations with serious internal conflict. His string of experiences was so striking that I began to explore whether his calling involved bringing people together around a middle ground. When he realized that his circumstances were preparing him for his life mission, he stopped resisting and began to lean into them as part of God's plan for his life.
2. **Things are stuck and practical steps aren't working**
When practical solutions don't work, it's time to look at inner obstacles. If something seems much harder than it ought to be, look for internal obstacles connected to allegiance issues.
3. **The person is in a transitional season**
The primary focus of God's activity in transitions is inward. He brings what we are doing to an end to make room in our thoughts (and our schedules!) for reexamining our inner world. Therefore, it is hard to go wrong in taking the conversation about almost any significant occurrence to that level!
4. **The reasoning seems irrational**
Recently, I listened to a coachee disqualify himself from working with parents of teens (even though he'd been a youth pastor for 10 years!) because his children weren't that old yet. My challenge was, "So Jesus has nothing to say to us about marriage, because he's not married yet?" After a good laugh and a little reflection, he began to tune into the underlying fear that was the real obstacle. When we say something that even *we* know doesn't hold water, reexamining the belief behind it seems natural.
5. **The person is experiencing major adversity**
Asking the allegiance question is costly, so it takes unusual circumstances or high stakes to get us to go there. Clients who are experiencing pain, loss or intense frustration are more likely to want to ask the allegiance questions.

Allegiance After the Lordship Decision

God is always pursuing our hearts to bring about a fuller union with Him. We respond by making Him Lord of whatever each new day brings to the surface. So the process of making Jesus Lord is never truly finished: there are always new areas of the heart for even mature believers to bring to Jesus. As Paul says, we are to work out our salvation with fear and trembling; "for it is God who is at work in you, both to will and to work for His good pleasure" (Phil. 2:12-13).

A while back one coachee (Jeff) was entangled in a messy, cash-hemorrhaging business partnership. In a wide ranging conversation exploring how he'd gotten himself in that position in the first place, Jeff began to talk about his pattern of attaching himself to spiritual role models and then getting burned by them. As his most recent spiritual mentor crashed and burned, God asked, "Who is your rock?" Jeff's take-away from that experience was learning not to entrust himself so unquestioningly to people.[9]

Later, when the conversation got back around to his work, I remarked, "It seems like in business you are also looking to team up with people who give you a sense of certainty in decisions—"

"Oh!" he exclaimed abruptly, cutting me off. "That's it. I'm looking to them to be my rock in business just like I looked to pastors to be my rock. I need to reflect on that."

Allegiance issues can come up anywhere in the coaching conversation, with anyone. Here, Jeff discovered a need to lean on Jesus more fully in business decisions. Because he had already made the one-time lordship decision, Jeff was able to move quickly toward surrendering that area to Christ once he identified it.

This story highlights two important allegiance principles. The first is that God is actively taking every circumstance we experience and using them to shape us into the image of Christ (see Romans 8:28-29). No matter what we face, God will build our character through it if we let Him. So *every* coaching issue presents the opportunity to talk about allegiance, when we go to a deeper level and talk about *being* instead of just *doing*.

Allegiance and Hypothetical Questions

It is often helpful in allegiance decisions to examine the question hypothetically. Being able to weigh different options in theory moves you out of the fear realm and helps engage your mind and heart instead of just emotion.

- *"What could happen here if you threw self-interest to the wind and just choose to do whatever God told you? Give me a scenario."*
- *"If you looked at this like an investor, and you were going to arrange your life here for maximum return for the Kingdom, what could you do with it?"*
- *"What do you fear would happen if you went down this road? What's the thing that wells up when you think of doing this?"*
- *"Take your best guess: what do you think God might be asking from you here? Why that?"*

The second principle is an important balance to the first: convicting people of their sinfulness and need to change is the Holy Spirit's job (Jn. 16:8). He's very good at it: he's worked with billions of people over thousands of years, and he has much more experience at this kind of thing than you do. So let him do his job.

Thankfully, it isn't up to us to figure out where people haven't made Jesus Lord and get them to do it. Your part as a coach is to come alongside *once circumstances*

9 "See John 2:23-25 for how Jesus handled this.

already have coachees asking the fundamental questions, and help them go where the Holy Spirit is already taking them. So unless the change process has already begun, trying to coach someone into making Jesus Lord isn't going to work—that's your agenda.

Levels of Engaging

One tool that works well for coaching allegiance issues is the Levels of Engaging. Three change levels where we can function are:[10]

1. Endurance
2. Head Change (external)
3. Heart Change

Let's look at a scenario to explain the different levels. A person comes to you who feels stuck in his job and complains that he isn't going anywhere professionally. Someone functioning at the Endurance level might say, "My job situation is terrible. I am overworked, underpaid but I can't afford to quit. I guess I'll just have to soldier on." When you are enduring, the goal is simply to survive, and maybe win a little sympathy along the way to make you feel better.

While it can be worthwhile to let a person in a difficult situation vent a little, it's hard to create movement when someone sees their task as simply enduring. One way to break the logjam is to observe how they are responding and invite a different viewpoint: "When you talk about this, it sounds like there is nothing you can do about it. What would you do if you really believed this could change?"

The most common engaging style is at the Head level. This client might say, "My goal is to find a new job where I can really flourish," or "I've realized I'm lacking some key skills I need to move up in the company." The objective is practical and external—the client wants change, but sees it simply as a matter of doing different things, instead of becoming a different person. Many great changes take place on this level, but it doesn't touch the client's fundamental allegiance, because it doesn't require a change of heart.

The Heart level of engaging goes further: the problem is not with my circumstances, but with me. It isn't just that I *did* something wrong or I lack a skill. My performance is a natural outgrowth of who I am, and it won't change until I change. Engaging at the heart level might sound like this: "My boss told me last month that the reason I am not promoted is that I use people instead of relating to them, and I can't shake that challenge. I want to figure out why I do that and how I can change." When you get the level of motive (why I do this), the door is wide open to talk about allegiance!

Recently, one of my peer coaches challenged me on a pattern I have of minimizing pain by joking around at inappropriate times in the conversation. Going to the heart level on that issue means asking, "Why do I do that? What drives me to laugh when I

10 For more tools and examples of coaching the levels of engaging, see *Coaching Questions* by Tony Stoltzfus, pg. 94-95.

tell a painful story? And if I am doing it to manage my intensity in the conversation, what is it that produces an intensity that needs managing in the first place?" Managing my behavior is a head-level strategy. Heart change happens when I ask, "What does this say about me?"

Coaching in the Fullness of Time

The biggest challenge in coaching allegiance is allowing God to determine the timing, instead of trying to manufacture the moment. Scripture says that "A man's gift makes room for him, and will bring him before kings" (Prov. 18:6; RSV). I like to state the converse: "A man's flesh makes room for him, and will drag him through the mud." Our difficulties are often the direct result of the lordship issues in our lives. It's hard to watch someone keep doing the same thing that causes pain, and resist the temptation to jump in and try to save them.

It's helpful to remember that allegiance issues are fundamental decisions about our identity—and identity is not easily changed. My experience as a coach is that it takes extraordinary circumstances (often painful) to produce the level of motivation required for real heart transformation. I've worked with leaders who had to go around the same mountain half-a-dozen times before they were ready to deal with God. Just because I see something I think the client needs to change doesn't mean it is God's time to address it.

Coaching Allegiance

1. **Watch** for God to bring a teachable moment.
2. **Pray** that God sends the person the circumstances they need to change.
3. **Position Yourself** to be the go-to person when the client is ready to re-evaluate.

Think about it this way: how many things does God see right now that you could be doing better? (That's a big number!) Does He tell you all those things at once? No—He has you in a life-long developmental process that moves you steadily forward. So treating my coachees like God treats me means only addressing what's on God's agenda in that season of their lives.

Since we can't change hearts on our own, we must wait for God to bring a teachable moment that creates a context for change. A key coaching tool here is prayer. I may ask God, "Send him the experiences he needs to fully embrace you in this area," or "Do in her the things she can't do for herself." If I'm praying, I'm actively doing something with my intuitive insights, which helps me let go of trying to force them down the client's throat.

Another technique is positioning yourself for reevaluation. Rocky was an ENFP on the Myers-Briggs (highly relational, unstructured, future-oriented) who found it difficult to objectively evaluate the opportunities that came his way. His glass-half-full demeanor caused him to regularly overestimate his chances of success and underestimate the time it took to get there.

The first time I challenged him on this pattern, he was simply not ready to hear. The new thing he was interested in looked so good that he was convinced he could find a way to make it happen despite obvious obstacles. Instead of pushing, I said, "OK—I may be off on that one. Since it is going to take some work to fit this in, how about if we make getting it done part of our coaching agenda for the next few sessions?" That was fine with Rocky—and in the process of trying to pull it off together, *he* was the one who raised the idea of working on getting more realistic in his projections.

If a client *reaaallly* wants to do something that seems self-defeating, and isn't ready to hear differently, standing in front of that speeding train isn't a winning strategy. Instead, set things up so that you have a chance to talk about the outcome of that decision down the road. If you are working on it together, or set up some check-ins to evaluate progress down the road, if the teachable moment happens you'll be positioned right there to take advantage of it.

Coaching the Allegiance Checkup (4.1)

This devotional exercise helps us examine our hearts in five areas where we often seek to be our own masters. The idea is to pray the prayer in the *Allegiance Checkup*, watch our internal reactions and then journal on the experience. The exercise is about *observing* our responses, not about trying to control them or give the "right" answers.

This is a challenging step, so you may want to talk through how to do it honestly and yet experience God's love in the midst of human frailty.

Ask coachees to send you their journal for the exercise, and look for the feelings, doubts, joys, and fears they are experiencing. The raw emotions that surface are places to probe gently.

We are using emotion here as a window to the soul. By describing emotions, people can access information that is difficult to get at cognitively (our minds tend to create defenses around areas we feel are threatening or uncomfortable). But to take advantage of the insights emotion can give, *you must ask an emotion question*, like the first two in the list below. The third question is a cognitive question, the fourth is a will question. The last two questions are useful once coachees have entered into their interior world and experienced what is going on there. But if you ask one of the last two questions first, you are likely to get their analysis of what they think they should be experiencing instead of their true interior condition.

- *"You mentioned that this was discouraging. Enter into that emotion and describe it for me."*
- *"When you prayed the part about control, what were you feeling?"*
- *"What can you learn from this about what draws you or drives you?"*
- *"What would God say to you in this place?"*

When people are wrestling at this deep level, we want them to be able to resonate with our shared human condition (that we are all bottomless wells of unresolved issues) during the challenge. While some coaches feel that you should never bring yourself into the conversation, I believe that it can be very helpful at times to share *brief* examples of personal wrestlings in these places to maintain a feeling of safety and mutuality.

Needs, Losses and Bonds (4.2)

When an area surfaces where the client struggles with allegiance, that's actually a good thing—the first step in change is always becoming aware of the need to change. This awareness is evidence of the activity of the Holy Spirit. It can have a deep impact on people to celebrate consciousness of sin (not sin itself!) as evidence of the Spirit's work, instead of treating it as a reason for guilt or shame. Sometimes we expend so much energy feeling bad about ourselves that there is no energy left to change.

However, if a client already has made the lordship decision and the normal application of discipline still leaves them struggling,[11] I look for an underlying reason why discipline isn't working. Find the reason, and you can change the behavior.

An exercise I use (either verbally or as a reflective step between appointments) to help find the reason is called *Needs, Losses and Bonds* (4.2). These questions probe the inner motives and drives behind stress or a struggle to change. Needs are what you are trying to get by functioning this way, while losses are what we fear will happen to us if we don't. And bonds are why this issue has such a hold on us.

Earlier today I spoke with a pastor whose poor past decisions were creating a lot of stress in his role. As he was reflecting on them, he said, "I knew they weren't good decisions at the time, but I went ahead anyway. When people around me know what they want, I seem to just defer. Why do I do that?"

I used a "Needs" question to help surface what was going on in him: "What do you gain by trusting their discernment more than you trust your own?" That query became an action step for him to reflect on during the week. The answer to that question is usually a basic human need like approval, security, certainty or protection. There was something very important this pastor gained by deferring to the choices of others, and the pattern won't change until he discovers that reason.

Life Coaching for Leadership Couples

Keeping spouses on board is an important part of life purpose discovery. Ideally, couples go through this process together. In marriage, the two shall become one—and hence, their individual destinies are intricately woven together. I frequently encourage my clients to invite their spouses into our life coaching calls. Working at purpose as partners enriches the client's experience, provides excellent feedback along the way, and draws the marriage closer together. Some spouses stay in the background and comment every so often, some engage the process as a partnership (and even do all the exercises alongside their spouse), and some clients find that they cannot move forward in their own callings until the spouse is also clear on his/her life purpose.

When working with Christian leaders, the most common couple-specific issue is one partner's destiny inappropriately dominates the marriage. I often work with couples where the husband is moving forward in a clear sense of call while the wife is just following along with little grasp of her own destiny. This often surfaces when major decisions need to be made about the couple's future. Here's what it sounds like.

---

11 Obviously, areas like addictions and psychological illnesses fall outside the bounds of what we are talking about, since we shouldn't be coaching those situations anyway.

"OK. So you're feeling led to either go back to grad school or to start a business and you just need to sort out the alternatives."

"That's pretty much it, yeah."

"What's your wife saying about this?"

"I think she's pretty much on board. She's open to moving if we need to."

"What does 'pretty much on board' mean? Can you tell me exactly what she is saying?"

"Well, she's concerned about uprooting the family and all. I get a lot of emotional stuff from her and I'm not always sure how to take it. Some days she'll blurt out, 'We need to get out of here! This job just doesn't fit you!' Then a week later when I mention a school I'm thinking of she's all torn up about losing her friends again. But it always comes down in the end to her saying, 'I'm committed to you and I'll follow you wherever we need to go.'"

"So is what you are hearing from her when you talk about this decision her feelings, or her discernment?"

"Pretty much her feelings, I guess."

"What has she told you so far that the Lord has said to her about this choice?"

"I'm not sure she's told me anything that has the force of, 'here's what God is saying.' I wish she would."

"And what has she said that she wants in this decision?"

"Um… I guess I'm not sure. We've never really gotten to that place."

"Is that what you want? Does that pattern make you feel more secure and drawn closer in your marriage, or less?"

"Definitely less. It makes me feel really exposed. I think she thinks she's honoring me as a husband, but I really wish she'd just tell me what her heart is saying."

"Can you identify what you are doing that is feeding into this cycle?"

"I've let that go on, and not pushed for her discernment. And we've pretty much prioritized my destiny—I mean, she's kept the house and raised the kids and done everything in the background so that I could pursue my call. That seemed to work OK until the kids were gone, but now that we're empty nesters, she's floundering. In fact, I don't even know what my own wife's purpose is—that's not good, is it? I need to pursue her on this."

In our cultural context, it is common for male Christian leaders (especially ones in the ministry) to assume that their personal call is the priority in the marriage. They then fold their wife's energy and abilities into the pursuit of that call, instead of making it a priority to pursue *her* heart and draw out *her* unique destiny.

But this pattern violates Paul's most fundamental admonition to husbands: "Husbands love your wives, as Christ loved the church *and gave himself up for her,* to make her holy, cleansing her by washing with water through the word, that he might present her to himself as a radiant church without stain or wrinkle or blemish" (Eph. 5:26-27). The husband is supposed to exhibit sacrificial, *agape* love by giving himself up for the wife. Unfortunately, the pattern among ministry leaders is often the opposite: the man expects his wife to give up herself for *his* call.

This verse calls us to model the way we love our wives after how Christ laid down His life for us. Compared to Christ, who allowed Himself to be tortured to death so that we could have a future and a hope, husbands who don't aggressively pursue, promote and even find ways to defer to their wives' callings sorely miss the mark.

One of the oft-quoted Proverbs is, "Hope deferred makes the heart sick" (Prov. 13:12). And I've coached some heartsick spouses over the years. They've deferred, served and sacrificed for decades to advance their husband's call, but haven't been loved in that same way in return. That lack of love has left a hole in their hearts that aches for their husband to pursue them and help them become who they were created to be.

I've been deeply touched by men of God I know who have chosen to make room for their spouses' callings and loved them well in this way. A good friend who is a career pastor in his 50's chose his last pastoral position based on where his wife wanted to go to grad school—and then they moved to where *she* got a job. He was very clear before the move that she had sacrificed to put him through grad school and had moved around for his call, and now he was going to step back and sacrifice for her. He ended up substitute teaching in the public schools for several years to help make ends meet until he finally found a ministry position in their community. *That's* laying down your life for your wife!

Laying Down Your Life

- *"When was the last time you relocated or sacrificed on your own career future to allow your wife to pursue her life purpose?"*
- *"Of the time, energy and money you've spend on pursuing your callings in the last 10 years, what percentage has gone toward yours, and what percentage toward hers?"*
- *"What time, money or energy are you personally investing right now to help your wife do the things she was created to do?"*
- *"How much of your wife's time is spent doing what she loves? How much is spent doing what she has to do to keep things afloat? What do you want to do about that?"*

A Couple's Purpose

When working with married clients, life coaches need to be alert to how purpose is handled in the marriage. When we're working on major decisions, I want to know the spouse's role in decision-making:

- *"How do you make decisions together?"*
- *"What is the process you use to come to a place of unity?"*
- *"How is your spouse engaging this decision?"*
- *"Are you getting her discernment or just her deference (or her feelings?)*

It's a red flag when one partner is just going along with things or always deferring to the other's desires and decisions. When I'm working with a man (especially a high "D" on the DiSC™!) who says that his wife is on board, I'll often ask, "What exactly did she say?" or "What has she told you that she wants here?"

Saying "Yes" can mean everything from being totally on board to giving in to keep the peace. When you bring the spouse into the process: it makes it much easier to surface and troubleshoot obstacles within the marriage relationship.

4.1  Allegiance Checkup

Take these five areas and pray each one during your devotions. Use the words given or expand on them. The idea is to *observe* what goes on in you as you pray, not to try to make yourself into the perfect Christian. Use the reflection questions at the bottom to jot down the thoughts and feelings you experience as you pray. Then simply be present before God with who you are and what you wrote. You are His.

Control

"Lord, run my life. I let go of the reins—I want you to order my life and give me what you think I need. I let go of trying to control my circumstances—I will accept whatever comes from your hand. I let go of controlling the people around me, whether it is through anger or argument or exerting power. I embrace you as my master."

Money

"Lord, I want you to manage all my money, all the time. I will give it, keep it, spend it or save it just as you say. I give you my anxieties about money, too. You are my security and my provider. Thank you for all that I have: it is enough for me. I am content with you and what you've given me: I choose not to look to anything I can buy for my happiness."

Recognition

"Lord, be my reward. Hearing 'well done' from you is the only recognition I choose to work for. I let go of trying to please or impress anyone else so they will like me. I let go of the drive to be famous or accomplished or competent. And I choose to face into conflict and tell the truth, because I trust the outcome to you.

Relationship/Intimacy

"Lord, I trust you with my relationships. You are the protector of my children and the guardian of my heart in friendships. I put you in charge of every area of my marriage (or if I marry). You are the love of my life, and you are enough for me. I won't seek to get my relational needs met my way. My sex life is yours, too—in thought and action, I choose to do things your way and lead a life of purity."

Self-Image

"Lord, I admit that I am a sinner to the core. I utterly die to the need to look like I have it all together—I don't. I let go of needing to be a 'somebody,' of crafting a public image, or of spinning my stories so I look better. I choose to be open about my faults, apologize quickly, and be who I am instead of trying to polish my image. My identity is in your hands."

Reflection

1. How did you experience praying this prayer?
2. Track yourself as you pray through each area. Can you honestly say this? Was it easy or hard? Did it open you to God or make you want to hide?
3. What emotions came to the surface as you prayed? (i.e. joy, fear, relief, anger, etc.) What's behind those feelings?
4. What do these observations tell you about yourself?

Needs, Losses and Bonds  4.2

When it seems unusually hard to get something done or you struggle to change a behavior, it can be helpful to stop and look for an underlying reason instead of just trying harder. Set some time apart and reflect on the questions below to help identify what's going on under the surface when change is unusually tough.

Needs

- *"What do you gain by doing this?"*
- *"And what does that give you?"*
- *"What does this pattern (or behavior) give you that you feel you need?"*
- *"What desire or need drives how you function here?"*

Losses

- *"What are you afraid will happen if you go there?"*
- *"What will you lose if this changes?"*
- *"What are you holding onto or pursuing here that you don't want to lose?"*
- *"What's the worst case scenario?"*

Bonds

- *"What memory, desire, fear or drive has a hold on you here?"*
- *"What are you dealing with that feels bigger or more powerful than you?"*
- *"What holds you back?"*
- *"What kind of outside help would give you the best chance of breaking that bond?"*

Coaching Tip
Because this exercise is about becoming more aware of hidden, subconscious drives, you may need to come back to it several times or work on it over a period of weeks before the person begins to understand what is really going on inside.

4.3 Clarifying Your Allegiance

If you are grappling with pledging allegiance to God in your dreams, life goals or just in daily life, these reflection questions can help you plumb what's going on in you.

God's Touch

- *"Where is God asking more of you or bringing something new into your life?"*
- *"What's God's growth agenda for you right now?"*
- *"How can you adjust your perspective to better engage this as preparing you for God's purposes for your life instead of as a duty, annoyance or problem?"*

Your Heart

- *"What fears or hesitancies surface when you think about this new thing?"*
- *"What draws you on, and where do you hold back?"*
- *"How does God want to meet you or touch you there?"*

Your Sonship

Now, soak for a few moments in the idea that God is 100% for you—you are His dear friend, and He wants nothing except for you to do well, to leave behind the good for the best, and to come up higher with Him. Read the last section of Romans chapter eight where Paul asks, "Who shall separate us from the love of Christ…?" and reflect on these questions:

- *"What is God saying to you about His love for you in this area?"*
- *"How do you want to respond to God's heart?"*
- *"How do you want to be with God in this endeavor or decision?"*

Question 2: Who Am I? (Design)

"The glory of God is a man fully alive."
St. Irenaeus

Saul was between a rock and a hard place again. While his physical attributes garnered attention and opportunity, he'd always battled with fears and insecurities. On the day of his coronation, he'd hidden in the baggage to escape the responsibility of his new role. A few years later, worried sick as his army melted away in the face of the Philistine war machine, he'd stifled his conscience and offered the priestly sacrifice himself in a desperate attempt to keep up morale. Naturally, Samuel showed up just as he was completing the deed. With words that chilled his heart, Samuel announced that Saul's reign would not endure—God had chosen another king for his people. And the Philistine army was still camped right over the next ridge!

Somehow Saul survived that terrible moment, and things appeared to be going well in spite of Samuel's prophecy of doom. He had won victories on every border, and the people acclaimed him for safeguarding their homes and farms. His old mentor had even come back with a commission from God: destroy the Amalekites. Leading a crusade with Samuel's approval restored his popularity, and the recognition and acclaim held back the gnawing fears inside him. Then everything fell apart.

Instead of destroying the spoil, the people wanted to keep their Amalekite treasures. Saul compromised and kept everyone happy. But on the way home from his victory celebration, Saul ran into the prophet—who shredded his self-image by calling out his disobedience and telling him that God had torn away his kingdom. Saul managed to worm one concession out of Samuel—to save face by honoring him before the people—but it soon became clear that Saul and Samuel had had a falling out, and as the story of Agag's beheading spread, the people could easily figure out why.

Saul's old paranoia returned with a vengeance, and this time there was no Samuel, no promise from God and no sense of God's presence to withstand them. Things got so bad that courtiers suggested recruiting a musician to ease Saul's tormented soul.

In that moment, one of Saul's warriors remembered a young man he'd met named David. "I have seen a son of Jesse the Bethlehemite who is a skillful musician, a mighty man of valor, a warrior, one prudent in speech, and a handsome man; and the Lord is with him" (I Sam. 16:18). So David, youngest son of a poor sheep herder, secretly anointed king by Samuel, was plucked from anonymity, brought to the palace and became part of the king's retinue. He was the epitome of the up-and-coming man. Whenever the evil mood came on Saul, David would play and the king was comforted.

A Tale of Two Callings

I Samuel 16 tells the tale of two intertwined callings. Both men's innate qualities were tied to their roles. Saul's outstanding characteristic was his physical prowess: he was "a choice and handsome man, there was not a more handsome person than he among the sons of Israel; from his shoulders and up he was taller than any of the people" (I Sam. 9:2) Saul was a man of action: early in his kingship he exhibited the personality traits of a dominant leader who could think strategically, rally people to a vision, and get things done (see I Samuel 11). In other words, Saul's strengths and personality type fit his call.

The same was true of David. What got David noticed and brought him into national leadership roles were his innate strengths—his musical aptitude, his athletic ability (note his skill with a sling), his handsome appearance. As a songwriter, David was good with words. He also exhibited great natural charisma and relational instincts, which immediately attracted people. Saul loved him greatly, but soon regretted it—David's favor with the people rapidly surpassed that of the king himself.

While Calling, Passion, Preparation, and Allegiance were all part of his ascent to the throne, David's innate Design—his strengths, talents, gifts and personality type—was what initially launched his career. Because God created him for his life mission, David's design provided clues to what he was called to do and be. Similarly, exploring the gifts, strengths, and personality types of your coachees yields important clues to their destinies.

Here are a few universal principles we can glean from David and Saul's story:

- Many of their innate abilities were evident from young adulthood or earlier—just like yours are.
- Their strengths and personalities fit their God-given callings—just like yours do.

- These innate qualities were instrumental in moving them into their destiny roles—and so will yours.
- Their Design was the basic equipment God gave them to steward—just as your task is to maximize your innate strengths.
- Strengths alone aren't enough—building character is a must to fulfill one's call.

Understanding Design

Design is the starting point for life purpose discovery. It consists of two complimentary areas: *Strengths* and *Personality Type*. After a brief overview of each area, we'll introduce a Baseline Assessment tool that helps you decide where to focus the search. Next, we'll walk through a suite of exercises and coaching techniques used to find a person's design, and demonstrate them with examples and sample dialogs. Finally, we'll present tools for aligning the client's role with their design.

Design is the sum of the innate qualities you were born with: your *nature* (as opposed to *nurture*, which falls under the heading of Preparation). *Strengths* are the talents and aptitudes that make you naturally good at certain things. They let you perform at an exceptional level in a certain area, applying less effort and for greater results.

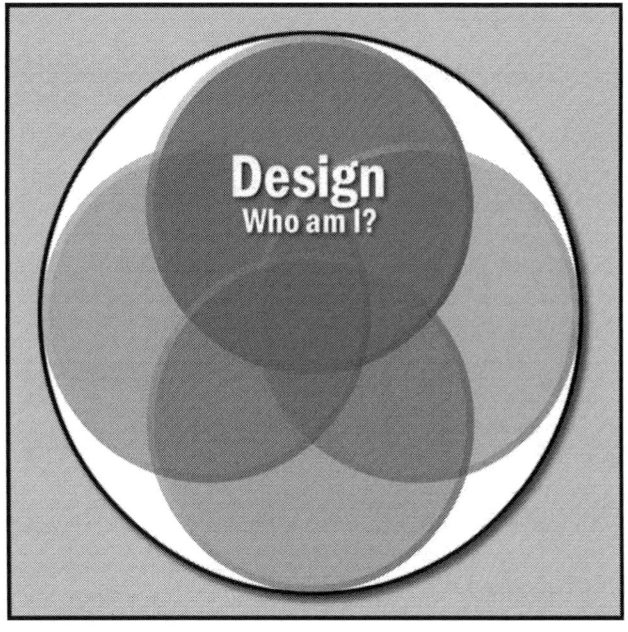

Strengths can be physical qualities like endurance or quick reflexes that make you good at sports, a pleasing singing voice or the fine motor skills of a surgeon. Strengths can also be aptitudes like an ear for music, a knack for foreign languages or the ability to visualize things in 3-D. Or you might be gifted at empathizing with others (an emotional aptitude), or be a former strong-willed child who can overcome any obstacle (a volitional strength).

Personality Types are shorthand language for describing our unique, inner traits. While strengths describe abilities and outward performance, Personality Types attempt to explain our soul's inner workings and how they influence our actions. They provide a model for understanding how different people think, take in information, make decisions, and relate to both their inner world and the world around them. They describe what goes on inside our heads. (Men, take note: learning personality types might actually help you understand what the women in your life are thinking!) Therefore, our type says a lot about where we excel, what we enjoy, and what roles and activities energize or drain us. Obviously, this is of real interest in life purpose discovery.

Launching the Search

So where should you start the destiny discovery process? While you can begin anywhere on the Purpose Diagram, it usually makes sense to start with what we began life with: the innate abilities that make up our Design. Design underlies what energizes and motivates us (our Passions), what needs and people we respond to (Calling), and influences where we gain credentials and accomplishments (Preparation).

There are other reasons to begin the search here:

- Design is the easiest area for coachees to get a handle on (Calling is the hardest).
- Design is age-independent: any teen can gain by looking at it, whereas Preparation and Calling tend to crystallize later in life.
- Objective assessments and powerful, well-developed tools for Design (like DiSC™, StrengthsFinder© or MBTI©) abound.
- Since innate qualities don't tend to change over time, Design insights are more easily retained, and stay relevant for all of your life.
- It's easy to generate a quick win in this area to energize the coaching process.

Creating a Baseline

If a client wants to discover and align with his or her destiny, a good starting point is a *Baseline Assessment.* Its purpose is to identify what the person already knows about his or her life purpose, so you can customize the life purpose discovery process client's unique needs. A baseline can be administered verbally, by asking the questions during a coaching session, or you can assign it as pre-work before an appointment.

On the following page is an example of a filled-out Baseline Assessment for Design (a blank copy is in the companion volume, *A Leader's Life Purpose Workbook* as exercise 6.1). Following it is a page on how to evaluate the client's responses. Similar Baseline Assessments and hints for evaluation are provided for Passion (exercise 9.1), Preparation (14.1) and Calling (17.1). You'll probably want the client to begin by doing all four. It's an excellent way to bring some overall structure to discovering an individual's purpose.

Design Baseline Assessment 1.1a

The questions below give us a baseline for creating your customized life purpose discovery plan. Take five to eight minutes to complete the assessment. If you don't know what to say on a question, or would have to dream up an answer on the spot, leave that question blank. This isn't a test where you try to get the right answers. We're trying to ascertain what you already know for sure about your life purpose so we know where to start.

1. What is your personality type (DiSC™, Myers-Briggs or other assessment)?

   I'm an 'S' on the DiSC

2. List several key characteristics associated with that personality type.

   I like to solve complex problems
   My fundamental drive is for competence and to make things better
   I like closure and I like to know what to expect (the J)

3. List the types of three family members or co-workers (if you know them). After each, give an example of how your personality type complements or conflicts with theirs.

   Don't know

4. Do you know your spiritual gifts? If so, what are your two top ones?

   Dreaming, Teaching

5. Name four in-born talents, abilities or strengths. What are you naturally very good at?

   I am good at strategizing things out into the future and making contingency plans
   I am great at soccer—have good reflexes, body control and speed
   Math comes easily to me
   I'm talented at organizing ideas and putting them into words

6. Name three weaknesses (places where you *aren't* naturally talented).

   None that really stand out

7. What percentage of the time does your job allow you to function in your best strengths?

   Maybe 10%

Evaluating the Design Baseline Assessment

The first three questions on the Design Baseline Assessment help you ascertain the client's knowledge of type. The five levels of personality type understanding (see box) help us quantify the client's understanding.

The first question reveals if the person knows their own type (Level I vs. Level II). Question two differentiates those who know what their type means from those who just know the letters (Level II vs. III). The third question identifies those who have learned to use type in everyday tasks and relationships (Level IV or V).

Once you know the level, it becomes much clearer what action steps to pursue. For instance, if the client is on Level I or II, doing a formal type assessment and validation with them might be a good first step. A specially-discounted on-line DiSC™ assessment is available through www.ALeadersLifePurpose.com. Or, clients operating at level III might want to learn the types of those around them (see exercise 6.2) and create steps to discuss different conflict, communication or working styles.

Type: Levels of Understanding

Level I: Don't know my type.

Level II: Know the letters but don't know what they mean.

Level III: Know my own type and understand what it means.

Level IV: Know my type and that of those around me, and use that understanding to communicate and relate more effectively.

Level V: Type expert. Can help others identify and understand their type and how it interacts with others' types.

By comparing the baseline results with the levels of proficiency they could achieve, you can show your coachees what exploring type could give them. Most people are at Levels I or II. Level III is usually sufficient for life purpose discovery, while moving to level IV or V offers the client powerful tools to work and relate more effectively. Organizational leaders benefit greatly from functioning at level IV or V.

The fourth question is about spiritual gifts. Look for whether coachees feel they have a gift and know what it is (only 60% of believers do), and if those gifts are actually listed in the Bible. In the example given, the individual has reported one biblical gift (teaching) and one that isn't found in the Bible (dreaming). That tells you something about the person's working knowledge of gifts! A gift assessment may need to be part of the growth plan.

The remaining questions inquire about strengths. Is the person listing innate talents or learned skills? Have they reported solid, valuable, prominent abilities, or are the strengths they list trivial or buried? Where they able to list their strengths at all? (If not, that's an interesting place to probe for obstacles.)

The fifth question on weaknesses is similar. Can the person confidently advance some significant weaknesses—areas he or she isn't good at? In the example given, the person hasn't listed any weaknesses at all. That should get your coaching intuition twitching!

The final question looks at alignment between Design and role. Lower scores can indicate a frustrating mismatch (maybe that's why they hired you as a coach), a lack of self-understanding of strengths and type or both.[12]

Creating a Growth Plan

Once you've reviewed the assessment together, you're ready to start planning how to explore the coachee's design. The information from the baseline keeps you from wasting time going back over ground the person has already covered. Coachees can also choose how far they want to go in exploring their design. In different seasons of life we need different levels of life purpose insight. Some may just want to learn enough to better make a career decision next month, while others are seeking to realign their whole lives around an ultimate legacy.

The next two chapters offer a series of exercises you can choose from to create a Design discovery plan that fits your client's agenda. Each chapter has several primary exercises, with secondary options for those who want or need to do additional work in that area. You don't have to do them all—just the ones that meet the client's needs.

To maintain high buy-in, involve the client as much as possible in creating the growth plan. Here are three possible approaches:

1. **Ask for a Strategy**
   Ask coachees to identify where they need to grow based on the assessment, and then solicit options and steps that translate those goals into actions.

While this option does a good job of keeping ownership with the client, it doesn't always work. The challenge is that the client may not know where the opportunities for growth are, let alone how to effectively pursue them.

In order to make a wise decision, you have to have a certain amount of information about the alternatives. These days, you wouldn't want to buy new a car without finding out the gas mileage it will get. In the same way, a client is going to need a certain amount of information about possible options in order to make good decisions. You have a set of life purpose tools the client doesn't know about (the options). So unless your client is pretty self-aware or has already done a fair amount of destiny work, you are going to have to provide that information for the client to make a wise decision. So our second possible approach is:

2. **Present Options**
   Come to agreement on the areas to focus on, present several tools that could move things forward, and ask the coachee to choose which ones seem most compelling.

I like to briefly describe several potential exercises or discovery steps, and then ask the client to choose the ones that seem most "compelling." To follow the analogy,

12 Role alignment should increase with age, so that leaders in their 50's and 60's function in roles that closely match their Design, while younger leaders may not. For more on convergent roles, see chapter 16.

I'm the car dealer showing you the different models we have on the lot (based on what you've said you want) and then asking you to decide which one best fits your needs. Another way to do this is to give clients the *Workbook*, point out the sections they might benefit from and ask them to choose which exercises to pursue. In general, the coaching technique is to present some options, and then stand back and let the coachee evaluate them and choose.

Note that you "come to agreement" on the areas to focus on. Often the client can identify *where* they need to grow ("I don't know my type") much more readily than *how* to produce that growth. The tools and exercises probably have to come from you.

Growth Plan Creation Strategies

1. **Ask** the client to develop a plan
2. **Present** options for the plan and ask the client for a choice
3. **Request** a response to a strategy you suggest

But there are times when even option two doesn't provide enough handles. Let's go back to our car-buying analogy for help. Normally when you buy a car, you'd have at least a mental list of features and qualities you want in a vehicle. But suppose a person who has never been in a car before goes into a dealership to buy one. In that case, they don't even know the *categories* of options they have to choose from. "I can get air conditioning? What would you use that for? And what is this lever on the floor between the seats?" If I'm the salesman, I have a *lot* of explaining to do before the person can really make an informed decision.

Or I can take a shortcut: ask the person what their overall goal is in buying a car ("I need to drive to work, but I can only afford $250 a month"), and then use my knowledge of the options on the lot to offer suggestions. That's option number three:

3. **Make a Request**
   Suggest several exercises, explain why you feel they would be beneficial, and ask the client to choose how to respond to your request.

I use requests when I get into an area that the client has never been before. For instance, if the person has never done a personality or gift assessment, they have no way of knowing what an assessment can do for them unless I explain it at length. Just like the car salesman, I may choose to do the explanation, or I may jump directly from their goal to the tools I have and make a request: "I believe a DiSC™ assessment and validation would help you reach your goal. Here's a request: how about if we take that first step, and once you experience what DiSC™ offers, you can decide how far to go with it."[13]

This goes back to understanding a life coach's role. It isn't our job to be a

13 At some point I always explain to my clients that they can respond in one of three ways to a request: they can say, "Great idea, I want to do that!" they can choose to decline and explain why, or they can modify it to suit them better. But a request demands a decision one way or the other.

discernment expert—figuring out what this person is born to do and telling them. Your job is to be a *process expert*: to understand the self-discovery journey and be able to offer tools and information about that process that will help clients reach the goal quicker than they can on their own.

The whole reason the client is coming to you is the expectation that you have something to offer to help them discover their life purpose. Once you have done the baseline, don't be shy about making recommendations for what type of *process* would lead to the clients' objectives.

If you are using the baseline as an action step, a good practice is to have the client send it before the appointment. That gives you time to review it beforehand and come up with a short list of exercise options you could offer to the client.

Chapter 5: Design/Strengths

"The unexamined life is not worth living."
Socrates

Strengths are natural, innate talents and abilities that can produce exceptional performance—an important component of life purpose. One person is good with numbers; another is adept at visualizing spacial relationships, while a third has a pianist's hands. These talents are what enable us to perform well right out of the gate, ramp up proficiency at an accelerated rate, and consistently operate at an exceptional level. The root of the word strength has to do with power—and strengths are your innate power to do something well.

My children's strengths were visible when they were only a few years old. Taylor is naturally athletic and loves to push the limits of his body. He's the one who had to crawl on *top* of the swing set instead of staying on the seats, who broke his arm trying to climb a tree with no hands. He was first to venture up into the playscapes at McDonald's restaurants, and he loved it. Even though our daughter was two years older, she wouldn't risk the tunnels until he went first.

Our daughter, however, was as fearless with people as our son was with heights. At a year-and-a-half old, she would walk up to people she had never met, crawl into their laps, hand them a book, and expect them to read to her. Her natural aptitude for words and communication has made her into a poet and songwriter as a teen.

Strengths and Personality Type

Strengths and personality type have much in common, because inward mechanisms and outward performance are connected. However, strengths can describe things that don't fit well under personality type ("he's really good with his hands" or "she picks up languages easily"), whereas personality types often explain inner functions that aren't strengths (the "NT's" primary drive is for competence; while a "D's" root fear is loss of control). I find it helpful to think of the two as an overlapping continuum (see diagram). At the far left end of strengths are purely physical qualities that aren't part of our personality at all, like hand-eye coordination. The right end of the spectrum features things like core motivations or a desire for privacy that aren't strengths or weaknesses, but simply portray our individuality.

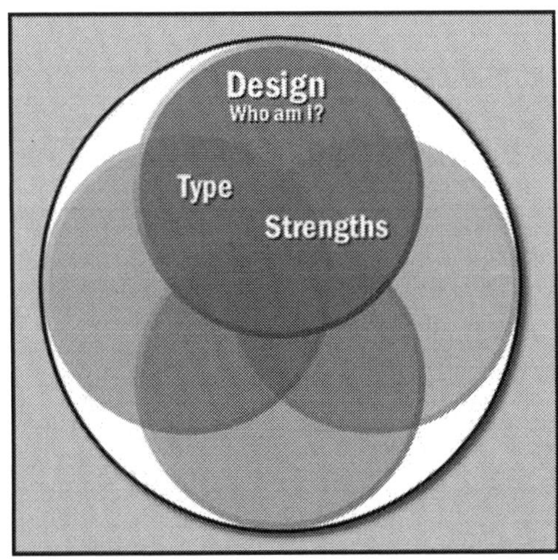

We might say that personality types describe our inner workings, while strengths describe aptitudes for doing certain things. For instance, a "C" on the DiSC™ is inwardly motivated to do things right and bring them to completion (their type), which tends to give them an aptitude for jobs like accounting that require precision with numbers (a strength).

Both personality types and strength systems create sorting categories that offer language to understand human differences. I find it most helpful to view these categories as continuums with fuzzy boundaries. Some clients (particularly "C's" on the DiSC™) can get sidetracked by trying to make sure every insight into their purpose is placed in the "right" category. Their insights are real; the categories are simply artificial constructs that help us remember and understand the insights. So whether something is a strength or a type quality is much less important than just knowing it is there!

Strengths vs. Skills

Sometimes clients confuse strengths and skills. A skill is the practiced ability to do a task well. It's proficiency. However, it is possible to be proficient in something that doesn't come naturally! Many clients seek coaching because they can do their jobs well but don't enjoy them; or can succeed at the tasks assigned to them but feel sucked dry by the extraordinary effort it takes to do so. Skills are not always strengths.

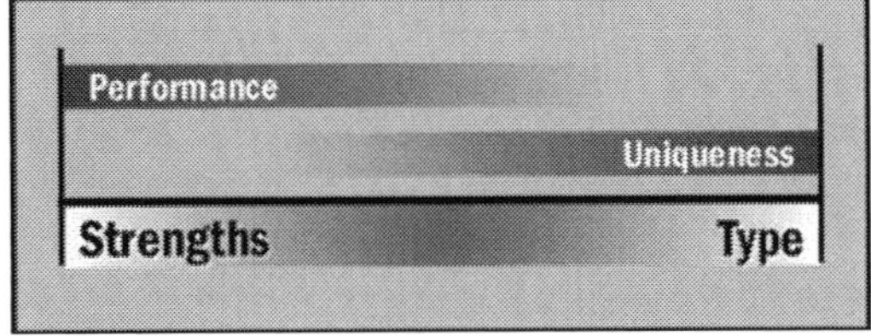

Weaknesses that you've been able to overcome or compensate for are also not strengths. We'll use the term "learned skills" for things we *aren't* innately good at but have become proficient at anyway. If you are naturally weak in an area, you may gain proficiency in it, but the level of effortless excellence displayed by those who are truly gifted in that area will forever remain out of reach. It's only when skills are built on top of natural strengths that truly exceptional long-term performance is possible.

And that's the importance of strengths in life purpose discovery. To maximize your life, you must be in a role that allows you to operate out of your strengths, because those are the areas where you can really excel.

A common assumption is that our greatest growth comes from identifying and correcting our weaknesses. For instance, job reviews often focus on pinpointing weaknesses as areas for growth, and tie one's career and compensation to overcoming them. But the authors of *Now, Discover Your Strengths* turn this conventional wisdom about strengths on its head. The extensive survey the book was based on found that *the greatest performance and growth potential comes from capitalizing on our strengths*. In other words, don't spend your energy trying to improve your natural weaknesses! Instead, find your inborn talents, invest most of your energy into making them world-class strengths, and reshape your roles around them. That process fits perfectly with coaching values: instead of fixing what is lacking in people, we help them discover their greatness and capitalize on it.

Unfortunately, the vast majority of people work in roles that don't allow them to regularly use their best strengths. It's been widely reported that only one in five workers at large companies worldwide use their strengths on a daily basis. And that's where a coach can help. By increasing leaders' conscious awareness of their strengths and helping them realign to spend more time in those areas, you automatically increase their satisfaction and effectiveness in the workplace.

> **Strengths-Finder™**
>
> The Strengths-Finder™ system is a powerful way to measure strengths and help clients refocus around their best. This assessment defines a strength as "consistent near-perfect performance in an activity." That's a broader definition than what we're using here: to attain near perfect performance means practice and skill development (what we're including under the heading of Preparation) built on top of innate talents. In fact, Strengths-Finder™ is in many ways a business-oriented personality typing system. By separating type and strengths here, we're allowing the client to ask, "What is my natural style?" and "What am I good at?" as two separate questions.

Character Weaknesses

There is one important caveat to the idea of focusing on your strengths. In this chapter, a weakness means simply the lack of a certain inborn talent. For instance, leaders who are strong at visioning are often weak at the skills that make for effective implementation. There is nothing wrong with that—focus on developing your visioning abilities and partner with people who are good implementers! But our talents also make us vulnerable to corresponding character issues. While Saul was a visionary man of action, the flip side of his strength was the fear of losing control. Saul's inability to deal with this character weakness grew into a debilitating paranoia that greatly undermined his ability to function as a national leader.

The lesson is this: when we are using the word "strength" or "weakness" to refer to inborn talents, the best results come from maximizing our top abilities instead of remediating our weaknesses. However, when we are talking about strengths or weaknesses of *character*, the opposite is true. Serious character flaws can destroy a lifetime of work with our best strengths in a moment. They cannot be ignored. So with talents and abilities, focus most of your effort on maximizing your best. With character, focus on dealing with weaknesses.

Strengths Are...

1. Natural, innate abilities. You were born with them and even display them as a kid.
2. Areas where you perform at an exceptional level without strain.
3. Things you have a knack for learning or pick up quickly.
4. Energizing and satisfying to function in.
5. Recognized by others when they are used.

Identifying Strengths

One potent method for identifying strengths is to do a formal assessment (like Strengths-Finder™). Or, the process can be done informally, by reflecting on one's experiences and drawing a list of strengths from them. One benefit of the informal method is it teaches clients to reflect on past experience and find life purpose clues there. The tools for the assessment process come directly from the characteristics of strengths (see box). We can construct an exercise around each characteristic:

1. **Natural, innate abilities**
   Self-inventory: What do you think you are naturally good at? (5.1)
2. **Areas where you perform at an exceptional level without strain**
   Look at successes and identify strengths behind them. (5.3)
3. **Energizing and satisfying to function in**
   Track what is energizing and what isn't in your current roles. (5.6)
4. **Recognized by others when used**
   What do those who know you well say are your strengths? (5.4)

Creating a Growth Plan

The *Baseline Assessment* (1.1a) will give you a feel for how far you need to go with your client in this area. For most people, the primary exercises will be enough to identify their strengths. We've provided additional secondary exercises for working with those who need more help.

So what exercises should go in your growth plan? For people who are highly self-aware or who have done strengths assessments in the past, the *Strengths Inventory* (5.1) plus the exercise on identifying weaknesses (5.5) are usually sufficient. Add any or all of the *Strengths Behind Successes* (5.3), the *Strengths and Energy* (5.6) or the *Strengths Validation* exercise (5.4) if the coachee is struggling with deciphering his or her strengths. For those who lack confidence in their own assessment, the *Validation* exercise can be particularly helpful—just be sure to solicit feedback from positive people who are for the coachee!

One way to apply what is learned is with the *80/20 Job Description* exercise (16.4). This helps surface the degree of alignment between role and strengths, and suggests where changes might be made to better utilize strengths. I like to mate this exercise with a personality assessment, since it provides another layer of information about the ideal role.

Limits on Functioning in Strengths

We'd all love to function in our strengths all the time. These factors place limits on our ability to do so.

1. **Failing to build skills on strengths**
   Your abilities are less valuable, and you'll tend to remain in low influence or entry-level roles
2. **Lack of credentials**
   Lack of education, experience, or sponsorship can limit opportunities
3. **Lack of character**
   Blind spots or past failings (like debt or divorce) can limit or eliminate choices
4. **Inability to exercise choice**
   Cultural, economic or political factors (like living under a totalitarian regime) can limit your options
5. **Life stage**
   It is far more likely that you'll be in a best-fit role in your 50's or 60's than in your 20's or 30's.

Normally, these exercises are done as personal reflections between coaching appointments. Encourage your clients to e-mail you their work beforehand—it is much easier to coach around the exercise when you have it in hand and have had the chance to review it. When I'm looking at a client's strengths list, I'm scanning for outstanding insights to affirm, obstacles to functioning in one's strengths (see box), whether the person is truly identifying strengths (and not learned skills or something else), and how able the individual is to name strengths and weaknesses.

One way to help those who are not as adept at reflection is to work through one strength in your session as an example. Use the exercise questions until a strength is identified, and then turn them loose to find the rest. For instance, if you are doing the *Strengths Inventory,* ask: "Give me an example. What's one of your best strengths?" Those who can name and unpack a strength can probably finish up on their own. With those who can't you have a chance to troubleshoot before they waste a week being stuck.

Some people struggle to name strengths because they are unreflective or simply not self aware. What I like to do in these cases is start with past successes and failures and find the strengths and weaknesses within those experiences (see exercises 5.3 and

5.5). Going back to childhood events is often particularly insightful.

For instance, I'll ask, "What's an award you won before you were 20? Then I'll draw out the details of the story with probing questions like, "What happened?" or "What made you a winner at this?" The key to the technique is the next step. Once you have a detail that seems significant, *generalize it into a strength statement and ask the client to respond.* So the dialog might go like this:

"I think won the Pinewood Derby in Boy Scouts because I wanted it badder than anyone else. I put a lot more time and energy into it. I analyzed the car, figured out that the most important part was the axles, and I spent hours polishing them so it would run smoother."

"You sound like a naturally competitive person. You want to measure yourself against the world and be the best, and that motivates you to perform at a high level. And when you want to, you can really focus a lot of energy on a problem. Does that sound like you?"

By generalizing the details of the experience into strengths statements you are helping the client make the connections they've been unable to grasp on their own.

Occasionally you'll run into someone who has an internal, obstacle in this area. I've coached people who had been told so often that they were no good that they couldn't verbalize one legitimate strength, and with others who were so afraid to look vulnerable or so lost in a dream world that they couldn't name any weaknesses. Often the best response is just to reflect it back to them and go a level deeper: "I notice that you named five weaknesses, but couldn't name a strength. What's going on there?"

For other ways to deal with obstacles, see Allegiance (chapter 4) and Dream Obstacles (chapter 9).

Strengths and Timing in Convergent Roles

While your strengths are innate qualities you have from the beginning, your ability to understand and function in them is not. For instance, which person is more likely to end up in a role that fits their strengths: a young woman fresh out of high school out looking for her first job, or a manager with 30 years experience in her industry?

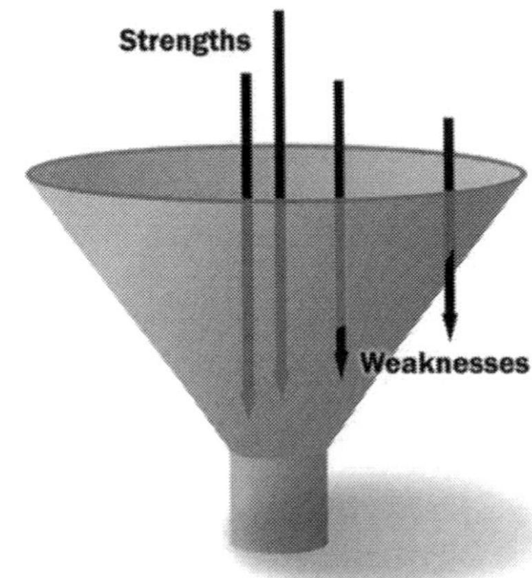

The ability to function in your strengths is also a function of life stage—an important insight for life coaches. J. Robert Clinton in his writings on leadership development theory (like *The Making of a Leader*) has identified the concept of *convergence*: a stage of maximum productivity, usually in a person's 40's to 60's, where your role is fit to your strengths, personality and call. This *Convergent Role* (see chapter 16) is often designed by the leader himself to fit his known strengths and weaknesses.

Clinton also identifies several earlier stages in life where we are being prepared by experience for this ultimate task. One way of visualizing your passage through these stages is moving downward through a funnel (see diagram). The walls of the funnel represent the boundaries of your understanding of your life purpose. When you are young, the funnel is wide: there is a lot you don't know about yourself, and there are many things you can do that move you toward your purpose. The guiding principle is, "whatever your hand finds to do, do it with all your might."

The objective in your teens and twenties is to *accumulate experiences that reveal your design.* In finding the places you fit and where you don't fit, you begin to determine the boundaries you must stay within to fulfill your destiny. The more experiences you have, the clearer the boundaries.

The middle stages of life (often late 20's to 40's) are about clarifying your strengths and systematically developing them. You take on roles that build you into the person you need to be to fulfill your destiny. The contracting funnel means that there are fewer roles that fit what you need to learn—your sweet spot is much clearer. Later in life (50's on) the time of strengths discovery and development has been completed, and it is time to focus on getting into a "best-fit" role and maximizing your impact. This stage is represented by the spout of the funnel—the sweet spot no longer contracts, since you know who you are, and as you stay within that channel Christ flows through you to the world with maximum effect.

The importance of understanding these stages is that how you coach strengths varies radically with age. *You must coach toward the developmental process,* not just toward finding the ideal role that fits the coachee's strengths. A great plan for a person in his 50's (identify a convergent role and move into it) will probably not work for someone who is 25. At that age, the self-knowledge, character and skills needed for a destiny role aren't yet present. When I coach younger people, I focus on the process of learning from the roles and experiences they have instead of getting them into a "best-fit" role. And when I coach people in the middle stages (where often you have any idea what the destiny role is but aren't prepared for it yet), I help clients develop preparation strategies so they are pro-active about growing instead of just waiting for God to release them. Calling stages and how to coach toward the developmental process are covered in depth in the companion book, *The Calling Journey.*

Strengths Inventory

5.1

This self-evaluation helps you get down on paper what you intuitively know about your strengths. Do this exercise *quickly*, and try not to be especially neat or over-analyze what you write: we'll evaluate your jottings later.

> ***Coaching Tip***
> *This exercise is most useful for those who have already done some life purpose discovery work. Inventorying what they already know may allow you to skip most of the other exercises in this section.*

Step 1: Brain Dump

List your strengths. What are your natural talents and abilities? What activities come easily to you? What talents in you do people consistently affirm? They can be an athletic abilities, an aptitude for a certain kind of task, or something experience has shown you are really good at. Just jot down whatever comes to mind. When you reach the point where you can't think of any more, flip to the *Strengths Examples* (5.2) and scan for ideas.

> ***Coaching Tip***
> *This exercise is mainly about getting something down on paper as a starting point. Have the coachee send their jottings to you before the next coaching session so you can review it. Be alert for coachees whose lack of confidence or self-awareness shows up in a scanty list. You'll need to do some extra work to draw them out. One tool for drawing out those reluctant to share strengths is to go back to childhood:*
>
> - *"What were you good at when you were a kid?"*
> - *"What kind of contests or awards have you won? What strength is behind that?"*
> - *"Where did you do well in school? Socially? In athletics? Academics?"*

Step 2: Cull it Down

Now, step back and look over what you wrote. Eliminate anything that is a learned skill: something that you aren't naturally good at but can do if you have to. Feel free to combine similar items or cross out anything that on second though you don't feel is a strength—just give yourself the benefit of the doubt and leave it on the list if you aren't sure.

Step 3: Top Five

Put a star next to the ones you think are your top five best strengths.

5.2  Strengths Examples

Below is a list of generic descriptions of possible strengths. Make them your own! The best statements about your strengths highlight what is truly unique about you.

- ☐ Math/numbers
- ☐ Communication
- ☐ Making friends/networking
- ☐ Introspection
- ☐ Athletics
- ☐ Hand-eye coordination
- ☐ Physical strength/endurance
- ☐ Repetitive tasks
- ☐ Creativity
- ☐ Problem solving
- ☐ Multi-tasking
- ☐ Focusing on one big project
- ☐ Craftsmanship
- ☐ Writing
- ☐ Quick and dirty solutions
- ☐ Learning languages
- ☐ Identifying with people
- ☐ Listening
- ☐ Acting/playing a role
- ☐ Team player
- ☐ Eye for beauty
- ☐ Artistic
- ☐ Sense of direction
- ☐ Visualization
- ☐ Dreaming/brainstorming
- ☐ Getting others on board
- ☐ Facing conflict
- ☐ Good with tools
- ☐ Affirming
- ☐ Risk taking
- ☐ Reasoning
- ☐ Emotional sensitivity
- ☐ Intensity
- ☐ Letting go
- ☐ Living in the moment
- ☐ Music
- ☐ Inspiration
- ☐ Fixing things
- ☐ Building things
- ☐ Designing
- ☐ Managing people or projects
- ☐ Details
- ☐ Storytelling
- ☐ Making people laugh
- ☐ Giving
- ☐ Organizing
- ☐ Delegating
- ☐ Critical thinking
- ☐ Fairness
- ☐ Showing mercy
- ☐ Sticking with it
- ☐ Reflecting
- ☐ Planning
- ☐ Improvising
- ☐ Enthusiasm
- ☐ Decisiveness
- ☐ Seeing the future
- ☐ Having fun

Strengths Behind Successes  5.3

Our strengths are what give us the capacity for top performance, so usually we can find strengths behind our successes. In this exercise, we'll list some successes and try to uncover the strengths that made them possible.

Step 1: List Successes

List at least five significant accomplishments. What have you done that you're proud of? What have others hailed or appreciated about your successes? Where have you won competitions or awards, reached an important goal or made a real difference? Focus on a specific task, project, or event (not a role that stretched over months or years). If you can, pick things in different areas (work, family, sports, service, leadership) and different life stages.

Coaching Tip

This is a second inventorying exercise, useful for those who are doing life purpose discovery process for the first time, or who struggled with the Strengths Inventory (5.1). If the person can access a lot of information on the Strengths Inventory, they probably don't need to do this one too.

Clients who are younger or more insecure may draw a blank on accomplishments, or be shy about stating them. You can usually break through this barrier by starting with informational questions about their life ("Tell me more about what you do at work."), and gradually drilling down toward what they've done well.

Step 2: Identify Strengths Behind the Successes

Now take each of your successes or accomplishments in turn. Which of your talents and abilities does this story highlight? What did you bring to the table that made this a success? Which parts came naturally to you or had a big impact with what felt like little effort?

Coaching Tip

Here are some additional debriefing questions for drawing strengths out of a success story:

- *"What did you do that made this thing succeed?"*
- *"What skills were needed to do this?"*
- *"Which part energized you or came naturally to you?"*
- *"What did you see or do in the situation that others couldn't or wouldn't?"*
- *"What did others affirm in you when you accomplished this?"*
- *"What did you do that made the most difference with the least effort?"*

5.4  Strengths Validation

Getting feedback is a great way to flesh out your strengths list or gain confidence in what you've already identified. Find a person you know well, with whom you have a strong relationship (your spouse, a family member, or a close colleague), and who is willing to spend 20 minutes helping you. Explain that you'd like honest, objective feedback on your strengths. Then take the following steps:

Step 1: Ask

"What would you say are five natural talents or abilities that I have; that are my best strengths? Where have you seen those abilities in action?" (If your friend is drawing a blank, show him/her the *Strengths Examples* worksheet (5.2)).

> ***Coaching Tip***
> *Younger individuals benefit most from this, because they have fewer experiences to base their understanding of their strengths upon. Parents or siblings (who have known them all their lives) can be a great resource.*

Step 2: Review Your List

Show your friend the strengths and weaknesses that you identified in exercises 5.1 and 5.5, and ask for comments. Add any new insights that seem accurate to your list.

> ***Coaching Tip***
> *For the shy or retiring client, asking if the feedback they received is accurate or valid can empower them to make their own judgment instead of just accepting whatever others think of them.*

Identifying Weaknesses  5.5

Knowing what you *aren't* good at is an important part of knowing your strengths. Remember, we all have weaknesses. If nobody else was weak where you are strong, you wouldn't have a life purpose!

Step 1: Examine Experiences

Think of several roles or situations where you felt you didn't do well. (Often frustration, stress, ineffectiveness or a lack of confidence are signs of functioning outside our strengths.) In each situation, what were you doing that *wasn't* a strength, didn't come naturally or sapped your energy?

> ***Coaching Tip***
> *Be alert for coachees whose lack of confidence or self-awareness shows up in a long list of weaknesses and a short list of strengths. I like to see a strengths list at least as long as the list of weaknesses. Here are some good questions for identifying weaknesses:*
>
> - *"Where in life have you said, 'That was too much work—I'll never do that again?'"*
> - *"In what areas of life do you look at others and say, 'Wow! They're really good at that?'"*
> - *"Take a look at your strengths. All strengths tend to have corresponding weaknesses. What are yours?"*
> - *"This weakness may well be the flip side of a corresponding strength. What do you do well in another area that makes it tough to do well here at the same time?"*

Step 2: Self-Inventory

Now, step back and start to draw from what you already know about yourself. What could you add to your list of things that de-energize you or don't come easily? Where in life do you expend a great deal of energy to get adequate results? Add these items to your list. When you can't think of any more, flip to the *Strengths Examples* (5.2) and scan for ideas.

> ***Coaching Tip***
> *Weaknesses are the flip side of strengths—for you to be highly observant and tuned in to the world around you, you can't always be creating new visions in your head. And to be a visionary dreamer, you can't be burning all your neurons paying attention to every stimulus around you. In other words, the weakness is part of the strength, and you can't have the strength without it. However, many people think of weaknesses as personal failings, so they avoid inventorying them. To get around this, practice expressing weaknesses as a function of strengths: "You really have a knack for reading people. Completing tasks is a weakness because you put your best into relating to those around you."*

5.6 Strengths, Type and Energy

This workplace exercise helps you identify strengths and explores the fit between your roles and your strengths and personality type.

Step 1: Keep an Energy List (Daily)

Start two lists side-by-side on your laptop, PDA or by placing this *Workbook* page in a place where you will see it throughout the day. One list is what energizes you, while the other is for energy drains. As you work, stop periodically for a few seconds and jot down what you've been doing that energizes or drains you. Keep adding to your list for at least a week.

> ***Coaching Tip***
> *Some people have a hard time doing this type of exercise without regular reminders. Putting alarms in your PDA or noting it as a short appointment three times a day in a date book can help. Leaders who actually do this during their workdays tend to generate more "Aha's" than those who throw a list together the night before the coaching appointment.*

Step 2: Evaluate (10 minutes)

Since functioning in your strengths tends to be energizing and satisfying, while functioning outside of them is draining, your two lists should tell you something about where your strengths lie. Take 10 minutes to ponder the things that are energizing. What innate strengths are you using in those tasks? Jot down those strengths below. Then go through the same process with the things that drain you. What does that tell you about where your weaknesses are?

Energizing Strengths	Draining Weaknesses

> ***Coaching Tip***
> *Here are some evaluation questions to help unpack this exercise:*
>
> - *"What are some of the common elements in things that energize you? How about in things that drain you?"*
> - *"What items did you come up with that you hadn't been aware of before?"*
> - *"What one step could you take this week to move away from functioning in an area that drains you and toward a strength that energizes you?"*

Chapter 6: Design/ Personality Type

"It makes you wonder. All the brilliant things we might have done with our lives if only we suspected we knew how."

General Benjamin in *Bel Canto*

Personality type is a specialized language created to describe human differences. Personality systems categorize people in areas like thinking patterns, decision-making style, what kinds of information we tune into, how we exert influence, etc. These differences are grouped into "types," usually organized by theories about what makes up human personality. The first recorded system was developed centuries before Christ by the Greek philosopher Hippocrates, based on his observations of human behavior. He postulated that people have four basic bodily fluids, and that an individual displays one of four personality types (Choleric, Sanguine, Phlegmatic, and Melancholy) depending on which of these four "humors" is dominant.

While the science behind it has long been discarded, this personality system is still in use over 2000 years later, testifying to the utility of personality types. After the basic coaching toolset (listening, asking, goal-setting, etc.) personality type is my most-used coaching tool. If I know a client's type, I automatically understand the person better. I know what they'll tend to expect of me as a coach, where the coaching process might most help them, some of the places they'll struggle, even how to adjust my coaching style to maximize the impact of the coaching process.

Here are a few quick for-instances. If I am coaching a leader who is a "D" on the DiSC™ profile, I know I am working with a hard-charging, task-oriented individual who likes to cut to the chase and take action. With a high "D," I move the conversation along quickly, speak directly, and I can safely omit many of the little relational touches that mean so much to an "I" personality. I challenge this client more than other types, speak it in a very direct manner and asking for more in the way of action steps. I am also aware that many "D" leaders' Achilles heel is running over people, so I'm more likely to ask them to play out how important decisions will impact those around them.

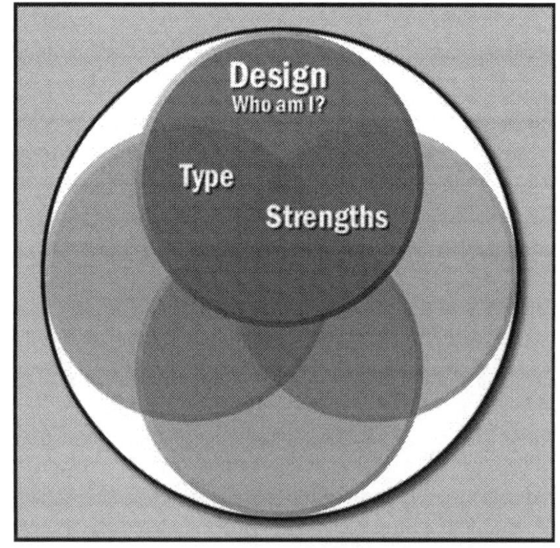

If I happen to be coaching a "P" on the Myers-Briggs around focus and time management, I know I'm working with someone who has a play ethic—if you're a "P," you either play first and then work, or you make work into play. "P's" like to continue gathering information and keep their options open as long as possible, which can make it a struggle for them to adapt to the deadline driven "J" working world. Most time-management tools were developed by "J's" (the opposite of the "P" type) who love clarity and closure, and they can drive "P's" nuts.

One of my "P" clients had an especially tough time with this. He'd vacillate between trying to time-block everything and work from a to-do list, to feeling so tied down by the structure that he'd let his life and his calendar spiral out of control. Talking about managing his time according to the natural tendencies of his type was a revelation. He discovered that what worked best for him was a varied schedule, not rigid time blocking. As long as he had adequate opportunities to choose in the moment what to work on, he could schedule things and get them done without feeling boxed in.

Aligning with your type's natural working style tends to raise the energy level, improve performance, and often leads to insights like "I'm not the lazy, can't-meet-a-deadline time-management failure I always thought I was!" Because the client finds real understanding of what makes them tick in the coaching process, the relationship is of much greater value.

These kinds of eye-opening results are a powerful rationale for starting the life purpose discovery process with personality type. The reason it is so easy to get a big win here is that so many people know so little about it. For instance, 70% of people have no idea of their type on the most widely used personality system (Myers-Briggs). Spiritual gift knowledge is just as poor: one recent study found that only about 30% of adult believers can identify a spiritual gift they feel they have—while almost as many claimed a spiritual gift that doesn't appear anywhere in the Bible! My experience with ministry leaders is that while some "know the letters," few can explain what those

Personality Systems

Here are a few of the better known personality systems:

- **Myers-Briggs (MBTI©)**
  Developed 60 years ago from the psychological theories of Carl Jung, this system is administered millions of times a year. It is the most used, best validated and most richly documented personality system.
  For Coaches: While spin-offs are available on-line, special training or academic credentials are required to purchase and administer the assessment. Whole catalogs of books and resources are available, on topics like MBTI and leadership or type and prayer styles. Professional report generating tools are available.

- **DiSC™**
  Originally created by William Marston in the 1920s, DiSC™ profiles four fundamental behavioral styles. It is one of the more widely used systems.
  For Coaches: Since the original work was not copyrighted, many versions of DiSC™ have evolved, making training easier and less expensive than for MBTI. Versions are available using biblical illustrations, as are professional report generating tools.

- **Temperaments**
  Popularized by Keirsey and Bates' bestseller, *Please Understand Me*, these are the original four categories of Plato/Hippocrates correlated to four basic letter pairs in the MBTI.
  For Coaches: There are many systems based on these categories with a variety of type names (for instance, Lion/Otter/Golden Retriever/Beaver). It is a simple, low-cost system with free on-line tests.

- **Motivational Gifts**
  The seven categories are based on the gift types listed in Romans 12. Popularized in the 1970s, the best known version by Don & Katie Fortune describes seven types with different motivations and styles.
  For Coaches: Very low cost, biblically-based and fairly simple, this is a good system for working in churches or with ministry leaders. The "God language" means it has less utility in the business world.

- **The Enneagram**
  A system of nine types displayed in a geometric relationship fully developed in the 1960s, it has been used in a variety of spiritual contexts.
  For Coaches: The "official" assessment is free on-line—you can even post the actual assessment on your site. This is a less-well-known system with fewer available resources.

letters mean or how to apply any knowledge of type to their roles or relationships.

Whether or not you are doing life purpose discovery, a good practice is to start the coaching process with a formal assessment. Many type systems allow you to create a personalized log-in that lets your clients take a pre-paid on-line assessment and receive a personalized report (which is also copied to you). Once you have the assessment results in hand, you'll want to follow up with a validation session where you talk through the report, resolve any anomalies in the results and verify the individual's type.

If you'd like to have clients or class participants find their type, an on-line DiSC™ assessment is available at www.ALeadersLifePurpose.com. Each person who takes it will receive a 25-page, personalized report on their type. We've negotiated a special group rate of almost 40% off for readers of this book and their coachees.

To use type, you first must pick a personality system and master it. I recommend that a professional coach's first skills training investment beyond their coaching certification be personality type (unless you've already mastered a system).

And I can't overemphasize the idea of attaining mastery instead of just dabbling.

Type Practice for Coaches

Once you've taken some basic training on your personality system of choice, how do you reach true mastery of it? Here are five ways you can work toward type mastery:

1. **Practice.** Do free assessments and validations with 10 to 20 people. Share your knowledge and improve the lives of your friends, family, church, or small group while you learn. Practice builds proficiency.
2. **Find Exemplars.** A great way to remember the characteristics of a certain personality is to pick an exemplar (someone you know who fits that profile to a tee) for each type. When you remember that person, the characteristics of that type will immediately come to mind.
3. **Get a Type Buddy.** That's a friend who is as interested in type as you. Spend time talking about the type of your mutual friends or well-known political, business or religious figures. Trade anecdotes about your own personality. Can you learn to roughly type people together without using a formal assessment?
4. **Have a Type Night.** Invite two or three friends or couples you know over, give everyone an assessment, and then validate the results by having each person read their type profile aloud from a book. You'll get lots of laughs and learn a lot.
5. **Teach on Type.** Offer an interactive personality class at your church (whole books of interactive learning games exist for some personality systems—it makes doing a workshop a blast). The learning activity that produces the highest retention is teaching others.

If you are going to help others with type, Level II or III mastery (see pg. 78) isn't enough—you have to move to Level V, where you can help coachees identify type and understand how their type interacts with others'. Master type the same way you master your coaching skills and you'll find you become an even more valuable resource to your clients.

An on-line DiSC™ Assessment at a special discounted group rate is available through www.ALeadersLifePurpose.com

Gift Systems

One type area of particular interest to Christian coaches is biblical gift systems. There are three main streams of thought about biblical gifts. The first says that all the New Testament gifts can be placed in the same list, because they are all gifts. Another school of thought lumps the four gift lists in the New Testament together with other "gifts" (like celibacy, craftsmanship, or music) from throughout the Bible. A third says the New Testament describes several types of gifts (charismatic gifts, office gifts, and motivational gifts) with completely different characteristics and functions, and you don't mix the lists.

Although they are the most widely used, I think the first and second approaches muddy the waters as much as they help. One problem is the sheer number of gifts (often over 30) that are described. To understand 30 gifts and how they interact with each other is literally orders of magnitude more difficult than mastering a system like DiSC™ with four basic types.

Second, let's say one of these assessments indicates that a person has gifts of prophetic utterance, apostleship and exhortation (one from each of the three main New Testament lists). An immediate problem is, can you even "have" a gift like prophetic utterance or miracles (from the I Corinthians 12 list)? I don't know anyone who can conjure up a miracle whenever they want. The Corinthians list is not of gifts that you "have," in the sense that they are within you and under your control. The Spirit manifests these gifts *through* you "as He wills" (I Cor. 12:11).

Similar problems exist with the Ephesians list. If the person in our example has the gift of "Apostleship" (starting and overseeing churches and organizations), and he is only 15, is he going to be able to function in that gift? Pastoring or apostolic ministry are *callings* that you mature into, not natural gifts you can deploy at will.

The only list of gifts we are told we actually have is the Romans 12 list[14]. These seven gifts (some call them the "motivational gifts") are what I call "the personality types of the Bible." They are innate traits that distinguish how we think and make decisions, what motivates us and what goes on in our head. It makes a lot of sense to treat the Romans list separately, instead of lumping it together with different types of gifts.[15] So instead of creating a whole separate category of spiritual gifts, I am going to treat the Romans list as a personality type system.

---

14 "Having gifts... let us use them" (Rom. 12:6; RSV).

15 For a fuller discussion of this topic, see *Discover Your God-Given Gifts*, by Don & Katie Fortune.

Case Study I: Type in Conflict

Jenny, a 27-year-old office manager, sought out a coach to improve her job satisfaction and move forward in her career. As a normal part of the intake process, her coach (Nancy) had her take an on-line DiSC™ assessment. The assessment generated a 15-page report which was e-mailed to both Jenny and her coach. One of Jenny's first action steps was to read the report, underlining the qualities that she felt fit her and noting those that didn't. A second step was to identify five key insights from her type that she might be able to build on to improve satisfaction with her work (see exercise 8.3.).

Confirming the results of an assessment was important (since no tool is always accurate), so in their next appointment, Nancy spent time validating Jenny's type. Did this feel like her true self? How much of the report seemed to be on-target? Were there any places where it didn't seem to fit? Jenny thought it was a pretty good description (she came out as a high "D"), but there were several areas she felt she didn't understand or didn't fit well. To firm up her self-understanding, Jenny penciled in a step for the following week to talk through the report with her mom and her best friend (see exercise 6.1) to get their perspective.

Meanwhile, Nancy began to coach Jenny around her job satisfaction issue. One area that quickly came to light was Jenny's relationship with her administrative assistant.

"She can be so frustrating *sometimes," Jenny declared. "Everything has to be done just so. If I'm missing one receipt on my expense report she is after me right away about it. She asks all these questions and has to know every step of a plan before she'll act. And whenever I launch out into something new, she spends the first two weeks digging in her heels before she gets on board. Granted, when she says she'll do a task I know it will get done and get done right, but sometimes she is so afraid of getting it wrong that she moves like molasses."*

"Well, this sounds like an interesting place to apply some concepts from your type report. What did it say about your preferred working style?"

"Let's see... as a 'D' I am fast moving and results-oriented. It says I tend to juggle a lot of balls easily, that I decide quickly but don't like a lot of details and administration—that's certainly true—and that I tend to cut to the chase in conversations."

"That's great. So what is your assistant like in these same areas?"

"She is slow to decide and to move. She doesn't multi-task very well. She isn't oriented toward results as much as... perfection, I guess. Sometimes I think if she only got one thing done in a day but did it right, she'd be happy. She actually likes the little administrative details that drive me crazy—she can just sit there and plow through that stuff for hours."

"That's a good description. We don't know this for sure, but based on what you've said, I'm guessing she might be a 'C' on the. DiSC™. 'C's' are the people who help make sure that things are done well. They tend to be slower at change and decision making than 'D's' like you because they want to think things through and do them with excellence. They tend to be good at details, very reliable and dogged about meeting their commitments. Does that sound like her?"

"Pretty much."

"When you are working with different types, the key to turning frustration into an effective working relationship is being able to play to their strengths and complement their weaknesses. It might help you if we take an area you are frustrated with and work through how to apply type principles to it. How does that sound?"

"If it makes a difference, I'm all for it. Can we talk about the slow decision-making thing? That's what bugs me the most."

"Sure. OK. If you are a 'D', you want to do it now, whereas if she's a 'C', she needs more time to assimilate information and think it through. How could you change the way you communicate so she has time to think about decisions without slowing you down?"

"Um... I guess she'd have to hear about things a ways before we are ready to act on them."

"How could you do that?"

"Well, one way would be to just drop things on her gradually instead of all at once. I tend to communicate everything at once at the staff meetings, because it is most efficient. Would it help if I gave her a heads up earlier in the week about what we're going to talk about?"

"Sounds like a great idea. What else could you do?"

"Actually, I could give her the staff meeting agenda to type up. That would save me a little time plus give her some notice of what we're going to talk about."

"Sounds like another great idea. Now let's take this a step farther. So far, we're working at ways to compensate for her being slower at decision making. How could you play to that strength as an asset *instead of seeing it as a* weakness?"

"I'm not sure what you mean."

"OK—let me say it a different way. Are there places in your life where slowing down and thinking things through more thoroughly would help?"

"Yeah," Jenny replied ruefully. "Sometimes I stick my foot in my mouth and it takes me three months to put things back together again."

"So how could your assistant help with that?"

"That's an interesting thought. She tends to focus on what could go wrong, and I tend to see what could go right. She probably could help me there."

"How? Give me an example of a project you are working on now where that thoughtfulness could be a strength."

"Well... We have to reorganize the way we handle customer service calls. I was going to

Coaching Exercise: Type-Switching

Here's an exercise to help you improve your service as a coach. Start with a personality system you are familiar with. For each of the types in that system, jot down at least five things that that type appreciates in communication. Look through a book chapter or report on that profile if you need ideas. What communication style would this type most want and need in a coach?

Next, identify two or three top things that you could supply (or learn to supply) to that individual type.

Finally, go through your client list, note each person's type, and jot down a reminder of how you can alter your own natural personality/ coaching style to best serve that individual's needs.

throw together a plan and announce it Thursday. But maybe if I ran my ideas past her first, and asked her to give me three things I'd have to take into account for this plan to work—I bet that would get her on my side and give me some practical suggestions to boot. I like that!"

This case study used a combination of several exercises and a DiSC™ assessment to help the client apply type to a work conflict. By figuring out her own style and that of her assistant, she was able to draw out the strengths of her team while minimizing the clashes. The coach's level V mastery of type was crucial—the coach helped Jenny reframe the conflict in terms of personality differences instead of personal failings, and create strategies to make those differences work for her.

This is another example of an area where the coach's expertise with relational tools adds value to the process. The solutions and the choice of where to use the tools still come from the client, but by introducing type the coach reframed the situation and opened up a whole different realm of solutions.

Case Study II: Type and Leadership Roles

Paul was the long-time senior pastor of a large, multi-staff congregation. At 55, he had begun to ponder how to maximize his impact in the years he had left—a common issue at this stage of life. Paul sought out a coach to sharpen his focus and realign his role for greater effectiveness.

One area we quickly targeted in his coaching sessions was re-orienting roles and communication patterns of his core team around personality type. Paul had reached Level II understanding of his profile: he had some knowledge of his own type, but not enough to use it effectively in his role or team.

Since it had been many years since he'd done an assessment, the coach repeated the process with him. The results were validated by getting feedback from his wife and several of his core leaders. As Paul grew in understanding of his "ENFP" style, he gained insight on his drive for relationship, his propensity to go back and reopen decisions that had already been made, and his tendency to think out loud (and then find to his chagrin that his staff implemented ideas that he was merely tossing around). The coach helped Paul identify what tasks and roles fit his personality strengths, what kind of team he needed around him (see *My Ideal Team*, exercise 6.4), and how to off-load tasks that weren't his strengths to his team.

Paul was also in the middle of terminating a long-time friend on his staff—a very painful exercise for a relational "ENFP"! The coach helped him navigate his tendency to delay and to gloss over the difficulties of the situation. By this point, Paul had gotten so much out of personality types that he wanted to do them with the other two members of his core team.

Assessments of these two team members revealed that one was an "ENTJ" (Jim, the executive pastor) and one an "ISTJ" (Dean, the staff director). The coach had an individual session with each one to validate their types and discuss communication patterns on the team.

Jim and Paul got along well—they connected at the dreaming/visioning level (their common "N") and the bias for action springing from their common extroversion. One sticking point was the changing agenda of "ENFP" Paul. "ENTJ" Jim got frustrated when he'd planned something out and then the objectives changed. His "T" decision making style (rational, principled, and willing to make tough calls) clashed at times with Paul's intuitive, relationship-oriented "F" style—for instance, Jim thought Paul should have fired his friend long ago.

The bigger challenge was with "ISTJ" Dean. As the only introvert and sensor (practical and present-oriented) on the team, Dean often found himself stuck carrying out the impossible dreams of the other two leaders, who hadn't adequately thought through the resources needed or the practical impact on day-to-day schedules. As a loyal "SJ," Dean simply swallowed his reservations and found a way to cope. But the team was losing out because the two fast-paced extroverts didn't allow enough time for introverted Dean to process the team's decisions, so he tended not to speak into them even when asked.

After cataloguing these issues in the individual sessions, the coach brought Paul up to speed on the main issues before meeting together with the whole team. For several hours these three leaders focused on understanding each other's strengths and crafting communication styles that worked for everyone. For instance, the two "J's" learned how to ask for final decisions from an "ENFP" boss, and "P" Paul agreed to be more accountable to stick to decisions once they were made. The "J's" learned to see Paul's adaptability as a strength, and they talked about when his "P" approach of keeping the options open worked better than their own natural style.

To fully engage Dean in the decision-making process, the two extroverts agreed to get an agenda to Dean before their meetings so he had more time to think about upcoming decisions. They also learned to put something before Dean and ask him to get back to them by a certain time, instead of asking for a decision on the spot.

The team also looked at their job descriptions and re-allocated several tasks based on gifting. For instance, as an "ENFP," Paul found it very difficult to hold a firm line in conflicts over staff privileges. Procedures were created that channeled those questions to Dean and Jim (who weren't so susceptible to relational manipulation), eliminating a huge energy drain for Paul.

The end result was Paul core team functioned more smoothly and effectively. The resulting efficiency freed up time to concentrate on mentoring a next generation of leaders (one of Paul's core passions) as less energy was given to the draining task of keeping the systems running. Paul felt that working with his coach was a "very valuable" experience that will make a big difference in the legacy impact of his key ministry years.

In this case study, the coach used personality tools to identify each team member's personal design, to troubleshoot sources of conflict and to help realign team roles to fit their types. The solutions still came from the clients—the coach provided tools and background information on type they could use to find those solutions. Coaching organizational leaders on personality type naturally evolves toward coaching the team, because there is so much to be learned from type about best roles, communication, conflict styles, and more.

6.1  Peer Validation

The people who know you well almost surely have valuable insights to offer about how you operate in your type. This exercise helps confirm what your type is and offers insight on how others see you.

Sit down for half an hour with a close friend, family member or spouse—someone who has known you for many years—and discuss your personality profile. Have your friend read through your profile (from a book or report) with you. Use these questions to guide your discussion:

- Have your friend point out the four or five characteristics that best fit you in this profile.
- Ask what insights this profile provides about who you are and how to relate to you.
- Can your friend think of a story or two that illustrates some of these type characteristics?
- How do these qualities influence the way you lead and do your job?
- What does this profile explain about you that most people don't understand?

Coaching Tip
When you learn a personality system, you'll generally be taught a validation process that goes with it. If coachees are still unsure of their type even after a validation session, or are having trouble connecting their type with how they operate in real life, this exercise can help.

Some questions for reviewing the peer validation exercise:

- *"What did you learn about yourself from talking to some peers about your type?"*
- *"Did you get any feedback that bothered you or you felt didn't apply? Why?"*
- *"Think of a conflict you had with one of these individuals in the past. How did your type play out in that situation?"*

Type Night

This is a great game to play at extended family gatherings and reunions, with your immediate family (when your kids are old enough), or with a team at work. It will help you understand each other better, and provide a lot of good laughs along the way!

You'll need a book on a personality system you are somewhat familiar with that includes several-page profiles of each type (Try *Type Talk* by Kroeger for MBTI©, *Discover Your God-Given Gifts* by Fortune for motivational gifts, or *The Personality Code* by Bradberry for DiSC™). Your group will need to be comfortable and secure with each other. This game may not work well in dysfunctional families or teams!

Step 1: Agree on Ground Rules

Create a set of ground rules like those below that everyone can agree on:

1. Focus on positive qualities, instead of negative ones. Make this a time that draws you closer and builds everyone up.
2. Honor each other. Don't tell stories that embarrass or hurt people.
3. Be honest if the discussion gets into a sensitive area of your life you'd rather not have others talk about.
4. If you feel like the description of another type fits you better, you can switch at any time.

Step 2: Figure out Your Types

If the book includes an assessment, have everybody take it. Some type books have word-choice lists that everyone can look at to make a tentative determination of their type.

Step 3: Validate

Have each person read their type profile out loud. After each sentence or two, have the reader say whether they think that characteristic fits them or not. If you aren't sure or want feedback, ask the rest of the group for input. The idea is to validate whether this is actually your type. If the description isn't a great fit, try looking at some other types that are slightly different and see if they fit better. Make sure you go first on this step and take the risk of being vulnerable first!

Step 4: Tell Stories (Optional)

Once everyone has validated their type, see if you can think of some family history stories or humorous examples of how different members functioned in their types or interacted with each other. Remember to follow the ground rules, stay positive and build each other up!

6.3  My Ideal Team

Teams can benefit greatly from understanding type, because it allows them to adjust roles to fit each person's natural style. This exercise helps team leaders identify their strengths and what their type brings to the table, then lists the strengths and types needed as complements.

You can also use this exercise to form teams or create convergent roles. If you aren't certain what types would best compliment you, ask your coach for help.

1. What does this team need to be able to do with excellence? What strengths or type characteristics do those tasks require? List them on the left.
2. Which of these qualities does your type provide? Underline them.
3. Identify any learned skills in your role—things you can do but don't come naturally. What types would love to do that kind of thing and could take it off your plate?
4. Which abilities do you lack? What types would provide them? (For ideas, you may want to leaf through the profiles of different types, and ask yourself what unique abilities of each type are most needed on this team.)
5. What are the weak areas for my type? Which types could complement those weaknesses?

Quality or Strength Needed on Team	Types or People that Offer It
Missions Fundraising Team	
Networking, meeting new people	*Me ("I")*
Making the Ask	*Paul or Melissa? Get-it-done "D's"*
Financial record keeping	*"C" - need someone*
Creating forms and procedures	*"C" - precise, dependable*
Writing a Newsletter, ad copy	*Me + ?*
Team building	*Me*
Writing a grant proposal	*Have "D" Paul outsource*
Staying connected with missionaries	*Sally or Lou - relational "S's"*
Prayer team leader	*someone passionate re: prayer*
Annual fundraising dinner - planning	*Me + team*
Fundraising dinner logistics	*More "S's" and "C's"*

Conclusion:
I need more "C's" on my team, so administrative and financial tasks get done.

Coaching Tip
A system like MBTI© which uses dichotomies (either/or choices) is also great for this exercise—simply look at the opposite of each letter to find the complementary strengths.

This is a coach procedure for typing a team and helping the group integrate those insights into their team process.

Step 1: Start with the Team Leader

Most opportunities to type a team will start with the leader of the group. Typing the leader first and helping him or her apply type insights within the team will increase motivation and position the leader to launch the team-typing process. Work with the leader to develop some clear objectives for the process:

- *"What do you hope to gain from typing your team?"*
- *"What would make this process a success?"*
- *"How do you need to grow personally through this process? Would you be willing to share that desire with your team up front?"*
- *"What do I need to be aware of as I work with individuals on this team?"*

Since this will be a group process, team members need to be aware up front that you'll be discussing each others' types and how they relate.

Step 2: Assess the Team

Assess each team member, provide a profile or report to each person on their type, and ask them to read it before you meet. With everyone's profile in hand, some potential communication issues and conflicts should already be apparent.

Step 3: Individual Validation/Role Fit Sessions

Schedule individual interpretation sessions with each team member. These are times to help the person understand their personal style and how it interacts with the styles of others in a safe, one-on-one environment. During this session, you will want to:

1. Talk through the report and answer general questions.
2. Validate the person's type.
3. Have the individual describe their role, and discuss how their type interacts with it.
4. Discuss how their type fits into the team process (as opposed to how they get along with individuals). Begin to unpack communication problems, conflicts or differing work styles and reframe those situations in terms of type.

Step 4: Report to the Leader

Before you meet as a group, it is usually wise to go back to the leader and summarize some of the results and main issues you've identified. The team leader is often the target of a lot of the members' frustrations, so meeting alone gives the person a chance to digest the findings and understand how to respond. Create a strategy together for how you'll handle any thorny issues during the group session. The team leader needs to be prepared to lead in personal vulnerability, responding well to feedback and willingness to change for the process to produce maximum results

Step 5: Team Type Session

Lead the team in a group session that explores each person's type and begins to troubleshoot communication or reorient roles based on type insights. You'll want to:

Round 1

1. Have each person share their type (ask the group leader to go first) and some key things they've learned about themselves in the process.
2. Highlight some of the strengths of that type and what it brings to the table after each person shares. Take some time for affirmation from the group of that person's strengths.

Round 2

3. Choose an example of how the leader's type affects the group (for instance, he's a dreamer and the more practical people don't know how to take that).
4. Help the group reframe their view of that quality in terms of the type dynamics involved. Coach them through the process of learning to communicate across that difference in ways that are effective and honoring. If needed, develop concrete communication steps that make the process work for everyone.
5. Repeat several times with issues you've discussed with the leader ahead of time.

Round 3

6. Once the group is in a good flow, allow them to start bringing up challenges that they identify and solving them together. Or, identify additional challenges you see and let them develop solutions.

Question 3: Why Do I Desire *This*? (Passion)

"The giants of the faith all had one thing in common: neither victory nor success, but passion."

Phillip Yancey

For coaching demonstrations, I'll often ask for an audience member to share an unrealized dream as a coaching issue. Once after a lengthy wait for a volunteer in a pastor's group, one man shared a dream that he thought was financially impossible: to take whole his family on an extended trip to Israel. John hesitated to even bring it up, because he also questioned whether it was right to put so much money into what was basically a family vacation.

John's choice to explore an impossible dream led to a memorable demonstration of coaching around passions—and to that dream coming to pass! Watch how the coach helped John flesh out his dream, understand what's behind it and tackle the obstacles to pursuing it.

"So tell me a bit more about that dream."

"Well, I've always wanted to go to Israel and see where Jesus walked—the places that I've spent so much time studying in Scripture. And I've dreamed about taking my family with me.

But I've got four kids, and when I think about time off and airfare and how much it is going to cost, it just doesn't seem like that's ever going to happen."

"We'll come back to the money issue. But first, tell me more about this trip. What would you do, where would you go—paint me a visual picture of it."

The coach uses the *Ideal Future Technique*[1] to help the client experience his desired future through visual language.

"OK. We'd go to all the key sites: Bethlehem, Jerusalem and the Mount of Olives. I can see myself walking over the grounds, meditating on the passages that took place at that very spot. But most of all"—and here John's voice rose and the words began gushing out—"I see myself sitting on the ground with my kids in a circle, making the Bible come alive to them! What a wonderful way to share in Jesus' life story, and to understand that our faith is rooted in history and it isn't a myth."

"That sounds like that's something you really care about. Why are you passionate about making the Bible come alive?"

The coach follows John's passion to discover his values.

"See, I have this love for history—it's what my undergrad degree was in. And we get so distant from it. We read the Bible and it all happened 2000 years ago and half a world away, and somehow it doesn't seem real. Seeing history makes it real. I can show that reality to my kids. And not just with any history, but the story of my savior—that's powerful to me. It would be like downloading a piece of my heart into my family."

"Let me see if I can sum that up. What I'm hearing is that grounding faith in reality through history is something you highly value."

"That's right. I never really thought of the trip in those terms. It's about a lot more than just sightseeing to me."

"And what about the idea of pouring your heart into your family? What makes family important to you?"

"I just think family ought to be a top priority."

"Why?"

"Oughts" and "shoulds" are often *aspirational values:* things we aspire to but don't really live, because they don't spring from our hearts. The coach probes to see if this is a true value.

"Too many pastors put ministry before family, and I don't want to do that."

"And what's behind that idea? Where does the motivation come from to make family a top priority?"

"Well, I was a pastor's kid myself. My dad was a good man, but if there was ever a conflict between family activities and a need at the church, he was at church. I've done some inner healing work, and I've been able to forgive him and let it go. But his mistakes are a big motivator to do it right. I'm committed to my kids having a real father who's an important part of their lives. I want them to learn from me, draw from me and know my heart, and not just see me as the breadwinner."

"So investing in family is an important value to you, too?"

The coach recounts the value and asks for confirmation.

"Absolutely"

"Now, you were wondering earlier if following this dream deserved to be a priority in life. What do you think of that question in light of those values for family and history?"

"That's a good question. This idea is connected to some of the themes in life that I care most about. I guess it's a lot more important than I thought it was... But there's still the money issue."

"OK, then let's brainstorm on that for a bit. Give me five options for how you could make this doable financially."

"Well... one possibility would be to take a chunk of money out of savings. Or I could combine it with some kind of ministry trip or speaking engagement, so I'm not paying for all of it."

"What else could you do?"

"Maybe we could arrange our summer so we could use one of those last minute, cut-rate airline deals..."

When the client discovers the deeply-held values behind the dream, it removes the internal obstacle.

Coach and client begin to explore practical solutions to overcome the money obstacle.

John took the true measure of his dream when he asked the passion question: "Why do I desire *this*?" As a result, he began to explore ways to make that dream a possibility. Only a few months later, he was invited to speak at a conference in Israel—and the conference organizers agreed to fly his family over as well! It was an amazing convergence of passion and practicality.

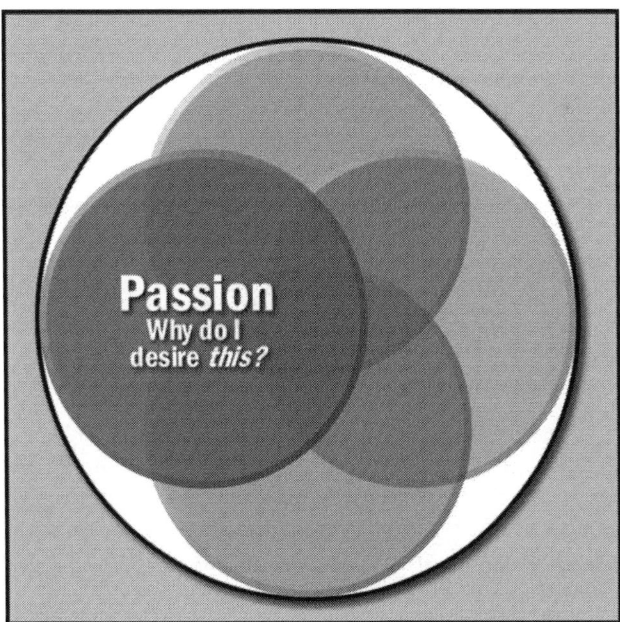

Passion Principles

Passion is the underlying motivation and energy behind our life purpose. Our passions define what's most important to us, what we really care about, and what we energetically pursue. They're the urges that compel us to *do* something.

Passion for justice is what led Wilberforce to get slavery outlawed in England. A passionate desire to show mercy kept Mother Teresa working a lifetime in the slums of Calcutta. Without the dynamism of passion, we never engage our calling with the drive and enthusiasm necessary to pull it off. John had yearned to go to Israel for years, but his internal obstacle (wondering if it was a valid end) held him back from applying his passion to it. Once that obstacle was removed, it unleashed a creative energy that helped John find a way to do what had seemed impossible.

John's story reveals a number of keys to understanding the place of passion in life purpose:

- **Passions motivate and energize us**
  Once John realized he really cared about his dream, he found the energy to pursue it.
- **Passions align with values**
  We are most passionate about what we hold to most deeply.
- **Dreams are a window to the heart**
  Even dreams that seem frivolous or impossible draw back the curtain on our passions, our deepest desires and our values.
- **Obstacles block passion**
  When we do dream, we often tend to see the immediate obstacles and get stuck, like John did. If instead of stopping we allow our passion to energize us, we (or God) might find a way to realize our dream.
- **Obstacles can be external or internal**
  John was initially stalled by finances, but the deeper obstacle was internal: is this a legitimate dream to pursue?
- **We can test dreams by their motivations**
  Looking at *why* we want to pursue a dream and what drives it helps us make a sound decision on whether or not to pursue it.

As the motivation behind our most important pursuits, passion is an essential part of purpose. So we want to tap into it. John's story also demonstrates the three main areas of passion we'll mine for these life purpose clues: *Energy*, *Dreams* and *Values*.

Assessing Energy is easy to understand—you help the client become aware of what kinds of tasks and roles create energy and satisfaction, and which ones leave the person feeling tired, drained or unproductive. Energy is connected to our sense of significance: accomplishing things that are really important to us yield a much greater sense of being on-purpose then the mundane or the urgent but not important.

Dreams are a broader arena. We'll look at the big, life-time objectives that can be scary just to voice, as well as smaller, just-for-fun dreams we might accomplish on a weekend or during a vacation. The various obstacles clients hit in the dreaming process are a key issue in this area. We'll also touch on topics like dreaming styles (different personality types dream differently), vision, and the picture of who the client wants to be in life.

Finally, we'll look at core values. Values describe our fundamental beliefs about what is meaningful and significant in life. They are the basis of our decisions and the root of our passions. Because people tend to have difficulty wrapping their minds around the concept of values, we've provided several different avenues for discovering them and some additional values information in the *Workbook*.

The section ends with a pair of summary exercises that help coachees create a lasting set of value statements and distill down what they are most passionate about.

Baseline Assessment

A good starting place for working at Passion is the baseline assessment. Again, this is designed to help you and your clients identify what they already know and where more work could be profitable. On the following page is an example of a filled-out baseline assessment for Passion (a blank copy is in the *Workbook*). This exercise can be done verbally, by asking the questions during a coaching session, or you can assign it as homework before an appointment. Following the example is a page of evaluation criteria for coaching the baseline.

1.1b Passion Baseline Assessment

These questions will give us a baseline for creating a customized life purpose discovery plan. Take five to eight minutes to complete the assessment. If you don't know what to say on a question, or would have to dream up an answer on the spot, leave it blank. This isn't a test where you are supposed to get the answers right: we're just trying to determine what you already know for sure about your purpose.

1. What is your core passion in life?

    To be an exemplary man of God in my generation

2. Have you ever made a list of life dreams? If so, name two or three dreams either from that list or ones you'd put on it if you had one.

    I have some dreams I'm pursuing, but I have never done a formal list.
    Go on two short term mission trips to Kenya or Madagascar with my spouse.
    I want to own my own business someday.

3. What are two areas of your current role that energize you, and two things that drain you? Were those easy or difficult to think of?

    Energizes me: *Motivating my team toward our yearly goals.*
    Training other staff for future management positions.
    Drains me: *Writing quarterly reports.*
    Firing or disciplinary proceedings.

    I had to think about that one a bit.
    It was harder to think of things that drained me.

4. Have you ever written out a set of personal or leadership values? If so, state two below:

    Sort of. We did that in our church once.

    I value the Bible as the word of God and the source of truth and direction.
    I want to be an example to my kids of what a loving father should look like.

5. How well does your primary role align with your core passions and what energizes you? What would need to change to make it a great fit?

    Pretty well, I guess. Most days I look forward to going in to work. It could be better, although it is hard to pinpoint exactly what.

Evaluating the Baseline Assessment

Our purpose is to get a sense of how far the client has already gone in exploring Passion so we can create a discovery plan that fits their needs. The first question examines the person's grasp of their core motivation. Here's what I'm looking for:

- **Well said** and tightly worded—as if the person has thought this through and used these words before, instead of making something up. This example has that flavor.
- **Unique**: Your passion is your own, uniquely fitted to you. The example seems to be worded in fairly generic language—I'd want to probe that and see if this is a genuine, personal passion or just a good Christian idea or stock phrase.
- **Passionate**: I'm looking for strong, emotional words like "exemplary." You get animated when you talk about your true passions—they energize you.

The next question covers dreams. Dream lists are common enough that a person who has done some formal life purpose work has probably completed one. Since we are trying to get a sense of how far the person has already gone in this area, look for responses that evidence some forethought instead of sounding off-the-cuff. The example dream about short term mission is very specific (two trips, to two particular countries). The dream about owning a business is vague—I'd like to ask more about it and see what's there. A good follow-up question is to ask for dreams in several different *Life Wheel Categories* (8.2) to check for balance.

The energy question (3) focuses on awareness of what energizes and de-energizes a person. Clients who have to think for a while to come up with an answer would likely benefit from some additional reflection in this area.

The fourth question touches on values. Although many leaders have been exposed to values concepts through their organizations, most have never created a personal value set. When the person does offer value statement examples, look to see if they fit the definition of a value—sometimes you'll get theological statements or aspirations (what the responses on the example appear to be) instead of lived-out core values. Since values are most useful when they are memorized and accessible at a moment's notice, I also look for short succinct statements instead of rambling ones.

Question five checks role and passion alignment. Vague satisfaction or dissatisfaction with the role tends to indicate a lack of self-awareness. People who strongly like or dislike their roles and can tell you exactly why know more about their passions than those who are fairly satisfied but have difficulty telling you what would need to change to make things really great.

Creating a Plan

Once you've reviewed the assessment, create a plan together for exploring this area further. Your plan should take into account how much effort the client wants to put into passion discovery. Exercises for creating a discovery plan that fits the client's agenda can be found in the next three chapters. See the Design section (pg. 79) for more on creating a discovery plan.

Chapter 7: Passion/Energy

"That which dominates our imagination and our thoughts will determine our life and character."

Ralph Waldo Emerson

Paul discusses his passion—preaching the gospel to the entire known world—as something that drove him, that energized him , even as a "compulsion" (I Cor. 9:16). "For this I toil, striving with all the energy which he mightily inspires in me" (Col. 1:29; RSV). That passionate energy took him across the then known world, ignited by the desire to preach the gospel to the far reaches of the Roman Empire.

When you add up the sufferings and sacrifices Paul made in pursuit of this goal, it is unmistakable evidence for a consuming passion behind what he did. He gave up everything in his prior life as a Pharisee for it ("Whatever gain I had, I counted as loss for the sake of Christ" (Phil 3:7; RSV)), and arranged his entire existence around preaching the gospel to those who hadn't heard it. Paul's passion was not just a good idea, or a human dream, or self-aggrandizement, but something God-inspired.

Recognizing Energy Cues

So how do you coach a person to discover their passion? One key technique is becoming aware of the client's energy. When we speak, our voice tone, volume and emotive content vary over time. For example, read the following two sentences aloud:

- “I’m not sure what is causing us to misunderstand each other.”
- “I am *so frustrated* with her! Every time we talk it feels like we are hurling grenades at each other.”

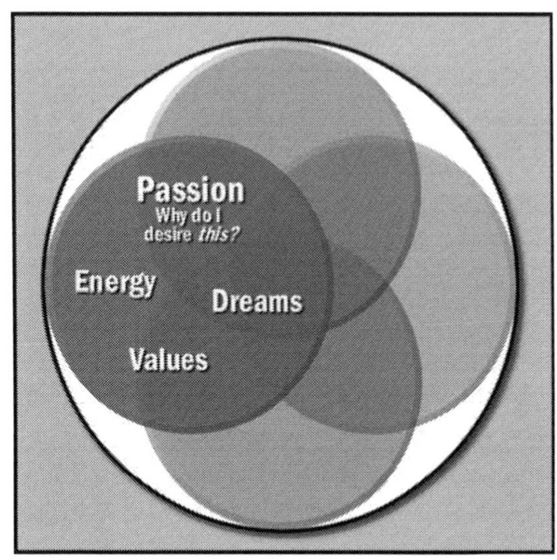

The energy in these two sentences is very different. The first is cool and analytic, while the second is animated and emotive. The person in the second sentence is talking about something he is passionate about. If he was reporting a chance meeting with a casual acquaintance on the street, you wouldn’t hear this level of emotion. This relationship is important enough to really affect him.

When we talk about our passions, we want others to get it—to understand that this is something we care about, and to know why we care. So consciously or unconsciously, we change the way we talk to communicate that energy. Here are several passion signals illustrated using the example sentences above:

- **Pace.** We tend to talk at a different pace (usually faster) when our passion surfaced. For instance, the second sentence above would tend to pour out in a rush of words.
- **Volume.** We talk louder when we are excited, softer when we are pensive or touched in a place that hurts.
- **Repetition.** Bringing up the same word or theme repeatedly can signal passion.
- **Tone.** Emotions affect the quality of our voice. It might quaver when we are moved, be accompanied by sighs when we are discouraged, or have an edge if we’re angry.
- **Confidence.** When we are passionate we tend to express ourselves more directly and with greater confidence in the rightness of our ideas. Notice that the first example sentence is tentative (“I’m not sure…”) while the second is declarative.
- **Word Choice: Emotive Content.** When we are passionate, we tend to use hyperbole or inflammatory language—we are “hurling grenades” instead of just talking. We turn to graphic metaphors and analogies to convey the strength of our feelings.

If you are meeting in person, there are also visual cues to look for:

- **Facial Expression.** People become animated when they talk about their passions. You'll see the energy in their expressions of joy, anticipation, grief or anger.
- **Body Language.** If you are meeting face to face, you'll often see a person sit up, become more alert, lean forward in their chair or motion more with their hands when they get into their passions. The energy they feel is expressed in their body position.

To turn these clues into life purpose discoveries, reflect back what you see to the client:

- *"I noticed that you got really animated when you started talking about the school bus problem. It seems like you hit on something important there—what makes you passionate about that?"*

Naming these energy areas as Passions can help the client unearth where their heart truly lies. The general rule is, follow the energy to identify the passion—the values, dreams and desires about which the person cares most deeply.

One way to follow the energy to Passions is a technique I call *Listening for Significance.* This works great for getting to the bottom of a dream or value. It's very simple: you watch the client for the energy cues, pick out the word or phrase that seemed to have the most energy behind it, and ask the client to expand on it. Here's an example.

Coaching Exercise—Cultivating Your Energy Awareness
Here are two ways to work at becoming more aware of energy in a conversation.

1. **Listen for Energy.** Listen to someone talking about something important for three to five minutes. You can ask a friend or spouse to share about something that is going on in their life, watch a speech on TV, or listen to a teacher or preacher. Have the list of energy cues on page 117 in front of you. How many cues you can find in five minutes? Take notes as you listen, and debrief together afterward on what you saw and what it means. Or try having two coaches list to the same speech and compare notes at the end.

2. **Listening for Significance.** Ask a friend or your spouse to share an important dream or desire. Listen for energy cues, and use the *Listening for Significance* technique to ask follow-up questions. Can you bring out the passion or core value behind that dream? Use a simple question like this repeatedly so you can focus on listening:

   "You mentioned that ____. Tell me more about that."

"What's one of your dreams?"

"Well, I've been thinking about getting involved with Habitat for Humanity—you know, building houses for people who can't afford them. Getting out there with a hammer and a bunch of guys and helping put a whole house together in a week sounds like an awesome challenge. I like the idea of doing something to help someone out, too."

"Awesome" is a high-energy word. "I like helping" has less oomph behind it.

"You mentioned that it would be 'an awesome challenge.' Say more about that."

"Say more" is a great question for this technique: it is totally neutral and lets the client go in whatever direction he wants to.

"It just sounds cool. I mean, you get 20 guys together, and we're all competitive, but to do something like that you can't just have everyone going off on their own. It's got to be a team effort. I used to be a football player in high school, and I always loved that locker room atmosphere of everybody giving it all for the same goal."

"Love" is a strong word—that's what we'll ask about.

"Say more about that locker room atmosphere. What's important to you about that?"

"I don't know... I guess you just feel like you are part of something significant when you are all pulling together for something bigger. Sometimes life can get pretty mundane at the office, just pushing paper around day after day. It's not that it's a bad job—I just want to do something different sometimes."

"Part of something bigger" is an important idea to the client.

"You mentioned that being on a team pulling together for something bigger is important. Expand on that a bit."

"It's like... I guess I'm a team person at heart. I'd much rather work with a group on a big goal than accomplish something on my own. I ***like*** *sharing the credit; I* ***like*** *being part of others' success and their being part of mine."*

The client repeatedly emphasizes the word "like"—as if others expect something different of him but this is who he is.

"It seemed that there was a lot of energy around your desire to share the credit for success. What's behind that?"

"One of my biggest joys is succeeding together. The Habitat thing for me is less about building a house for someone than it is building a successful team..."

As the conversation goes on, the energy and significance levels continue to rise. Pursuing the energy cues and asking about what is most significant quickly takes this client to one of his "biggest joys"—and that likely reveals a core passion.

Finding Your Energy

Clients can also use reflection exercises to look at their lives and find places of passion. Since heightened energy often points to passion, these action steps involve looking at various activities and seeing which ones energize or drain a client, as in the *Energy Activities* exercise (7.2). Some clients can do this during one sitting, while others may need to keep a list by their phone for a week or have someone talk them through the exercise. People don't often hit obstacles when trying to identify what energizes them—they just haven't been paying attention.

This is a good exercise for "S's" on the MBTI©—it starts with hands-on, practical experience and uses those concrete mileposts as jumping off points to reach the abstract. The *Energy Activities* exercise can also be used for an immediate payoff—take the list of energy drains and eliminate or reduce the amount of time spent on them one by one.

Following the Energy
Here are some queries for following the energy to the value or passion that underlies it:

- *"Why does this energize you?"*
- *"What about that draws you or engages you?"*
- *"What does it give you when you pursue this?"*
- *"Why is that important to you?*
- *"What's behind that?"*
- *"What makes you passionate about this?"*

The *Passion Bull's-eye* (7.1) aims to identify passions directly without first looking at energizing activities. This tends to be easier for older or more mature clients, and conceptual thinkers ("N's" on the Myers-Briggs).

The Passion Bull's Eye

This exercise explores the causes, ideals, and themes that you are passionate about. Use the questions below to identify them, then place each one on the Bull's Eye with the strongest toward the center. We're looking for ideals here, so if you think of an activity you love (like windsurfing), try to name the underlying passion (fitness, being outdoors). Think of passions within each of the *Life Wheel Categories* (8.2) to get a balanced view.

- What *causes* have I invested in long term? Where have I volunteered or contributed over the years, because I cared deeply about the cause?
- What are my *soapbox issues?* These are the issues and ideas I talk about all the time, argue over with people, get animated or upset about.
- What *needs* tug at my heart? What's the need I can't keep myself from meeting?
- What in my life brings my *emotions* to the surface? What do I see or think of that gets me choked up or compels me to take action?
- What am I most excited and joyful about in life? Most grieved over?

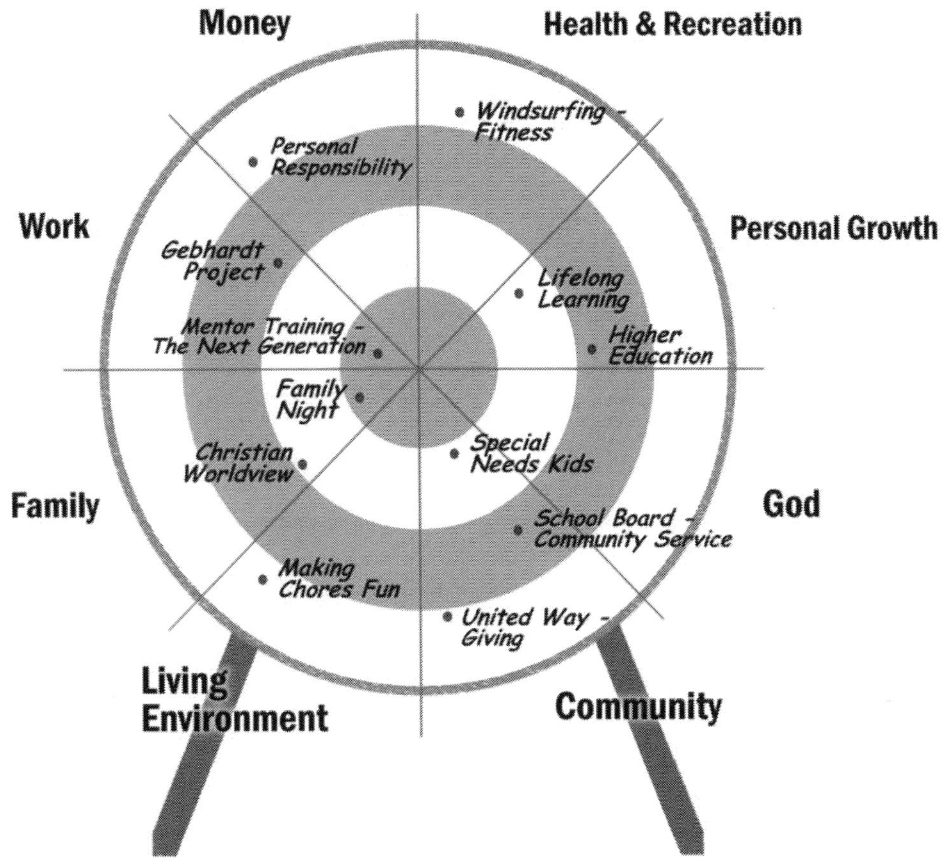

7.2  Energy Activities

This reflection (similar to *Strengths, Type and Energy,* 5.6) gives you another way to identify what gives you energy, and therefore may connect to your passions. We'll create a list of what engages and energizes you in life, and then mine it for insights.

Step 1: Roles and Responsibilities

Start by thinking about the different roles you fill in life: employee, student, spouse, friend, parent, or volunteer. What activities really stoke you? What do you think about or anticipate even when you aren't doing it? If it's hard to think of examples, pull out last month's calendar and look it over. Don't over-analyze—just try to get some examples down on paper.

Step 2: Fun and Fellowship

Add to your list from other areas of life: hobbies, church involvement, recreation, interests. We're not looking for what's productive, but what you are drawn to. What things in life do you give your best energy to and get the most energy back from?

Step 3: Find the Themes

Now we'll examine this list for clues to your core passions. Here are some reflection questions to help:

- *Why* do you care about these things? What is behind them that energizes you?
- What stands out or surprises you as you look at this list?
- What themes do you see repeatedly on this list? (For instance, "working with kids.")
- If you had to sum up what energizes you in all these different things in only three or four phrases, what would they be?

Coaching Tip

The most challenging part of this exercise is finding the passion themes underneath the activities. For clients who aren't good at summarizing or seeing patterns, naming what you see in the client's reflections can be very helpful.

The Passion Bull's-eye exercise asks about passion themes directly, while this exercise takes an indirect route by starting with the activities that energize a client. If the person has not done any life purpose work before, this two-step process is sometimes easier to navigate.

Chapter 8: Passion/ Dreams and Desires

"I am not unmindful that some of you have come here out of great trials and tribulations. Some of you have come fresh from narrow cells. Some of you have come from areas where your quest for freedom left you battered by the storms of persecution and staggered by the winds of police brutality. You have been the veterans of creative suffering. Continue to work with the faith that unearned suffering is redemptive. Go back to Mississippi, go back to Alabama, go back to South Carolina, go back to Georgia, go back to Louisiana, go back to the slums and ghettos of our northern cities, knowing that somehow this situation can and will be changed.

Let us not wallow in the valley of despair. I say to you today, my friends, that in spite of the difficulties and frustrations of the moment, I still have a dream. It is a dream deeply rooted in the American dream.

I have a dream that one day this nation will rise up and live out the true meaning of its creed: 'We hold these truths to be self-evident: that all men are created equal.'

I have a dream that one day on the red hills of Georgia the sons of former slaves and the sons of former slave owners will be able to sit down together at a table of brotherhood.

I have a dream that one day even the state of Mississippi, a desert state, sweltering with the heat of injustice and oppression, will be transformed into an oasis of freedom and justice.

I have a dream that my four children will one day live in a nation where they will not be judged by the color of their skin but by the content of their character.

I have a ***dream*** *today!*

I have a dream that one day the state of Alabama, whose governor's lips are presently dripping with the words of interposition and nullification, will be transformed into a situation where little black boys and black girls will be able to join hands with little white boys and white girls and walk together as sisters and brothers.

I have a ***dream*** *today!*

I have a dream that one day every valley shall be exalted, every hill and mountain shall be made low, the rough places will be made plain, and the crooked places will be made straight, and the glory of the Lord shall be revealed, and all flesh shall see it together.

This is our hope. This is the faith with which I return to the South. With this faith we will be able to hew out of the mountain of despair a stone of hope. With this faith we will be able to transform the jangling discords of our nation into a beautiful symphony of brotherhood. With this faith we will be able to work together, to pray together, to struggle together, to go to jail together, to stand up for freedom together, knowing that we will be free one day."

Dr. Martin Luther King Jr., 1963

Dreams are powerful. Dreams and those who dream them can change cultures, redirect nations and move mountains. Dreams animate our hearts with passionate energy, spur us to action, and offer the hope that a better future is not only possible but imperative. Dreams are the images of our passion overlaid on the future.

In the context of coaching, dreams can be defined as "*pictures of the future we hope to live in someday.*" They are snapshots of what we desire life to look like.

Since goals are a big part of coaching, it is helpful to clearly distinguish between dreams and goals. A goal is an end that you have committed to accomplishing. Dreams simply look at the future and say, "This is what I wish for."

The currency of dreams is hope; visions run instead on faith.

A dream becomes a goal when you commit to reaching in within a certain time frame. But part of the power of dreams is that you *don't* have to have practical plans to reach them. You don't have to be committed to making a dream happen—it is simply a picture of what the future might look like if it is in accord with your desires. The fact that we don't have to have a realistic plan frees us to imagine what we really want, instead of being bound by what we feel is possible.

"Vision" is another term that gets confused with dreams. A vision is a dream-goal that reaches out to capture others to work for its fulfillment. It is a visual picture of a desired future that a visionary has committed to make happen by bringing others on board to help. That means a visionary has no business recruiting people to a vision if he or she is not personally committed to seeing it through to completion. If your visions are ideas for a neat future that you may or may not act on, you are a dreamer, not a visionary. The currency of dreams is *hope*; visions run instead on *faith*, the substance of things hoped for.

If a vision is truly from God, it exists to bring into being the greatest of the three virtues, *agape love*. A biblical vision is a picture of a future God passionately desires and calls us to reach. Therefore, biblical visionaries are not vision-owners who mobilize others to do their vision: they are bondservants to God's desires for the sake of others. So if you hear a leader say something like, "You are here to serve my vision," run in the opposite direction. That's a leader who is most likely building a personal empire, not the Kingdom of God.

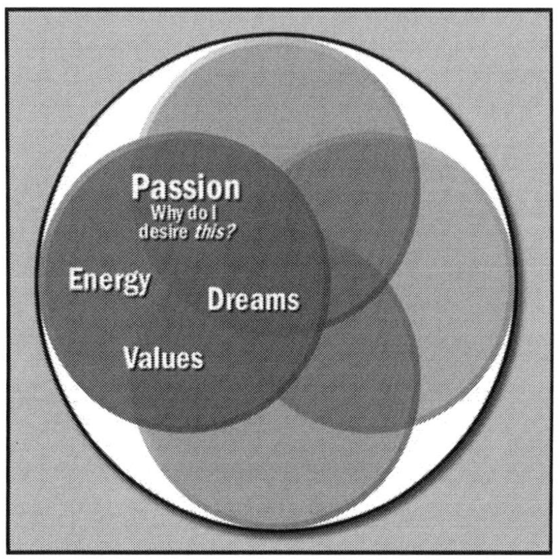

Dream Principles

Martin Luther King's "I Have a Dream" speech illustrates a number of important dreaming principles[16] we can apply to the life coaching process. Take a moment to reread the speech to fix it in your mind, and then we'll dive in.

1. **Dreams are visual images**
   Notice the abundant imagery in King's speech. He carries you to "the red hills of Georgia," to a future where "little black boys and girls will be able to join hands with little white boys and girls and walk together as brothers." You don't hear King's speech so much as you see it. Visual images affect us much more deeply and are more powerfully motivating than words. Therefore, we'll encourage clients to use the process of visualization to turn the skeleton of important dreams into fleshed-out pictures using the *Envisioning Your Dream* exercise (8.4).

2. **Dreams reveal deep desires**
   King's dream touches us at a visceral, emotional level because it expresses the heart-cry of an entire people for freedom and justice. Dreams are like that: they resonate with the passions of our hearts. One service we offer our clients is to help them find the deep desires that lie beneath their dreams (see *Dream Themes* 8.5).

---

16 King is also functioning as a visionary here. He was certainly committed to this dream—he gave his life for it!

3. **Dreams motivate**
   Martin Luther King spoke about his dream of a better future to motivate African Americans to keep working for equality and keep hoping for non-violent change. Dreams motivate because visualizing them activates the hope that they can be reached. A well-pictured dream makes the desired future real enough that we are willing to do pay a price to have it. In this chapter we'll explore two techniques for increasing motivation: *Envisioning* the dream fulfilled (8.4) and looking at the cost of not reaching a dream (see the *Regrets* exercise (9.2).

4. **Dreams ignore obstacles**
   Part of the power of dreams in the coaching process is that they overlook present obstacles. Notice how King urges his audience to "*Go back... knowing that somehow this situation can and will be changed.*" The dream is that inequality will be changed somehow; that we don't know how it will happen is immaterial to the fact that this is a dream worth pursuing. This quality of dreams leads us to an important coaching technique. When a client is stymied by present obstacles (like a lack of time or resources), ignoring the obstacle and picturing the dreamed-of future has an amazing power to re-motivate people and help them engage their creativity to get unstuck.[17]

5. **Dreams connect us to heaven**
   Because they describe an ideal world, dreams have a certain otherworldly quality. King states, "...we will not be satisfied until 'justice rolls down like waters, and righteousness like a mighty stream.'" An imperfect world doesn't lend itself to the perfection of dreams. King's dream is in fact a picture of heaven—and in that sense, every true dream is grounded in heaven, because every true desire was created to find ultimate fulfillment there (Heb. 11:16).

> **Change vs. Letting Go**
> One technique for helping clients deal with external circumstances is to explore changing their expectations as well as changing their situation. If change is not on the horizon, ask clients to imagine what it would be like to just make peace with circumstances and move on. Conversely, if the person is settling for less or just coping, challenge them to imagine a future where the thing they are coping with is totally eliminated.

Dreams and Limitations

It is important that we keep in mind that dreams are remembrances of Eden. We can imagine an ideal life where all things turn out well, but we cannot fully reproduce it in this broken world. A dream is an echo of the eternal, running down through time to a fallen race. Although we may pursue them here, our deepest desires only find ultimate fulfillment in heaven.

---

17 This "Ideal Future Technique" is covered in more depth in *Coaching Questions*, pg 42.

Does that mean we should stop dreaming or pursuing dreams? Absolutely not! We must dream, to keep heaven in mind and to understand how this world falls far short of it. Without dreams, we easily settle into pragmatic worldliness.

But, contrary to what some teach, dreams do have limits. There is only so much you can do. We in North America can believe that all creation ought to bow to our personal desires and fill all our needs, but that doesn't mean it will happen. Any honest appraisal of reality would show that even the best dreams of the best people don't always come true.

But to stop dreaming altogether swings us to the opposite pole—to let go of the hope of a better tomorrow. And hope is integral to biblical living. It moves us from simply making peace with sin and injustice to doing something about them. So how do we strike the balance?

In *The Power of Purpose*, Peter Temes remarks that the Western impulse is to change the world to fit our expectations, while in Eastern thought we change our expectations to fit what the world gives us. The Western dream is unlimited personal power to rearrange circumstances to match our desires (see the self-help section of your local bookstore for a roomful of advice on how to unleash your personal power). The Eastern dream is to enter a nirvana so at peace with the universe that nothing can shake us.

The historical Christian faith, born in the East and nurtured in the West, admits the truth of both approaches. For everything there is a season. There are times to work for change no matter the cost, and there are times to let go and be at peace with the way things are. There are times to chase your dreams, and times to release them. As coaches, we need to learn to deploy both approaches (see box).

Life Purpose and Dreams

The specific future you dream about says a lot about your life purpose. If you dream of opening a Bed and Breakfast and having the chance to host and serve all kinds of people, that dream may be a container for your deepest desires in life. So an important part of the life purpose discovery process is getting these dreams out on the table.

A great place to start is with a *Dream Inventory* (8.1). This version is broken into two sections: one for Big Dreams, and a second for Fun Dreams. Big dreams are desires depicted in larger pieces: getting a master's degree, starting a business, mentoring five young leaders or going to the mission field. Many fall under the second level of God's purposes—working to bring his Kingdom to life in the world (see diagram). Fun dreams aren't so much about legacy as about joy. They fall under the third level of purpose. Maybe you've always wanted to hike down the Oregon coast with three friends, take a hot air balloon ride or visit the grandchildren regularly.

Separating these two lists encourages coachees to engage the innocent desires that give spice to life. With just one big dream list, Christians tend to get embarrassed about putting level III dreams like "Take a fall color vacation in New England" next to "Lead 10 people to the Lord in my lifetime." We discount the fun desires as "not spiritual enough." Yet these dreams *are* part of God's good will, as long as we keep them in proper proportion with the entirety of God's purpose. That means holding them more lightly, and often allowing God to bring them as a gift instead of making them the focus of your life.

Fun dreams are very useful in situations where coachees don't yet know what bigger dreams they want to pursue. Looking at the desires underneath these fun dreams (see 8.5) can often access core passions as well as examining big dreams.

Creating a *Dream Lifestyle* (see 8.3) is another way to uncover fun dreams. Describing a living situation, workplace, home, schedule and relationships that you'd really love to live with can make it easier to voice what would bring joy in life.

I've included my own dream inventories from years ago in 8.1 and 8.5 to show what a list looks like and how it changes over time. Some dreams have been realized, and some I lost interest in and removed from the list. I am still working on a few, and some I haven't made any progress toward at all (like building a house) and I'm OK with that. A dream list is not a rule-book to follow. In fact, your lists *should* change as you grow older and become more fully aware of what God has placed in your heart. A part of aging is learning to let go gracefully of dreams you've passed by and allow the true dream, the dream of heaven, to take root in their place.

Dream Bigger

Believing in people helps them do more than they could on their own. It is easy to shortchange our dreams and limit them to what seems manageable with our current resources. But we grow in the course of pursuing a God-given dream—so we need to dream in terms of our potential, not our present. Here are several ways to challenge those who dream small to think bigger:

- **Ask for More.** "What if you really stretched yourself? What about going for double this impact, or even ten times as much?"
- **Remove Failure.** "Imagine that you couldn't fail—that you knew God was behind you on this. How big would you dream then?"
- **Envision.** Visualizing the fulfillment of a dream in detail is highly motivating. Often if you spend time there, the client will find the courage to think bigger.
- **Request Faith.** "Can I challenge you to push this beyond your current abilities? What if you made it something that requires God's hand for success?"

These exercises are generally used as reflective action steps. Most people like to think about an ideal future, so that isn't usually an obstacle. However, it is fairly common to have areas of the heart walled off, which keeps those desires from coming to the surface. When I get a dream list back, here are some cues I scan for:

- **Freedom to dream.** Is the person able to list both big and fun dreams? Do they have more than a few items?
- **Balance.** Do these dreams touch many life areas, or are some categories absent? For instance, on an over-spiritualized list everything is ministry-related.
- **Energy.** Ask about a few of their dreams and look for passion and energy. If it is missing, what's going on there?
- **Partnership.** How does the person's marriage (or singleness) affect their dream? Do partners dream together, does one dominate? Have singles put all their dream eggs in the Mister-Right basket?

Dreaming Styles

Another thing I look for is a person's dreaming style. The most striking difference is between "S's" and "N's" on the Myers-Briggs. "N's" are natural dreamers: they are future-oriented, conceptual thinkers who easily create dream pictures that are disconnected from the present (in other words, they can dream without needing a plan to get there.) "S's," on the other hand, are practical and present oriented. They dream by extrapolating concrete experiences into the future. Dreaming without a connection to present reality is frustrating and meaningless for them.

Years ago we had dinner with a wonderful older gentleman who did service calls for a manufacturer. His company was going to be bought out, and he was trying to figure out what he wanted to do with the rest of his working life. So I started asking him questions about his future. Time after time, he drew a blank. He had no unrealized dreams to pursue (he was happy with what he was doing), there was nothing from his childhood he always wanted to be, and he couldn't conjure up a picture of an ideal future much different than his present circumstance. Nothing in my life purpose toolbox was working.

Finally it dawned on me that he was an "S," and all of my questions were asking him to dream in an "N" style—creating an ideal future out of nothing. So I started asking him about past experiences. "What have you done in the past that felt like it really fit you? What roles have you flourished in? What are you doing now that really stokes you?"

He had much more to say when asked about concrete experiences. At one point I asked what he loved best about his current job. He responded, "Well, every day I go somewhere that really needs me. If I can't get that one crucial part to work, maybe the whole plant is shut down. So I get to be the hero every day: I solve their problem, everyone is happy, and then tomorrow I get to do it again." The next question was the key to the conversation. "What kind of job would let you to do more of *that*?"

So find out how your client dreams. Dream exercises come more naturally to "N's" (they are the dreamers, after all), but "S's" can enjoy them if they concentrate on mining past experiences for what they love, and extrapolating that into a picture of their desired future.

Finding Passions under Dreams

One way to follow up a *Dream Inventory* is to pick a dream and go for it! If the client wants to be coached on pursuing a certain dream, like starting a Christian school, often a first step is to *Envision* it (exercise 8.4) in detail—create a full-fledged dream image of daily life at that dream school. Once you have a clear picture of what you want and are motivated to pursue it, you can move into the basic coaching process of creating goals, options and actions.

However, if your objective is discovering the client's life purpose, the path to take is finding the passion that underlies those dreams. Why do you want to start a school? What would it give you, and the people you want to serve? From big, hairy audacious goals that change the world to innocent wishes for fun experiences, all dreams are a window into our heart's desire. They are *containers* that give form to our Passions, so we can visualize and talk about them. Life purpose coaching uses the details of dream image to unearth the desire hidden beneath it.

> **Freedom to Dream**
>
> Here are some tips for dreaming freely:
>
> - **Dream in pencil**
>   Dreams are containers for your passions. You can always change the container.
> - **Create a "Dream Space"**
>   Give clients permission to dream. Give them unlimited resources, or the knowledge that you can't fail, or whatever else they need to dream boldly.
> - **Don't worry about implementation**
>   Dreams don't need a plan—they are a picture of the future you desire.
> - **There is no "right" answer**
>   You don't get extra points for having things turn out exactly as you envision. Just put it down on paper!

If you look at a set of family photos, you'll see the same faces popping up time after time. It won't take you long to figure out who the brothers and sisters and grandmas are. Since dreams are snapshots of what our passions would look like lived-out, they are the family photo album of our hearts. If you leaf through your dreams, it won't take long to identify the "family" of underlying passions that keep popping up in the pictures.

Dream Themes (exercise 8.5) provides a structure for that process. It can be especially interesting to work with *Fun Dreams*. People are often amazed at what the fun experiences they are drawn to can tell them about who they are and what they value.

Dream Themes can be done as a reflection, but I prefer to coach it. New insights about themes come easier with an objective observer helping you name the connections. First, identify a theme (for instance, "Many of your dreams have to do with being in nature"). Then begin asking, "What does that give you?" or "Why is that important to you?" until you arrive at the core of the underlying passion. A coach who is experienced at this process can quickly move the conversation through dreams to deep desires without getting distracted by pragmatic questions about how feasible the dream is.

Coaching Beyond the Container

Treating a dream as a snapshot of an underlying desire is also a great way to engage clients whose dreams don't seem to fit with Kingdom values. Watch for how the coach moves the conversation from dream to true desire, and how that changes the tenor of the conversation.

"It sounds like you've made a lot of progress on your original goal. What else would you like to tackle today?"

"Well," Antoine said, "I've been dreaming about finding a faith that is more about God than about religion. I want to enjoy being with him without a bunch of do's and don'ts, and be about treating people right instead of believing the right things. I still believe in God, but I'm through with organized religion. I want to create a new kind of spiritual life that doesn't include church."

Instead of reacting to Antoine's emotion, the coach probes to understand what is behind this dream. (That's also a great way to buy time while you decide how to respond!)

"OK—that sounds like something you are pretty passionate about. Could you tell me a bit about what got you dreaming down this road?"

"I just get tired of all the pettiness, and people not walking their talk. Last week we found out that one of the elders was having an affair. Even though two of them knew about it for almost a year, nobody did anything. It's the same old same-old—we're more worried about how it looks than whether it is right. I finally decided I'd be better off going it alone."

"So what I'm hearing is that walking your talk is important to you."

"Exactly."

"And what's behind that?"

The coach begins asking about underlying motivations.

"Well, things like honesty and integrity are important to me. I don't want to be the kind of person who says one thing and does another, and I don't want to be in a group that does that."

"OK. So what would going it alone give you that you aren't experiencing now?"

"The ability to be part of something I believe in. No more of the frustration of dealing with all the religious crap. I get all upset when we do such stupid stuff to each other, and it isn't worth it."

You get frustrated with things you care deeply about.

"That's reasonable. So if you stop going to church, and you don't have the frustrations—is that your real objective?"

"Um... I don't understand. Can you ask that a different way?"

"Sure. Here's a scenario. Let's say you found a church out

there that really did walk their talk—people were honest, they dealt with things as they came up, you didn't have all these frustrations. If the choice was between going it alone or joining a great church, what would you do?"

"Well... yeah, I'd join. I just don't believe that kind of church exists."

"But leaving that question aside, what's your deepest desire? To live your faith alone or to be in a community that really walks it out together?"

The coach challenges Antoine to relook at what he really wants.

"I'd love to be part of that kind of community. I just haven't been in anything that works."

"So if you put the choice in terms of your deep desires, what is it?"

"It seems like I have two options: I can go ahead and do God alone, which is not my deepest desire but would get me out of this frustrating situation, or I can keep trying to find a real community, which is what I really want, although I'm losing hope that I can find it."

The dream's underlying desire is to be part of a true community. That *is* biblical.

"So what I'm hearing is that the best part of you wants community?"

"Yeah. The more we talk, the more I realize how important that is to me. I just don't know how to find it."

"Well, that sounds like something we could work on."

"OK—I'm game."

(And if the reason the church isn't perfect is because you joined it, we'll figure that out along the way, too.)

In this dialogue the coach helped Antoine reconfigure his dream in a way that let him move toward God and find his heart's desire at the same time. What makes it work is the belief of the coach that dreams are containers for desires that were

Separating the Factors

The dialog with Antoine illustrates a technique called "*Separating the Factors.*" When there are two or more contributing factors for a decision, the coach creates scenarios that let the client evaluate the decision one factor at a time.

In Antoine's case, there are two motivations expressed: the desire to go it alone, and the desire to leave his frustrating situation. Which one really reflects his true desire? So the coach creates a scenario that separates the two factors: what if the choice was a great community versus an individual faith? By removing the frustration factor from the choice, we can see how strong the desire is to go it alone.

Another way of posing the same question would be, "If living an individual faith turned out to be every bit as frustrating as staying in the church, which would you choose? This equalizes the frustration of the two options—it's just that posing two negative outcomes is less motivating for the client.

originally made to point to God. Instead of opposing the client's dream, the coach helps Antoine explore what's behind it, then challenges him to reach for that desire instead of settling for second best. So the steps for this technique are:

1. Take the dream seriously,
2. Find the deep desire under it that points to God,
3. Invite reorienting the goal around the true desire instead of the container (the dream).

Coaching beyond the container to the true desire can even work with overtly fleshly desires. If a client wants to have an affair, what does he hope to gain from that? What is his true heart's desire in a romantic relationship? It may be intimacy, or being respected, or excitement, or an escape from criticism at home. I'm not going to coach someone to have an affair, but I can coach him toward true intimacy, respect or a meaningful life within God's plan for him The closer you strike to the true heart's desire (which was created for fulfillment in heaven), the easier it is to create a Kingdom-oriented goal.

I use a variation of this approach when dreams are frustrated by external circumstances. For example, the dream is to go on a Caribbean cruise with your husband, but you can't because you have two toddlers at home. One way to get around that roadblock is to identify the underlying heart's desire. If it is to have a special time alone with your husband to make a lasting memory, then I can ask, "What are five other ways you could satisfy that desire without leaving home for a week?"

The visual image of the dream (going on a cruise) is a *container* for the underlying desire. But desires can fit in many different containers. If clients can separate their passion from the dream container, it opens up many new options for its pursuit.

It's How You Play the Game

If some dreams lead to true desires and others don't, it may be helpful to have a framework for understanding which is which.

I'd like to go to Bora Bora some day, and stay in one of those bamboo cabanas that are built out over a blue-green tropical lagoon. I'd sit with my feet dangling in the clear, warm water, watch the sun go down, see the moon rise over the surf and rock to sleep on the waves.

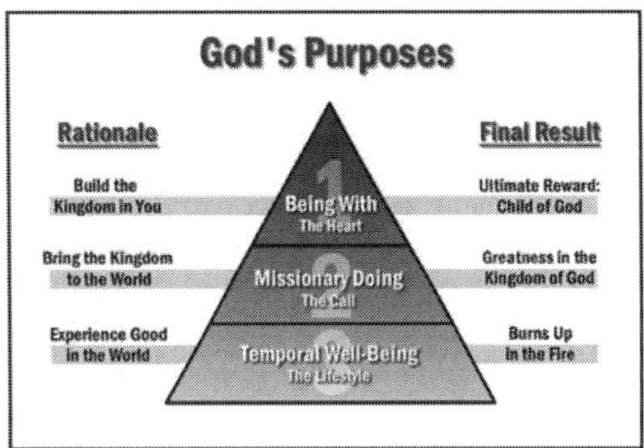

Sounds wonderful, doesn't it? There is nothing wrong with dreaming about it—in fact, that kind of dream gets me thinking about heaven, if I hold it loosely. But if I cling to it, and make Bora Bora my passionate pursuit and the focus of my life, not only will that trip fail to satisfy me, but it will mess up the rest of my life, too. This goes back to the purpose diagram: a desire for temporal happiness (level III) has grown out of proportion and displaced being with God and bringing in His Kingdom (levels I and II) as the focus of life.

Money and sexuality are similar. They are not intrinsically bad things, but they can be pursued in destructive ways. Much of the content of our dreams falls into this neutral ground, where the object of the dream is neither good nor bad; it is how we go after it that makes the difference. Any temporal pleasure elevated to the status of a primary purpose brings death, not life.

Our passions fall into three categories:

- **True Desires**, which reflect the image of Christ and point us toward heaven.
- **Innocent Desires**, that are part of being human and are neutral.
- **Corrupt Desires** are true or innocent desires that are twisted into sinful, destructive forms.

When our desires get messed up they tend to be either True Desires pursued in the wrong way, or Innocent Desires taken out of proportion. Sex out of wedlock is often a true desire for intimacy pursued in the wrong way. Arranging our lives around getting to Bora Bora is an innocent desire taken way out of proportion. The book of James teaches that desires tend to become corrupted when they are unmet, and they are unmet when the focus is on fulfilling our temporal desires instead of being with God:

> *"What causes wars, and what causes fightings among you? Is it not your passions that are at war in your members? You desire and do not have, so you kill. And you covet and cannot obtain, so you fight and wage war. You do not have, because you do not ask. And you ask and do not receive, because you ask wrongly, to spend it on your passions." (James 4:1-3; RSV).*

Desire itself is not wrong. James (who is about as hard-core as they come) actually says that the right thing to do with a desire is ask God for it! But he offers one caveat:

Blind Pursuit

Blind Pursuit happens when we are pursuing something that we know we shouldn't, and we intentionally ignore the warning signs so we can keep running after it. Here are four indicators of Blind Pursuit, with a question for each:

- **There is pressure to have it now**
  "What is driving the urgency for this? Does it need to happen now, or could you wait?"
- **The beneficiary is me**
  "Who except you benefits from this dream?"
- **Ignoring the impact on those around me**
  "How will this affect your spouse? Your kids? How will it impact your friendships?"
- **I avoid examining future implications**
  "Play out the impact this course of action will have on the next few years of your life."

passion is not meant to help me get mine, but to lead me to serve.

So passions can be tested in terms of *proportion* and *pursuit*: is this dream in proper proportion with other things in life, and is it worthy of making it a primary pursuit? Those are great questions to ask in life purpose coaching! Here are several more:

Proportion

- *"Evaluate this dream's significance. How much of your life is worth giving to it?"*
- *"How does this fit in with your other priorities in life?"*
- *"If the accomplishment of this dream was the most significant thing you did this year, would that be great, or a disappointment?"*
- *"What does it give you if you reach this dream?"*

Pursuit

- *"Talk a little about how you could best line up this desire with biblical guidelines for how to live a great life."*
- *"Where does this lead you? What kind of life will you have in the future if you pursue this dream in this way?"*
- *"What is driving the desire to pursue this?"*
- *"Who else benefits from this dream? Is that enough to make it truly significant?"*

The key to asking about proportion and pursuit is believing in the person. When you start asking questions like, "How could you even *think* of following this fleshly desire?" the dialog will pretty quickly come to halt.

8.1  Big Dreams Inventory

Begin jotting down as many of your dreams for your future as you can think of. Dreams are what you'd like to do someday. Are there big things you've wanted to accomplish, significant milestones to reach, or a difference you dream of making in the world? Put them under "Big Dreams" below. Fun Dreams are what would bring joy to life. Is there a place you've always wanted to go, an experience you'd love to have, or something cool you want to do just for the sake of doing? Jot these down under "Fun Dreams."

To fill out your list, try thinking of dreams in the *Life Wheel Categories* (8.2): *God, Work, Money, Living Environment, Personal Growth, Health and Recreation, Community* and *Family.*

Big Dreams

My List from 1990

Be able to work half-time by the time I'm 45.	*Done! The original thought was working a regular job half-time so I could do ministry half-time. I've revised that to do work actively half-time and spend half my time in writing and reflection. I reached that goal when I was 45-1/2!*
Own our house and have no debt.	*In Progress. We own about half of our house, but still have a long way to go!*
Create a community setting for artists.	*Partially fulfilled in a year-long residency internship program I created and led. Early in life I saw my passion unfolding through the arts, whereas now it is through leadership. I am currently working on a similar community for coaches.*
Share with others through my creativity the intimacy you can have with God.	*I'll do this all my life. The desire to connect people to God and each other morphed into writing and teaching instead of music and art.*
Make a professional tape of Kathy and my songs.	*Partially completed. I set out to do this and never finished. Several of our songs have appeared on CDs, but this is no longer an important goal and is off the list.*
If I have kids, raise them in the Lord.	*In Progress. We are currently home-schooling and feel our kids are in a great place. This has been a big investment!*
Live in community and help others to do so also.	*Since I created this list we've spent over five years living in intentional communities and plan to continue in the future.*

Fun Dreams Inventory  8.1

My List from 1990

Build a house.	*Not yet. I was thinking, 'build a house with my own hands' at the time. I still dream of designing a house and having it built, but doing all the work myself isn't a priority any more.*
Build a 16" telescope.	*Done! I was a physics major in college and love astronomy and cosmology. I built an 18" scope about 10 years ago, had a lot of fun with it, and then sold it.*
Take a balloon ride	*Off List. What was I thinking? I'm scared of heights. Dangling 1,000 feet up in a wicker basket wouldn't be fun!*
Learn to play piano	*Off List. I bought a keyboard and started to learn, but discovered music was not a primary call, so I let it go.*
Have a home studio: synth, four track, mikes, computer	*Done. I did this and had fun playing with it. It was what helped me see that music wasn't the direction for my life.*
Decorate our home to show our faith and creativity.	*Done. We really did this when we bought a house next to a college and ran a student ministry: funky wall hangings, a hand-painted backdrop, a bulletin board of current event clippings, etc. After we had kids, home became more of a sanctuary than an outreach and this wasn't as big a priority.*
Take a long retreat somewhere idyllic.	*Done. Kathy and I took a three-month sabbatical at a silent retreat center. I've now started to dream about finding some place on a beach where I can stay for three months and write.*

8.2  The Life Wheel Categories

Breaking life down into categories can help you identify a balance of dreams in all areas and minimize the tendency to forget something important. We're going to use the same eight categories from the *Life Wheel Assessment* found in the book *Coaching Questions* as our dreaming, values and Preparation categories. Consult the list below to see what might fit in each area.

Work

Your job, career or vocation. (For stay-at-home parents, keeping the family running is your vocation!)

Money

Finances, retirement, investments, spending and saving habits, giving, etc.

Living Environment

Your physical surroundings: house, car, yard, bedroom, and the things you own that make up that environment

Personal Growth

What you do to develop yourself: education, training, learning projects, reading, personal accountability—anything that expands your world, develops new abilities or creates personal change.

Health and Recreation

Hobbies, sports, fitness, diet, health care, sleep, Sabbath, vacations—the things that take care of your mind, body and emotional health.

Community

Relationships with friends and neighbors, plus your community service: PTA, politics, volunteering, boards, service projects, etc.

Family

Your spouse, children and extended family relationships.

God

Your personal relationship with God plus involvement in religious activities: devotions, church involvement, leadership roles, retreat, spiritual disciplines, etc.

Dream Lifestyles

8.3

What's your dream lifestyle? Picture your surroundings and daily patterns in the future when you are living what you think would be a great life for you. The object is not to pick whatever's most expensive or comfortable—dream about a lifestyle you could actually live, that fits your design and lets you do what you love. Have fun with this: envision where in the world you'd live, your home, your ideal workplace, your schedule, your activities, the people you'd be working with, or your average day. The idea is to get what you really want out on the table in detail so you can see what's there. If you are not a natural dreamer, look to the past and present for ideal situations and put them together to build a picture of your desired future.

My Ideal Lifestyle

Living in the mountains - on top of a ridge, with a great view across three or four ranges.

A simple house, two bedroom, low maintenance yard. Basement storage space for my wife to stash her projects so they don't clutter the house.

My office—desk under a big window. Neat. Plenty of bookshelf space. Doors where I can walk out onto a shaded patio and work outside. An inspiring view. An office for my wife, too.

Travel not more than once a month for work, short trips. Control over my schedule. Balance of reflective and active time.

A tiny, rough cabin with a small desk and a chair in the woods 100 yards from the house where I can go to be alone with God. No phone, no water, no bathroom needed.

Physical labor for exercise. Creating gardens, fountains or beautiful spaces.

Several good, life-long friends. Some who live close by, where we share possessions and meals and take walks together. Others that I talk to regularly by phone, and we get together and do something for a weekend twice a year.

Regular chances to see the grandkids.

Coaching Questions

- *"How does this lifestyle help you accomplish your mission in life?"*
- *"What does this lifestyle eliminate that would get in the way of your mission?"*
- *"What's in here just to bring you joy in life?"*
- *"How do your deep desires come out through what you listed?"*

Group Option: Collages

Get a bunch of magazines, cut out pictures that represent your ideal life, and paste them to poster board. After an hour or so of cutting and pasting, share your collages with each other. Explain why you chose each picture and what it represents.

8.4  Envisioning Your Dream

Take a big dream or vision, and picture what your life will look like when you have accomplished it. Don't worry about *how* you'll get there—just envision what life will look like when you do! Visualize where you'll be living, your surroundings (home or office), the ages of your family members, what kind of people you'd be working with, and any other details you can think of—the more the better. Walk through an average day in a future where you'd reached this dream and record what you see.

Coaching Tip
People often struggle on this exercise with being too general. Words or general concepts have little emotional impact compared to pictures, and to create a picture, we need details. For instance, when asked to visualize the dream future, a client might offer something vague, like, "I'll be working in management." Use your questioning skills to press that out much further: "What position will you hold? How many people will report to you? What will you be responsible for specifically? What will your office look like? Your team? Your daily routine?" These kinds of details will make the dream come alive.

Here are some additional coaching questions for envisioning the dream:

- *"Look five or 10 years down the road—describe what life would be like then if you had reached this dream." (This question places people within the future of their dreams and helps them see beyond the present obstacles in their way.)*
- *"Picture that for me in detail—your work setting, your team, your clients, your daily routine. Put yourself into that future and describe it in detail."*
- *"How old will you be at that time? How old will your kids be? What does that mean?"*
- *"Talk about the people around you. What kind of team or end users or partners will you be working with?"*
- *"Pick a specific person you know from your target audience, and tell me exactly how fulfilling this dream will impact that person's life." (Thinking about real people, places or situations can make it easier to describe the dream future.)*
- *"How will you be a different person because you pursued and reached this dream?"*

Dream Themes  8.5

This exercise identifies themes in your dreams and the underlying deep desires that animate those dreams.

Step 1: Identify Themes

Look over your *Dream Inventory* (8.1). Do several dreams seem to work toward the same end? Which dreams are connected, and how? (Glance at the *Passion Bull's-eye* exercise (7.1) as well, if you did it.) Find the themes that run through your dreams. If you aren't seeing the connections, sit down with a friend and ask what connections they see in your dream list.

Step 2: Name the Passions

Look over your themes, and name the underlying passions that animate each one. Why do I dream these particular dreams? What does each theme give me? What does this say that I care about?

Sample Dream List with Comments on Themes

Dreams	Comments
▪ *Share with others through my creativity the intimacy you can have with God* ▪ *Make a professional tape of our songs*	*A theme that connects many of my dreams is music and the arts. However, music is the* **container** *for the underlying desires (transparency, intimacy). I eventually let go of music, but am still deeply passionate about transparency and intimacy.*
▪ *Create a community setting for artists* ▪ *Live in community and help others to do so.*	*Community is a theme that runs through many of these dreams, growing out of my passion for relationship and the place I see it has in personal transformation. The containers around that passion may change, but the passion remains.*
▪ *Build a house* ▪ *Build a 16" telescope* ▪ *Write a book*	*Do you get the idea I like to design and build things? It's a joy to me to figure out how to do something I haven't done before—to envision it in my mind and then create it in reality. Designing and prototyping is central to my call.*
▪ *Take a balloon ride* ▪ *Take a long retreat somewhere idyllic*	*Several of my dreams reflect an underlying passion for enjoying God in nature. That is an important value that comes out in things like taking balloon rides or building a telescope, or where I choose to live.*

Coaching Questions

- *"What common themes do you see that run through your dreams?"*
- *"Several of your dreams seem to focus on ___. What does that mean?"*
- *"What does this dream give you? Are other dreams about the same thing?"*
- *"Why are you passionate about this dream?"*
- *"And what does that give you?" (Keep asking until you reach the desire.)*

Chapter 9: Passion/Dream Obstacles

"If at first the idea is not absurd, then there is no hope for it."

Albert Einstein

Jack and his wife were at loggerheads. "We took a family vacation back to North Carolina last month," he declared with exasperation. "And now every day they keep talking about going back. I don't want to rain on their parade, but I don't see how that's possible."

"What's behind those feelings?"

"For Joyce, she's always loved the North Carolina weather, the scenery and the culture. She's had a hard time fitting in here, so that's been an issue, too. With the kids, it's probably friends and the familiar versus another new place."

"So if you asked her what she wants, what do you think she'd say?"

"That she wants to go back. She'd say it in a heartbeat."

"And I take it you see things differently?"

"Well, I thought we decided this is where I was called to go. We prayed together and came to agreement, it's a dream position, it is right in line with my career goals—but now she's dug in her heels and there doesn't seem to be any middle ground. I'd be willing to do it for her, but there's no job for me in North Carolina, and who knows what I'd have to take to find one in a month. A 50% pay cut is not going to make her happy, either. And I've already resigned, so we can't stay here."

"So either way, you have some big obstacles to surmount. I'm curious—if your wife really wanted to live in North Carolina, did that come out when you were deciding on this position?"

"That's what really frustrates me. I felt like this was God's call, and she agreed with it—but now she's off on a different tack."

"So have you talked about this?"

"Tried to," Jack said despondently. "If I start talking about the hard facts, she starts into the 'you care about your job more than me' thing, gets in a passive-aggressive mode and things go downhill from there. I really want to be together in this, but I don't know how to make it happen. This is the third time now we've been through something like this—where she believes in one choice but then can't be happy with it—and I don't want to go through that again."

Obstacles affect all areas of the purpose diagram, but they are most prominent with dreams. In this story, Joyce submerged her dreams in preference to Jack's—until the vacation brought her desires back to the surface at full force, and their prior plans and agreements (plus their finances) stood in the way of her dream. From Jack's point of view, his ideal job seemed within his grasp until agreement with his wife became an obstacle. Neither of the two seemed in touch with the internal obstacles that were making the conflict so intractable.

An obstacle is something that stands in the way of thinking rationally about and pursuing your life purpose. Coaches talk about two major types of obstacles: external and internal. An external obstacle is a circumstance that seems to block progress—like Jack finding a job in North Carolina (for Joyce's dream). It's anything outside of you that keeps you from your dreams and goals.

Internal obstacles block us when our thinking patterns throw a wrench in the gears of forward progress. Where external obstacles tend to be fairly easy to identify, internal obstacles are buried deep within our psyche. What keeps Joyce from being able to identify and articulate her true desires to Jack? Maybe she was disappointed so many times growing up that she decided not to hope for things anymore. Or maybe she doesn't think its important to God for her to live in a location she loves. These are examples of internal obstacles.

Sometimes internal obstacles can even be dearly held principles or beliefs. One of my own inner obstacles was the belief that "if the relationship is broken, something is wrong with me." That belief kept me from letting go of broken relationships, led me into unhealthy situations and prevented me from standing up for what was right. My obstacle was so closely related to core values like dealing with God and relational leadership that I never fathomed that there was a stronghold mixed in with them. Even after contributing to several extremely painful situations, it took a year with a counselor to bring it to light and realign that area of my heart with Scripture.

Dealing with External Obstacles

External obstacles don't usually lurk in hiding. Most clients can tell you exactly what they are: "I don't have time to follow that dream"; or, "I don't have the credentials for that." I hear some of these obstacles so frequently that I have taken to calling them "The Big Five":

1. **Money:** There is never enough
2. **Time:** Ditto
3. **Opportunity:** You have the ability but not the chance to show it
4. **Ability:** You lack some particular knowledge or skill needed to pull this off
5. **People:** Either you need them to get on board, or you need them to get out of the way

Questions for the Big Five

- *"Give me some options: where could you come up with the money you need to pursue this?"*
- *"What changes to your schedule, your resources or your timeline could give you the time you need to do this?"*
- *"Where could the opportunity you need come from? What actions could increase your chances of getting it?"*
- *"Who do you know that has the answer or could teach you to do this?"*
- *"Could you accomplish 80% of this dream on 20% of the resources? What might that look like?"*
- *"What does this key person need from the situation? How could you help them win, too?"*

Practical tools work well for external solutions. Options techniques are a good place to start.[18] For example, a client asks for coaching on creating a convergent role that fits his calling. In the process of identifying strengths and passions, you come across the fact that he strongly dislikes conflict and tends to avoid it. But the leadership situations he loves include organizational conflict as a matter of course. In the past, he has even refused roles in his area of call because of his aversion to conflict. (Conflict avoidance can also be an internal obstacle—we'll start by treating this as an external obstacle, and go down that road next.) So what do you do as a coach to help him?

Overcoming One-Dimensional Thinking

To overcome a practical problem, we need practical solutions. Stating the problem simply and clearly is a great starting point. In this situation, the question is, "Given that there is going to be conflict in this role, how can you rearrange things to best play to your strengths?"

The client will likely respond first with ideas that reduce the amount of conflict. While he might be able to come up with several ways to do that, thinking only within this box limits the potential solutions. When we look at a problem from one only perspective, that's when we tend to get stuck. The obstacle itself becomes less a hindrance than our own one-dimensional thinking.

The key to a breakthrough is pushing the client to think in new dimensions. The coach names the problem solving strategy the client is using, takes it away, and then challenges him to solve the problem another way. "So far you've talked about solutions that try to reduce the total number of conflicts. What else could you do

---

18 A variety of options techniques can be found in *Coaching Questions* beginning on pg. 41.

to spend less time and energy on that area?" How many more possible categories of solutions can *you* think of? Brainstorm for a couple minutes, and then check the footnote for a list of possibilities.[19]

How do you know when other types of solutions are available? Often what tunes me in to one-dimensional thinking is when solutions occur to me that are outside the client's box. For instance, I might think "Why not delegate some of this to your staff?" As a coach, I'm not usually going to just blurt out my own solutions. But when I can think of options that are clearly outside the client's box, maybe a question that will expand the box is in order: "What kind of people resources could you draw on to help you?"

> **Categories of Solutions**
> Here are several general categories of solutions for external obstacles:
>
> 1. **People.** Who could help? Who would know the answer?
> 2. **Objectives.** What if you changed the dream or your timeline for it? How could you realize 80% of it with 20% of the resources?
> 3. **Dream vs. Desire.** What is the desire under this dream? What other ways could you pursue that desire?
> 4. **Learning.** Where could you find an answer? How could you learn this?
> 5. **Expectations.** How can I realign my expectations with what is realistically possible?
> 6. **Self.** What am I doing that is causing this? What could I change about me that would make a difference?

The key to this question is that I haven't asked about my idea (delegation), but about *a whole category of solutions involving other people*, of which delegation is one possibility. I take my insight and expand it into a broader category that the client can then explore. Here's another example—I think, "Why not let these people sort out their own conflicts instead of jumping in to save them?" But instead of offering that advice, I ask, "It sounds like you think dealing with these conflicts would be your responsibility. How could that change?"

This is one of many brainstorming and options techniques that work with obstacles. Once the client has settled on a potential solution, a final step is to make a plan to get around it. With dreams, a plan tends to get in the way; but with obstacles, it is a hopeful, freeing thing to have a step-by-step stratagem to overcome them.

Regrets

Another coaching technique for dealing with obstacles is regrets. Most of us have

---

19 Other options: 1) Let go. Just refuse to deal with the conflicts or allow them to play themselves out; 2) Delegate. Give the conflict management role to someone else; 3) Team. Take a group approach to working with conflict; 4) Outsource. Use outside facilitators to resolve conflicts; 5) Rethink. Identify the desires under this dream role and see what other roles might be a better fit.

done at least some thinking about the cost of pursuing our dreams. We make budgets, estimate the time it will take, wrestle with the sacrifices that dream might require. However, it is much rarer to find a person who has truly examined the cost of ***not*** following a dream. That's the idea of regrets: you ask the client to evaluate the cost of *not* moving forward. Here's an example:

"...So what I'm hearing is that you'd like to go back to school and prepare to be a teacher."

"Yeah, that's what I want—it just doesn't seem possible."

"What's standing in the way?"

"Well, I'd have to go back to school—three years if I did it part time. I don't know if I could even do that and work the same hours. So in addition to the time issue, we're going to see our income go down right at a time when we'll be spending a lot extra on tuition. I figured out how much it's going to cost, and it pretty much wipes out our savings."

"OK—so this is going to involve some sacrifices. But let's look at the other side, too. Imagine for a minute that you are 80 years old, looking back on your life, and you never pulled the trigger on becoming teacher. Would that be a minor thing, or something you'd really regret?"

"Oh! I'd definitely regret it. I'd feel like I'd missed something."

"Say more: what other feelings do you have about that choice?"

"Sort of an ache in the pit of my stomach. It would be like... like I'd chickened out on life or something. I'd be disappointed in myself."

"So what does that mean for this decision?"

"I've got to take this a lot more seriously. When you look at it that way, the money looks like small potatoes."

Regrets explore the cost of staying where we are at. While this technique is typically used in the coaching conversation, an exercise (9.2) is also provided for doing it as a reflection.

Obstacles and Expectations

The bigger your dream, the more you should expect obstacles. If this was easy, someone else would have already done it. We often forget that our life call is about becoming and not just doing. *The process of following your call will make you into the person you are called to be,* just as becoming the person you are called to be will enable you to accomplish your life mission. Obstacles are the training ground of your calling. They do not prevent you from becoming who you are called to be; on the contrary, they teach you to become that person. You cannot fulfill your calling without what your obstacles give you.

Frankly, one of the most debilitating spiritual obstacles Christians face is their expectations about obstacles. We expect that when God is in something, it will work—that the evidence of being right with God is when things go smoothly and succeed. Never mind that Jesus completely refuted this idea—the drive to gain control of our future by doing certain "right" things that ensure we'll meet with favorable circumstances is deeply rooted in the human psyche.

So when we hit obstacles in life, we are surprised and disillusioned. We thought the deal was that we'd found the right way in serving God, and in return He'd ensure we experienced favorable circumstances—so we'd live successful, healthy, happy lives. So when suffering comes, piled on top of what is already a bad experience is the fear that we've missed it and the disillusionment that springs from wondering if God is breaking the deal.

What the Christian walk is supposed to look like is a crucial theological issue for life coaches. Does God promise our clients a life of favor, happiness, success, prosperity, health and more, here on earth? In a word, no—and if you hear different on TV, don't believe it. Remember the levels of purpose. God is more concerned with having our hearts forever than making us happy in the here and now.

I expect clients to have trouble in this life, just like Paul. I know that they will be poor sometimes so that others might become rich, like Mother Teresa. I'm not surprised if God lets their businesses crater to get their attention, like with one of my current clients. And because I know that God's plan encompasses suffering as well as success, I can hold out to them the hope of glory in the midst of it all—that these difficulties are making them into the men and women they were born to be, and empowering them to bring many others to share in the eternal Kingdom. I believe this because it's been my life story, too. And I believe God's plan operates as much through pain as pleasure because that's Jesus' life story, too.

You do not serve your clients well if you hold out to them the promise of a good life devoid of difficulty or suffering. God did not set up his Kingdom to give us a way to control our futures and ensure ourselves of favorable circumstances. Instead, he promised that "***in*** all these things we are more than conquerors" (Rom. 8:37; RSV). God's promises are meant to come to us in the midst of life, not to take us out of it. "Many are the afflictions of the righteous, but the lord delivers him out of them all" (Ps. 34:19).

Bible Study: Success
Want to see how your picture of the Christian life matches with Scripture? Pick *any* three biographical characters in the Bible, and study each person's actual life experience (as opposed to what they said) in these areas:

- How "successful" was s/he?
- Where was s/he at in terms of physical and financial security?
- Was s/he receiving the recognition that was due?
- How comfortable was his/her life?
- How long was it from the time his/her destiny became apparent to when it was fulfilled? What happened during those years?

Try studying Hosea, Jeremiah, David, Naomi , Paul, Joseph, Moses, Peter, Jonah, Abraham, Sarah, Jesus, Noah, John the Baptist, Eli, or Daniel.

Coaching Up the Purpose Levels

When your clients become discouraged by obstacles, getting perspective on God's purposes is tremendously helpful. A great way to help them reorient is to coach them up through the levels of purpose. What this means is helping the person move from looking at the situation in terms of the first level (temporal comfort and success) to the two higher levels: bringing the Kingdom to others and building the Kingdom within.

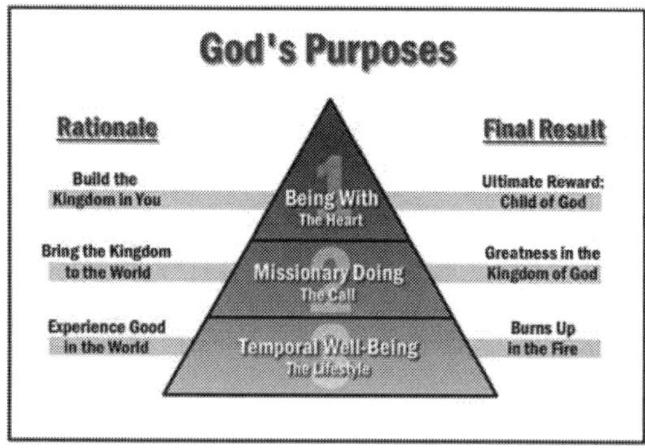

Several years back I worked with a client who was struggling with his relationship with God. In the process of running a family business, there'd been a relational breakdown and things had gotten to the point where he wasn't invited to family gatherings any more. Then his house burned down twice within the course of a year. He was stuck—wondering where God was in all of this, and how a loving God could be so capricious. None of it made sense.

When I first asked about what was going on inside him, he would just say, "I don't know." One of the initial action steps he did was to read a book I recommended on the life of Joseph. Certainly Joseph had his share of hard knocks, getting sold into slavery by his own brothers and then unjustly thrown into prison. Being rejected by family was something this client could relate to! But after it all Joseph could say to his brothers, "You meant evil against me; but God meant it for good, to bring it about that many people are kept alive..." (Gen. 50:20; RSV). I began to gently challenge him to try on a new perspective: what if God meant this for good? What would that mean? What is this creating in you? We talked about his calling and who he wanted to reach, and we also talked about God's desire for him. What part of Jesus' heart was opened to him by sharing in Jesus' sufferings?

In the process of reframing his expectations of the Christian life, he met God in a new way and got his work life back on track. About six months later he called to share something exciting: he'd given a copy of the book on Joseph that he'd read to his sister (the one he'd been estranged from) as a gift, she'd liked it enough to use it in a neighborhood Bible study, and one of her friends came to the Lord through it. She was all excited, and he was blessed to have been a part of it with her.

So why did his house burn down twice? You can say that we live in a fallen world and sometimes bad things just happen. Or you can say that all things are under the sovereignty of God, and God willed it. You could even say that God arranged the whole thing so that his sister's friend could be saved. I'm not smart enough to figure that out this side of the grave, but I do know this: no matter why such situations happen, *our response is exactly the same:* to come to God and say, "Lord, you said you'd take everything that happens in my life and leverage it for good, to build the image of Christ in me, if I engage it according to your purposes. How do you want me to meet you in this?"

To sum up, coaching up the levels of purpose means reframing the situation in terms of God's higher purposes—bringing His Kingdom to the world and forming

Christ in our hearts. To use this technique, pose a question that brings those other levels to mind and ask the person to ruminate on them:

- *"Instead of seeing this as an obstacle thwarting you, think of it as an opportunity. How could this work to increase the domain of Christ in your own heart?"*
- *"How is God forming who you are through this situation?"*
- *"Who would benefit if you met God in this?"*
- *"If God sent you this situation because it is exactly what you need to prepare you for your destiny, what do you think He would be doing?"*

An *Identifying Obstacles* exercise (9.1) has been provided if you want to get clients reflecting on what is stopping them. It usually takes help from a second party to overcome obstacles (if we could do it alone, we'd have done it already!), so instead of providing exercises, this chapter focuses on handles for addressing obstacles in the coaching conversation.

Dealing with Internal Obstacles

We hit internal obstacles when our inner beliefs, principles or healing issues get in the way of a dream. Unlike external obstacles, which are right out in the open, internal obstacles are usually hard to see. They show up first as subtle clues in our behavior or responses. Usually we can't name our own internal obstacles until we bump up against the blockages they produce. So the process starts with a block. Here are some common examples:

1. **Inability to dream or unusual limitations on dreaming**
   "When you start to think about your dreams or having a better future here, what holds you back from imagining what could be?"
2. **The person is stuck**
   "It seems like you're stuck here. What do you think is holding you back?"
3. **Irrational fears or beliefs that don't fit known facts**
   "You mentioned earlier that you have lots of experience working with this age group, but it sounds like you are disqualifying yourself from speaking to them. Talk to me about that."
4. **Inability to face something**
   "We've started talking about challenging this person several times, and I notice that each time you quickly changed the subject. What do you think is leading to that response?"
5. **Repeated playback of negative labels**
   "Several times now I've heard you use the phrase, 'I'm not a leader.' That doesn't seem at all consistent with what I see in you. Where does that idea come from?"

We often notice internal obstacles because they cause us to do things that don't make sense. For instance, "Why can't she generate any dreams that aren't ministry-related?" or "Why does he act like he's unqualified when he so obviously is?" But remember: people have a good reason for what they do. Emotions have a logic all their own. When a belief is damaging or self-sabotaging, it isn't that the person said, "I think I'll take on a self-defeating belief today!" Somehow that belief is useful or makes sense in that person's world. It's when you identify the *reason* for the belief that you'll have the most success in changing it.

Here's an example of coaching around an internal obstacle that starts with a blockage the coach has identified. Watch how the coach brings the obstacle to light.

"Question—you've been looking at ideas for a family getaway. Over the last month or two we've also been talking about finding more time in life for things that you love, like hiking, camping and getting out on the water. I've heard a number of options for doing things together that your wife and son like, but none for doing the things you love."

The coach sees a pattern in the client's responses and follows his curiosity.

"I'll just have to find time to do those things on my own," Matt replied. "I don't want to impose on them."

"What do you mean when you say you don't want to 'impose?'"

"Impose." Where's that coming from?

"Just because I like it doesn't mean they will. We'll all have a better time if we stick with something I know they'll enjoy."

"I appreciate your willingness to lay down your life for your family. But I'm also curious: what's happened in the past when you've gone camping or hiking as a family?"

"Well, we haven't ever really done that."

"So how do you know they won't like it?"

"It's just not the sort of thing I'd want to ask them to do."

The client is assuming he will get a certain response. When the coach checks, there are no facts to back up that belief.

"Your son Joey is in the Boy Scouts, right? Do they ever go camping?"

"Yeah."

"So last time he went—what did he think of it?"

"He had a really good time at Scout camp. He's been pestering me ever since to let him go again."

The coach searches for additional facts to test the client's belief against.

"OK—let's step back for a minute here. On the one hand, your son had such a good time camping that he's been pestering you to go back. On the other hand, you don't want to ask him to go camping because you don't want to impose on him. Those two things don't seem to go together—can you talk about that a bit?"

This looks like an internal obstacle: the client's assumption is irrational given the facts.

"Yeah, I guess that does sound a little weird. I just don't want to make them do something they don't want to do..."

"So what do you believe would happen if you asked them to go camping? What's the image in your mind?"

Drawing out the belief behind the behavior.

"It would be really disappointing. They'd say they don't like it and then I'd either have to push and start a fight or give up

anyway. It just sounds easier not to ask."

"That makes sense. Now go a layer deeper—what makes you believe you'll get a 'No' in the first place?"

"Now that I think about it, there were a couple times early in our marriage where Liz and I disagreed about where to go on vacations, and I just decided it was easier to not expect something I wanted, let her decide and not cause a fight. But that was 20 years ago."

"So the belief I'm hearing is, 'it's better to give in and not expect anything than cause an argument.' Is that belief serving you well, or not?"

"Well, Liz and I have had several blow-ups in the last few years where she gets mad at me for not telling her what I want. And I guess I'd have to say I'm losing, too—because I don't even bring it up, we never end up doing things that I really like. I think Liz knows that, and she feels bad about it, but I don't let her do anything about it."

"So do you want to change this belief?"

"How do you do that?"

"Well you decided to believe this. Is there anything stopping you from just un-deciding?"

"No, I don't think so. I can just un-decide?"

"Can you?"

"Yes, I think I can!"

Here's where the belief comes from. It *looks* rational to the client, but does it work?

We "name" the belief. Then ask if the belief is making life better or worse.

The client discovers that his belief is actually counter-productive—it gives him the very thing he is trying to avoid. That's a very good reason to change!

In this dialogue, the coach is alerted first by an interesting pattern in Matt's options. Exploring it surfaces an irrational belief that doesn't fit the facts and an inability to face family conflict. The coach was able to help Matt name the underlying belief, and that led to change.

When you are up against a real internal obstacle, things tend to get more emotional or irrational the deeper you go. On the other hand, sometimes when the facts come out they confirm the client's choice. If Matt had said, "We don't go camping because my wife's allergies are so severe that she might end up in the hospital," then there is a rationally good reason for a behavior that seems irrational.

Coaching Internal Obstacles

Here's the process used in this dialog:

1. Your intuition shows you a possible obstacle.
2. Find facts to test against the client's response.
3. If there is dissonance, juxtapose the facts with the client's response and ask for reflection.
4. Draw out and name the underlying belief.
5. Ask the client to choose what to do with the belief.

Because we are looking at a blind spot (something the client does not see), the coach will usually have to initiate examining it. If this obstacle seems to be blocking the client from reaching a goal, it's a good place to dive in. Listen to your intuition when you consider addressing an obstacle!

Strongholds and Ungodly Beliefs

This dialogue illustrates what the Bible calls a "stronghold" in II Cor. 10:3-6. In this oft-misinterpreted passage, a stronghold is a "thought," "argument" or "proud obstacle to the knowledge of God." In other words, strongholds have to do with wrong *thinking*, not spiritual powers. While the weapons that we use against them are spiritual ones, the stronghold itself is not something in your spirit but in your mind.

Strongholds (sometimes called Ungodly Beliefs) are identity statements, usually couched in the negative, that are based on hurt.[20] They have a hold on us because they are part of our identity; they are strong because the emotional wound they formed around is unhealed. Because we decide how we'll respond in similar situations in the future while we are still wounded, we build parts of our selves around reaction or self-protection.

Identifying Strongholds

Strongholds are characterized by:

1. **Negative Identity Statements.** Trying to *not* be like someone.
2. **Overreaction.** The emotion is out of proportion with the situation.
3. **Irrational Responses.** Strongholds are emotional, not rational choices. Often they just don't make sense.

In the example dialog we discover that Matt was hurt by disagreements early in his marriage, and he is still trying to protect himself from something that happened 20 years ago. Here are some additional examples of what strongholds sound like:

- "I'll never do that again!"
- "When I grow up I'll own lots of companies and I'll never be poor."
- "How can you own a house and still be a Christian?" (That was one of mine.)
- "My dad was never around for us when we were kids and I swore that I'd never be like that."

Notice that these are all negative messages. The error of a stronghold is that we are reacting: trying *not to be like* some person or situation that hurt us, instead of trying to *be like* Jesus.

There are two fundamental strategies to use when coaching a stronghold. Sometimes the hurt has been dealt with over time, and the coachee can just un-decide. However, if the hurt is still present, prayer, counseling or inner healing is

20 Study the Esau story (Gen. 25) and the "root of bitterness" passage in Hebrews 12 to learn more about strongholds. Esau experienced favoritism and conditional love from his parents, and his broken relationships with family rose out of this hurt. The selling of his birthright represented checking out of the family system that hurt him.

often needed to release the emotional wound before the belief can change.

So how do you know which of these approaches to use? It's always a good first step to just ask the coachees how they want to handle it. Healing usually falls outside the bounds of the coaching relationship, so if it is needed, create an action step around finding the resources to get it. An alternate approach is to just try the simplest approach (un-deciding) first. If that doesn't take, then you can always go back and explore the healing option.

Brute Force Approaches

Trying the simplest solution first is a reliable coaching strategy. If the client thinks it will work, they should try it. If the commonsense solution doesn't make any headway, little is lost. However, this "simplest first" strategy backfires when the client can't let go of a solution that isn't working. For example, in areas where change has failed repeatedly, clients will often default to a solution like "be more disciplined" or "try harder." I call that a Brute Force Approach: let's just apply more energy to the situation and force ourselves to change.

I'm not a big fan of brute force approaches. Discipline is supposed to get you to the point where something comes easily, and you don't have to keep putting effort into it. In other words, the purpose of discipline is to get you to the point where you don't *need* to be disciplined. Grinding your way forward in a way that uses up significant energy and isn't getting any easier looks like a losing proposition to me.

Brute force thinking can be challenged with questions like, "How has that worked for you in the past?" If you've already tried to lose weight, exercise regularly or have daily devotions by being more disciplined, and it has failed 14 times in a row, why would you have any confidence that that approach would succeed this time? If there is a pattern of failure, something significant needs to change about your approach to get different results. And one of the places to look for that change is internal obstacles.

If that approach has already failed 14 times in a row, why would you have any confidence that just trying harder would succeed this time?

Often brute force approaches contain an "ought" or a "should" that drives them. "I ought to be able to discipline myself to do this," or "If I were really spiritually on-the-ball I'd have mastered this already." The internal obstacle is the person's beliefs about the change process! Not only are those beliefs irrational (we've already proven this doesn't help), but they keep us from stepping back and saying, "This isn't working; what else can I try?"

When the normal application of discipline doesn't produce results, I want to step back and ask, "Why?" What's going on under the surface? Why is success so hard to come by? What is sabotaging you? Find the root obstacle, root it out, and change comes much easier.

For years, I struggled with healthy eating and exercise patterns. Even when I succeeded for a time, I soon dropped back into my old patterns. Food was a crutch that helped me feel good about life. I tried all kinds of ways to discipline myself—but trying harder wasn't working. I just couldn't muster up the energy to change.

Then I was diagnosed with dysthmia and got medication for it. Within weeks, I was sleeping well for the first time in 15 years. I felt rested, I had more energy, and suddenly I *wanted* to exercise. It was fun to do five or six hours a week of hard manual labor throwing dirt around in the back yard. After feeling rotten physically for so many years, I'd forgotten what it was like to feel good.

I tried the brute force approach, and just felt more like an idiot every time I failed. It was only when I finally uncovered the root obstacle that I was able to do what I wanted to do.

Stirring Up the Darkness

Sometimes we have trouble getting a handle on the motivations or fears that are lurking under the surface. A great technique for unveiling them is something I call "stirring up the darkness." If a client is avoiding or fearing something and doesn't know why, create an action step that has them do what they fear on a small scale and track what goes on internally as they do it.

The idea isn't to overcome your fears by force of will, but to do the thing you fear and observe how it affects you. It's a data-gathering exercise. For clients who aren't in touch with their inner world, the fresh picture that emerges can unlock the change.

A while back I was working with a client on assertiveness. He had a difficult time figuring out why he was so passive in conflict situations, so we decided to try stirring up the darkness. The client set an action step to pray for situations that would challenge him to be assertive. Two weeks later he reported on a conflict with his boss, a friend who was upset with him and returning a defective item to a salesperson who tried to brow-beat him into keeping it. Through those experiences the client began to get in touch with his lack of belief in himself—he habitually assumed that others were better or more knowledgeable than him, and so he deferred when he should have stood strong. That insight began a transformational journey of recasting his identity around who he really was.

Spiritualized Obstacles

The "shoulds" we live out of are often bound up in our need as Christians to project a certain image. These spiritualized obstacles spring out of human guidelines we create when we get religious about the Christian walk. For instance, we might fear that we haven't stated our calling right, or that we'll look arrogant if we voice a big dream (see box for more). For a coaching example, let's look at the question, "Is this dream of God?" This can be a major roadblock for a Christian client. We think that if we don't hear God just right, we'll fail, and shame ourselves and the Kingdom. Not a very motivating prospect, is it? So how do you coach around this obstacle?

One amazing thing I've learned about coaching people on hearing God: at least eight times out of 10, when a person says, "I don't know what God is saying," after 20 minutes of coaching it turns out that they *did* know—they just didn't have the confidence to believe that they had heard. I've even coached believers who said they'd never heard God speak to them in their entire life; yet when we explored past situations and decisions we quickly found places where they had met God.

So when coachees think they don't know what God is saying, I start by finding out what they *do* know:

- *"Tell me more about the situation."*
- *"What has God spoken to you on it so far?"*
- *"What do you know?"*
- *"What is your heart saying?"*
- *"If you weren't afraid of ___, what would you do?"*
- *"Take your best shot: what do you think God wants you to do?"*

> **Common Spiritualized Obstacles**
> Here are some common wrong beliefs Christians drag around.
>
> - Humble people don't talk about big dreams.
> - I ought to be able to conquer this without help.
> - I ought to be able to do [insert any skill] like [person who is gifted in that area]_.
> - God doesn't bless people who aren't living right.
> - Being in God's will means being at the right place doing the right thing at the right time.
> - When God is in something, it works.
> - Adversity is a result of sin.
> - I can't hear God.
> - If I do more God will be happy with me.
> - The desires of my heart are "just me."

If the person is really mired in the question, "Is this God or is it me?" there are other coaching options. Create an action step around taking the situation to God in prayer and asking for direction. As a coach, I want to help the person be intentional about that step: "When will you pray about this? What time are you going to set aside for prayer?" Going back to prayer can be amazingly effective—when we get serious about asking, God gets serious about answering. "If any of you lack wisdom, let him ask of God, who gives to all generously and without reproach, and it will be given to him" (James 1:5).

Sometimes it's the faith you communicate in the person as a coach. Just saying, "I believe God will speak to you" (and actually believing it!) raises the faith level enough to give the person a breakthrough. Like everything in the Christian life, hearing God runs on the fuel of faith. You have to choose to believe He is speaking and have faith in the still small voice in your heart. Often the voice has already come—the barrier is the person believing in themselves, that they have actually heard God speak to them.

I also find that different people have different ways of hearing God, and working with those historical patterns is good practice. Ask, "How has God spoken to you about major decisions in the past?" I've had clients whose important decisions are consistently confirmed by provision, others who hear through Scripture, and some who look for agreement with their spouse—even one who was very clear that the things he planned came to naught and what was of God simply dropped into his lap!

One quick note on obstacles in the spiritual realm: demonic powers are real, and they can erect difficult external obstacles. For example, Daniel's prayer was thwarted for three weeks by demonic forces. When it comes to internal obstacles, it's a different story. If I hear a client say something like, "The enemy has just been stealing my joy and making me discouraged," I'll ask, "So what do you think is the open door in you he is exploiting to do that?" or "Where's the point of vulnerability that this attack is coming through?" When it comes to our internal world, the only power the enemy has over believers is what we give him. If clients feel they are is experiencing "spiritual attack," that's a great opportunity to help them identify the place of vulnerability and close the door.

Exercise: Pray Both Ways
Another way to test a dream is praying for it both ways:

- First, pray: *"God thank you for letting me pursue this dream. Thanks for your favor on it. I want to do this with you and for you..."*
- Then pray: *"God, thanks for releasing me from this. I'm grateful that you are looking out for my best and I can walk away from it..."*

Track your internal responses as you pray. Where is the peace in this? With which prayer does your spirit bear witness?

Testing Dreams

Sometimes, the hearing God obstacle can be addressed by testing a dream. If you are going to uproot your family and move across country to get a graduate degree, you want to have confidence in that course of action. The Bible provides several tests coaches can employ to increase coachees' confidence in decision-making.

One has to do with Allegiance. Continuing with the passage from James, "But let him ask in faith, with no doubting, for he who doubts is like a wave of the sea, driven and tossed by the wind. For that person must not suppose that a double-minded man, unstable in all his ways, will receive anything from the lord" (James 1:6-8; RSV). Being double-minded means asking God for direction without having settled whether you'll follow it when you get it. If you are just looking for confirmation for something you've already set your heart on, or you want to hear what God has to say and then decide if you can pay that price, don't count on getting a clear direction. Those who hear, surrender the decision before they ask.

If my Christian clients are considering important steps, I want them to have the confidence and power of knowing that God has spoken. I want them to reach for the best. So even if the person is all excited about a goal, I'm still going to ask, "What is God saying to you about this?" If they haven't asked or haven't heard anything yet, I want to believe in them that they can hear, and challenge them to take the risk and ask. Here's what that might look like:

"She sounds like quite an individual. So how are you going to know if this is the girl God has for you?"

"Well, I really love her, and I want to marry her."

"Is that enough? Or would you want more clarity if you could get it?"

"If I can get more—sure. It's just hard to hear God in this kind of situation—I am so wrapped up in it emotionally."

"So how could you unwrap yourself? What would it take to reach the place where God could give you any answer and you'd be content, and know He had your best in mind?"

"Wow, I guess I'd really have to let go, and say, 'God, you're enough for me.'"

"Is that worth doing?"

"Yeah. Just not easy."

"But I believe you can do it! This can be a great moment in your life with God."

"I think I'm going to need to get away for a retreat or something and really wrestle with God on this one."

The key to this type of conversation is to hold up a great hope—you can hear God clearly and have real confidence in it—and by doing so communicate your belief in the client. Even marriage is a dream rooted in heaven—it can truly satisfy only if it comes completely under the lordship of Christ.

Another great dream-testing exercise is from I John 3:16-22. We can reassure our hearts before God and know we are of the truth if we are walking in sacrificial, *agape* love for our brothers and sisters in Christ. The testing question is, "*Who does this dream benefit?"*

If the only reasonable answer is, "Just me," you won't get a lot of assurance from this test! But this verse does suggest a way to move toward it: reconfigure your dreams so they serve others sacrificially and aren't just about you.

One other test I regularly apply is spousal alignment. "How is your spouse feeling about this decision? What has God said to him/her?" Surprisingly often, I find that spouses have not come to one mind on important decisions. It's one of those things that men especially know is wise but can easily forget to practice. (For more on life purpose and marriage, see pg. 57).

9.1  Identifying Obstacles

Most of us run into obstacles when we start pursuing our dreams. There is nothing abnormal about that—a dream that is worth giving you life *should* stretch you and force you to grow along the way. Obstacles come in two flavors, external and internal. External obstacles are circumstances that keep you from moving forward – things like a lack of money, skills or credentials. Internal obstacles are beliefs or thinking patterns that hold you back. If you believe that conflict is something to be avoided at all costs, for instance, you'll have a hard time dreaming about taking on roles or responsibilities that involve conflict.

External Obstacles

Get alone for a half hour or so and think about what external circumstances block the pursuit of a particular dream. It may help you to imagine moving toward your goal step by step. As you envision it, ask: "What do I need for this dream that I don't have and will be difficult to get?" The things you don't have but are confident you can acquire aren't obstacles—we're looking for the places you say, "I don't know how this could ever happen."

1. ______________________________

2. ______________________________

3. ______________________________

4. ______________________________

5. ______________________________

Internal Obstacles

Now, imagine again the step-by-step journey of pursuing your dream from the beginning, and this time observe your *internal* reactions. How do you feel when you think of the different challenges your dream entails? Where do emotions like fear or doubt rise up? What is your inner critic telling you? Record your thoughts and feelings below.

1. ______________________________

   ____

2. ______________________________

   ____

3. ______________________________

   ____

Regrets  9.2

When we think of pursuing our dreams, we usually have some idea of the costs and risks required to reach them. However, few people examine the cost of **not** taking the risk to pursue a dream. This exercise helps you weigh the price of both courses of action.

Step 1: Get Into the Dream

This is an emotive exercise, and for it to work you have to really get into the dream. Visualize yourself living it. See it, touch it and experience that dream. What would be different in your life? How would it change you? What would it be worth to reach it? Going through the *Envisioning* exercise (8.4) can help.

Step 2: Look Back

Now, imagine that you are 75, looking back on what you've done in life. If you had never pursued this dream—the risk seemed too big, or you couldn't find the time or money—how would you feel about that?

- What would you lose?
- What would you think of yourself for making that choice?
- Would you be profoundly disappointed, or would it not be that big of a deal?

Step 3: Compare

Once you've gotten in touch with the cost of not pursuing your dream, compare it to the cost of going for it. How does this change the equation? What's the best long-term choice?

Coaching Tip

Here are a few typical questions a coach might use with regrets:

- *"We often think about what it will cost to follow a dream. What would it cost you if you* ***didn't*** *pursue this?"*
- *"Imagine you are 80 years old, sitting on the porch and talking to your grandkids about this decision. What would you want to be able to tell them, and why?"*
- *"What, if anything, would you miss out on if you just put this on the back burner for five years?"*
- *"How does reflecting on regrets change your sense of urgency about this dream?"*

Chapter 10: Passion/Values

"Lives based on having are less free than lives based on either doing or being."

William James

The conflict between the two leaders was escalating fast. While they'd been putting the finishing touches on the travel arrangements for an extended mission trip, a disagreement arose over who should be included on the team. On a previous expedition, one younger team member had gotten homesick and left early, forcing a revamping of their plans. This time around, the team leader was firm: this trip was a crucial support for the new churches they'd planted, and they couldn't risk taking someone who'd bailed last time. His second-in-command was equally adamant: this young man had a big call on his life, and they needed to believe in him and get behind what God had created him to be. Finally, unable to resolve their differences, the two leaders parted ways.

This incident from Acts 15 is a values conflict between Paul and Barnabas over John Mark. Paul valued the task. Faithfulness and total commitment to the work are what he expected from team members, and those who didn't give their all needed to be replaced. Barnabas, the son of encouragement, valued developing people. He was the one who'd gone after Paul the outcast, brought him to Antioch and even stepped down from leading their first missionary journey to let Paul grow into his call. For Barnabas, developing people *was* the task. Unable to find a common ground on Mark, the two apostles parted ways.

As in this story, core values define our central Passions and form the basis of our decisions. Values have several shades of meaning:

- They are deeply held, enduring beliefs,
- Values define what is valuable or important to us in life,
- They are a framework for defining what we think is right and wrong,
- Values are understandings and expectations for how people ought to behave.

Values describe what we are most passionate about, what motivates us, and why we make certain choices. Values aren't aspirations about the future; they come out in everything we do *now*. If that seems a little fuzzy, you're not alone. Values are one of the tougher concepts for coachees to grasp. But they are very important because:

- It's hard to coach toward someone's values if neither of you know what they are!
- Since values capture what is most important to our clients, life purpose discovery always touches on values.
- Values are the "why" for our decisions. Since coaching is about making and walking out choices, knowing the values that drive a coachee leads to better decision-making.
- Convergent roles that fit our destiny are highly aligned with our values. Identifying those values is often the first step in finding the convergent role.

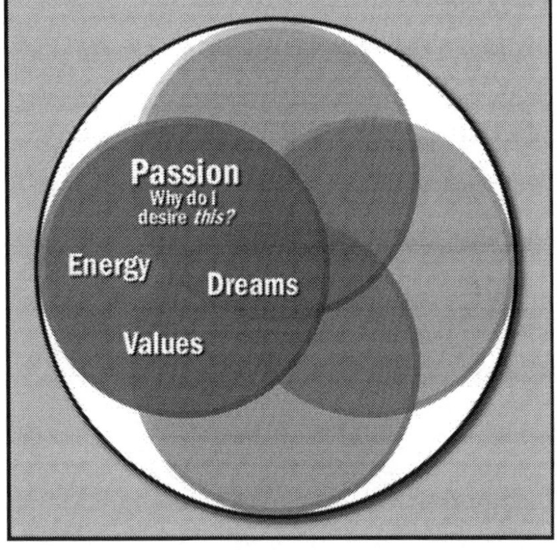

Of special importance to Christian coaches working with Christian clients is that we share a set of common values—things like *agape* love, service, or becoming like Jesus. This value system replaces the cultural framework of "life, liberty and the pursuit of happiness" which most coaches work within.

Our common Christian values begin to diverge at the finer points of doctrine that define denominations and religious groups. So to coach within a shared framework, Christian coaches must learn to major in the majors. Our unity is found within the historical creeds and understandings of Scripture shared by all denominations, not in questions like free will versus determination, women in leadership, or whether Jesus would be a Democrat or a Republican. We all have things that are non-negotiable to us (those are our own values!) But the ability to stick with the core principles of the Christian faith and let the rest be negotiable is what lets you coach believers outside of your own particular stream.

Values Education

If a client is unfamiliar with the concept of values (if so, it will be obvious from the Baseline Assessment), you'll need to do some educating before values can be discovered. Often the best values education is to be coached to discover one of your values and then debrief on how you got there. Here's what that might look like.

"I'm not sure I get this values thing. Can you describe that another way?"

"Sure, Nate. Would it help if we look at one of your own values?

"That sounds good. I'm just not sure what they are."

"OK. Tell me about a decision you made recently—something you care about."

"Let's see... a couple of days ago I talked to my wife about supporting a child in Africa—you know, through Compassion International or something like that."

"And why do you want to do that?"

"Well, things have been pretty lean for the last five or six years. Between my wife quitting her job for the kids and starting the business, we've been stretched thin. But now the business is doing better, and we can afford to go beyond the bare necessities. I want to use some of what God has given us to bless others."

"And what's behind that, Nate?"

"It's caring for the least of these. It's doing the right thing. It's making sure that my finances don't just become about me."

"Why is that important to you?"

"Well, these are things that I believe in. And when you really believe in something, you do it. To say I want to live my life in the service of God and then just take all that He gives me for my personal benefit—I'd be a fraud."

"And why do you care about doing the right thing and not being a fraud?"

"That's what integrity is! It's doing what you say. And being a fraud is not doing what you say."

"And what's behind integrity for you?"

"I just think, 'what kind of person are you if you don't have integrity?' I care about doing the right thing because it makes relationships work, or it's what makes the customers come back to my business, but even if it didn't bring in the business, I'd still do it. Integrity is its own reward."

Values Discovery Questions

- *"Why is that important to you?"*
- *"What things, if they were taken away or you couldn't do them, would make life unbearable? What makes these things valuable to you?"*
- *"When making your most important decisions, what are the fundamentals you base them on?"*
- *"Where do you invest the best of your time, money and energy? Why?"*
- *"What are your 'soap box' issues? Your deep concerns? Why?"*
- *"What do you take the most pride in? What most excites you in life? Why?"*

"And that sounds like a value for you, Nate. We started with a decision, because values are the framework we make decisions by. I kept asking you why your rationale for giving was important, until you got down to the bedrock reason why you are doing it: integrity. You know you are at a value when you ask "why" and there is no more why. Like you said, integrity is its own reward."

"And that's why I do a lot of what I do, in all different areas of my life. OK, I think I'm getting it now."

This dialog demonstrates how to coach values discovery in a session. Start with something important to the person, and keep asking, "Why?" to push the conversation toward the underlying value. When the coachee starts circling back around to the same idea over and over, you've reached the core value. Because the concept of values is difficult to grasp, I like to start the values discovery with this kind of experiential learning.

A second approach to values education is books. One I often suggest to ministry leaders is *Values Driven Leadership* by Aubrey Malphurs. It is oriented to organizational values, but does a good job of presenting the basic values concepts and has lots of examples. Laurie Beth Jones' *The Path* also has a section on values that is pretty accessible to the average person.

Another way to help people come to grips with values is to describe what they are and aren't. The *Values Characteristics Worksheet* (10.1) lists a number of characteristics of values that help the client know what we are shooting for.

Grouping and Summarizing
Clients who are "S's" on the MBTI© tend to have a harder time with summarizing information into conceptual themes. That's something "N's" naturally do well. It can be helpful for an "S" client to search for themes in values jottings with a friend who is an "N."

The Values Discovery Process

Values are the driving force behind our work and our passions. But because they are such deeply ingrained assumptions, we're often not consciously aware of what they are or how they shape us. Once a client understands values and their importance, a values discovery process is the next step. This process usually takes several coaching sessions to complete.

There are several types of value sets you can create. One option is to create values for different sectors of life, like work, family, or spiritual life. Using a framework like the *Life Wheel Categories* (8.2) forces clients to examine what motivates them in many different areas. Plus, it is easier to identify and create values in sectors of life than to try to cover everything at once.

A second option is a global set of personal values that apply to all areas of life. This is most suitable for more advanced clients or those who have done values work before.

A third type of value set is *Leadership Values* (see 10.8). Focusing in on why coachees do what they do in leadership is tremendously helpful to an organization or team environment. A fourth variety is an organizational value set: the core principles that underlie the norms and decisions of a team or organization.

The coaching process I use to do values is:

1. Do a portion of the exercise in the coaching session to make sure clients understand it,
2. Turn them loose to finish that exercise on their own and e-mail you the results,
3. Offer feedback on the results in your next coaching session (see next page).

Then I start this cycle again with the next step in the discovery process. Moving from jottings to themes to statements will take at least three sessions. Most people want to do revisions of their final statements after getting some feedback, so that makes four.

One way to begin is with an exercise where clients identify words or phrases that describe what is most important to them. You can use either the *Values Brain Dump* (10.2) or use a *Word Choice* approach (10.3). The advantage of the Word Choice approach is that anyone can do it. Giving lots of handles makes it easy to come up with value statements—you just combine words from the list. For clients who have a harder time grasping the values concept, this is probably the way to go.

The disadvantage of *Word Choice* is that selecting from pre-defined options limits the uniqueness of the client's value statements. When working with leaders or those who are more self-aware, the *Brain Dump* exercise (10.2) is a better starting point. It requires more thought from the client, but will yield richer, more personalized value statements that cover the breadth of one's life. If the results of the *Brain Dump* need some extra fleshing out, simply refer the person back to the *Word Choice* list for more ideas.

Values Practice

Evaluate the following statements: are they values? Why or why not? And if they aren't, what are they?

1. I want to be a one of those Israelites who understands the times and knows what to do.
2. I value the Bible as the inerrant Word of God, our guide to faith and practice.
3. I value reaching out to the poor, widows and orphans, so by the time I am 50 I want to be giving half of my income away.
4. I do business with generosity, in a way that looks not only to my own interests, but to the interests of others.
5. I value creating a retreat center in Cuba for pastors who need love and refreshment.
6. The value I live by is: the Lord helps those who help themselves.
7. In my relationship with God, my center is intimacy, continual conversation and finding God in nature.

Once you have a list of values words or jottings, the next step is grouping them into themes that will become the actual value statements (step 2 of the *Brain Dump* exercise). If you are creating statements around the life categories, at most two or three themes per category can go into a statement. For a global value set, five to eight themes is a good number.

Finally, value statements in sentence form are developed out of these themes using exercise 10.6. A page of example statements is given (10.7) to help guide the client in this process. Limiting your list to a few values and wording them in pithy phrases makes values more valuable—long, abstract statements filed away somewhere are of little use.

Occasionally you'll get a client who struggles to come up with something even with the word choice approach. One way around the logjam is creating an obituary (see exercise 10.4). How you want to be remembered after you are gone goes to the heart of what kind of person you want to be; and that exposes values. If the client is an extrovert who doesn't like to journal, do the exercise as an interview instead.

Offering Feedback

Once the client has done some initial work with the *Obituary, Brain Dump* or *Word Choice* exercises, it's time to offer feedback on the results. The key here is that your input should mostly be around format instead of content. In other words, your job is to make sure that clients are identifying actual, lived, passionate values, and they are expressing them in useful ways, not to tell them what their values should be.

Usually I'll check the client's jottings or themes against the four tests on the *Values Characteristics Worksheet.* For instance, are the person's values phrases unique and personal? Sometimes, quotes from Scripture make good value statements. But if I see a lot of standard Christian phraseology ("I want to serve God in my generation") I start to wonder if this is really a value. Because values are in your heart, your value statements should come out of your heart—in your own words, not someone else's.

Another way to check values is to take a phrase or theme and ask the person to unpack each word in it. In great value statements, every word or phrase is pregnant with meaning. If you ask the person about a word and there isn't much there to explain, that may not be the best example of a true value.

Here's an example of a client unpacking a value word.

"One word you chose here is 'Integrity.' Unpack that for me: what does integrity mean to you, and why are you passionate about it?"

"OK. Integrity means doing what you say. It's keeping your word, following through. It means that your words and your actions say the same thing about who you are. I care about integrity because doing the right thing is part of my relationship with Jesus—I want my actions to bring honor to my Lord. And your integrity is one of your most valuable possessions. No one can take it away from you—it's the thing that makes you know you've done well even when everyone says you blew it. I don't know who I would be without it."

Can you hear the passion and the power in that response? Integrity is deeply rooted in this person's identity: "I don't know who I would be without it." When people talk about a value, they naturally speak in phrases that can be incorporated into the value statement itself. Lines like "...your words and your actions say the same thing" or "bringing honor to my Lord" are powerful, personalized expressions of integrity what could become great value statements.

Here's what unpacking an aspirational value sounds like:

"You put down 'outreach' as a value. Describe that—why are you passionate about outreach?"

"Well, you know, every Christian ought to be reaching out to his neighbors and the people around him. I mean, it's the Great Commission. So that's something I think is really important for me to work on and get better at. I want to lead at least 10 others to the Lord in my lifetime—that's the kind of thing every Christian should shoot for. So reaching out needs to be part of my values."

"So how are you living out that value now?"

"Um... I'm trying to build some relationships with my neighbors, get to know them a little. That's going kind of slow because we don't see each other much. And work is a hard place, you know? There just isn't much opportunity there right now. I need to pray more about that."

When people explain an aspirational value (something they want to be but don't currently live out) you'll tend to hear lots of religious lingo, "shoulds" and "oughts," and future language. Aspirations look to the future—"I will" or "I need to." Values are in the present, and should be written in present tense: "I am...," "I value..." or "I believe..." The "ought to" and the "want to" that places outreach in the future alert us that this client may not be talking about a true value. So the coach checks by asking for examples of how the coachee is actually living it. The weak response confirms that this is probably a dream or a goal, not a value.

Writing Value Statements

Once the person has some good reflections down on paper, the next step is to convert them to *Value Statements*. Putting your values into memorable form is like moving your passport from a safe deposit box into your pocket. Your passport won't help you travel unless you carry it with you. In the same way, while it is good to have values reflections in your life purpose workbook, having statements you've memorized is much more useful. When you are actually making decisions about life, you want your values at your fingertips.

I like to coach the person through the process of developing one value statement during the session so they understand the process and the final product. Then I turn them loose to finish the others on their own using the *Writing Value Statements* exercise (10.6). The *Value Statement Examples* are a helpful reference for the client at this stage.

If the person is creating values for the life categories, ask which area came hardest or they are least satisfied with, and begin there. Work with the person to create their first value using the "why" technique (see pg. 162).

Coachees who use the *Brain Dump* (10.2) to create values reflections have a leg up on this step, because they've already been playing with phrases instead of just individual words. If you started with the *Word Choice* exercise (10.3), one option is to

go directly to *Value Statements (10.6)*. Just figure that you'll probably end up having coachees go back and rework them at least once to get a final version. Or you can have them do the *Values Clarification* exercise (10.5) first. In this exercise, coachees talk through their values out loud with a friend or spouse. The act of verbalizing the values turns individual words into phrases and sentences, which gets people closer to creating statements. If done with a spouse, it brings the partner into the process, too.

Evaluating Final Statements

Most of the time, clients want feedback on their value statements. The four key things I look for at this stage are listed on the *Values Characteristics* worksheet (10.1):

1. **Short**
   One memorable phrase or sentence is great. A cue word to remember the value by is also a big help. Rambling statements containing several different concepts should be edited down to what is most important.
2. **Unique**
   Your own words. Something that has meaning for you. Not standard blasé lingo or other people's phrases.
3. **Unpack-able**
   Every phrase has meaning. The client can easily unpack what they've written to describe it in more depth.
4. **Now**
   The value is written in present tense (i.e. "I value" instead of "I will"). It describes who you are, not what you want or will do.

The most common problem with Christian clients is using standard Christian lingo—"I value the Bible as the word of God" or "I want to be a good Christian parent." If you work with ministry leaders, it is also common to see doctrinal statements in place of values. When I see these problems I push people to reword values so they are personal and unique:

- *"Can you say that in your own words?"*
- *"Why is that important to you?"*
- *"That's something most Christians believe. What's unique about you in that area? How are you passionate about this in a way that is different or goes beyond the norm?"*
- *"Try to move away from what you believe in this area to what you live by. What's the passion that animates how or why you do this?"*

Here's an example what values feedback might sound like in a coaching session:

"The value statement I came up with for family is, 'I value being a great Christian parent, investing in my kids' future in

the Kingdom, raising them in the admonition of the Lord.' How does that sound?"

"Sounds good. Nice and brief. I like the phrase, 'Investing in their future in the Kingdom.' What's that mean to you?"

"I see our kids as a stewardship—something that God gave us that we have to give back. So I want the way we parent to bring a return to the Kingdom. That's why we've invested a lot in short term mission trips, music lessons, stuff like that. When the kids show a desire to do something they could use for God, we try really hard to support it."

"Excellent! That's a good example of what a value ought to sound like when it is unpacked. How about the phrase, 'Being a great Christian parent.' Talk about what that means to you."

"Well, part of it is the investing in their future thing. Another is just staying focused. Kids are a priority. There is so much in life that will distract you if you let it—money issues, TV, things. When we make decisions, we've always tried to think through how it will impact the kids, and our ability to stay focused on being great parents."

"That's some excellent thinking as well. Here's a thought: when you talked about kids as a priority, and staying focused as parents, that language was a lot more powerful and personal than 'being a great parent.' Does that better represent the core of this value?"

"Yeah, I think it does. I'll relook at that one."

"Sounds good. And talk to me about that last phrase— that's from Scripture, right? "

"That's sort of our life verse when it comes to parenting. When we get in a tough situation, my wife and I sit down together and ask, 'What does the Bible have to say about this?' It's amazing how many times God has spoken to us or an answer comes that leads to a breakthrough when we just go back to his Word."

"Great! That sounds like something you are really living out. So other than rewording the 'great parent" phrase, it sounds to me like you have a very well-thought-out value statement.'"

Focus on the positive first. The coach asks the client to unpack the most powerful, *Unique* phrase.

Clearly, this value is being lived *Now*.

This phrase feels more like lingo, so the coach checks to see if it truly expresses the value.

There's a lot under the phrase—it is a value.

The coach applies the "*Uniqueness*" criteria here. What the client verbalized is much more personal.

Another stock phrase that needs checking.

At times verses are just lingo or filler, but sometimes they're crucial touchstones for the client's lived values.

Values Characteristics

Core values are deeply held, enduring beliefs that define what is most valuable or important to us. Below are a few characteristics defining what values are and aren't.

Values ARE:

- **Passionate.** They define what you care most about and why you do what you do.
- **Unique**. Since they come from your heart, they're in your own words.
- **Assumed**. Values are so much a part of us that we forget that they are there.
- **Lived**. If you truly value something, your behavior demonstrates it.
- **Lasting**. Values don't change easily—they're deeply rooted in you.

Values Are NOT:

- **Goals.** Goals are committed future aims. Values are what you hold dear now.
- **Aspirations**. A value is something you already live, not what you aspire to.
- **Principles**. Values are not cause and effect statements of how life works, like "You reap what you sow."
- **Doctrinal Statements**. "I believe the Bible is the inerrant word of God" is a doctrinal statement, not a value.
- **Visions.** Values are rooted in the now; visions are pictures of an ideal future.

Four Characteristics of Great Value Statements

1. **Short:** One sentence, one phrase, or even a single word to keep it memorable.
   - *"Now, can you sum that up in one sentence?"*
   - *"Can you shorten that into some pithy, meaningful phrases that can be unpacked?"*
2. **Unique:** In your words, not someone else's.
   - *"The language you are using could be true of a lot of people. Can you say that in a way that captures what is unique about you?"*
   - *"Can you say that in a way that if your friends read it they'd know it was you?"*
3. **Unpack-able:** Every word and phrase has meaning.
   - *"Unpack that for me—what does each phrase mean to you?"*
   - *"Take the key words there and tell me what each one means."*
4. **Now:** Written in the present tense, to describe who you are.
   - *"How well is this statement reflected in your life right now?"*
   - *"Is that a value that you are living out already, or is it something you aspire to that we might set a goal to reach?"*

10.2 Values Brain Dump

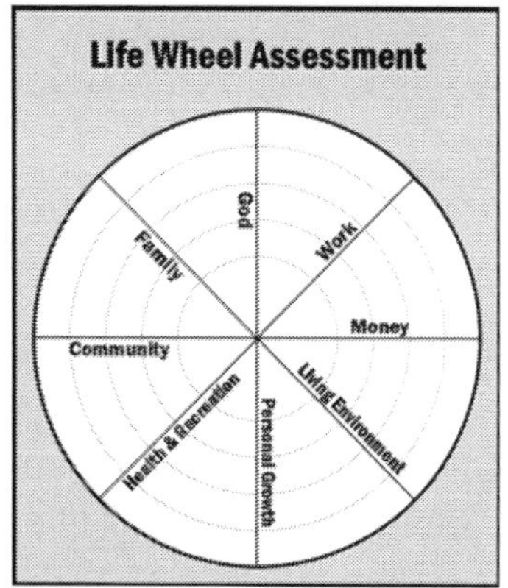

This exercise can be done in two ways: either as a general brain dump to create a global set of values, or by using the *Life Wheel Categories* (Work, Money, Living Environment, Personal Growth, Health and Recreation, Community, Family, God—see also 8.2) to create values for different areas of life.

Step 1: Brain Dump

Start with a stream-of-consciousness brain dump of words and phrases. What do you care most about in life? What's really important? Where do you invest the best of your time and energy, and why? What are the enduring priorities that drive your decisions? If you are using the eight categories, take each one in turn and brainstorm for five minutes or so in that area. Don't worry about organizing or evaluating your thoughts—at this point, you just need to get them down on paper

Family
Time together - vacations, fun nights, sitting around on the deck laughing and talking.
Fellowship. Depth and breadth.
Interdependence. We can count on each other to be there. Worthwhile relationship.
Doing your part. Family as a unit. Pulling your own weight. Easier together.
Sharing the responsibility. Making it fun.
Working together. Team. "Whistle while you work."

Money
Time is more important than money. Trading money for time.
Having enough, instead of being rich. God's provision. What you can do with it. A tool.
Free to spend or to save. Not having a hold on me. Using it for a purpose.
Income is from God. Paycheck comes from Him.

Step 2: Cull and Group

Now, take a step back and look at what you've written. Can you group your global value jottings into five to eight overall themes? If you are using the eight categories, try to cull it down to just two or three key phrases or concepts that you are most passionate about in each area. We are not looking for nice wording (that will come later), but to capture what best reflects your heart passion.

Family: *Doing it together makes it fun. Sharing the load makes it easy. Depending on each other makes it worthwhile.*
Money: *Money for time. Freedom: my paycheck is from God, and that's enough. A tool for a purpose.*

Values Word Choice

10.3

From the following list, circle the words that resonate most deeply with you and best describe what is important to you. Once you've picked out the ones that appeal to you, write them out on a separate sheet of paper. Are there some that are similar or could be grouped together? See if you can cull your list down to the five to seven themes or groups of words which are the "best of the best" in describing what you are passionate about.

Integrity
Honesty
Genuineness
Authenticity
Accountability
Do what you say
Directness
Sincerity
Strength
Character
Follow-through
Sacrifice
Legacy
Family
Marriage
Duty
Honor
Heritage
Responsibility
Harmony
Security
Stability
Peace
Home
Thoughtfulness
Practicality
Nurture
Love
Beauty
Romance
Volunteering

Freedom
Exploration
Creativity
Fun
Artistic
Spontaneity
Flexibility
Knowledge
The search
Meaning
Influence
Truth
Passion
Seeing the world
Adventure
Diversity
Travel
Change
Movement
New challenges
Opportunity
Enthusiasm
Starting things
Entrepreneurial
Motivation
Progress
Inspiration
Renewal
Healing
Nature
The outdoors

Relationship
Team
Community
Belonging
Depth
Being known
Intimacy
Commitment
Friendship
Communication
Gentleness
Compassion
Caring
Emotion
Spiritual life
Health
Devotion
Passionate pursuit
Worship
Generosity
Service
Reflection
Reaching out
Evangelism
Changing the world
Hospitality
Concern
Integration
Making a difference

Financial independence
Stewardship
Frugality
Overflow
Sharing
Benevolence
Life-long learning
Investment
Success
Recognition
Community involvement
Career advancement
Efficiency
Accomplishment
Focus
Purpose
Achievement
Building
Leadership
Mastery
Competence
Precision
Excellence
Planning
Being knowledgeable
Principles
Rationality

10.4 Obituary: Who Will They Say I Am?

Step 1: Write Your Obituary

Imagine it is right after your own funeral. Your best friends and family have gathered to remember you and celebrate your life. One by one, people stand up and describe who you were and the personal qualities they most appreciate about you. What would you want them to say? Jot down some phrases. If you need help, try looking at the *Life Wheel Categories* (8.2), and ask what you'd want people to say about you in each of those areas.

He was a regular guy.

He never got a big head. You always felt like you could talk to him.

He was a great dad—he just cared a lot about me. He used to tuck me in every night and pray for me, and some days when I was older I'd catch him still praying for me on his own before he went to bed.

He cared about the little things. I was often amazed at the needs he saw without being told, and how he would quietly go about meeting them.

He didn't leave a mess behind him.

When he committed to something, you knew it was going to get done.

He cared enough to pay attention and remember what was important to you

Step 2: Evaluate

Now step back and look at what you wrote. What are the common themes behind the responses you envisioned? Why are these particular phrases in your list important to you?

Theme: taking care of the little things.

Theme: being one of the guys. Being accessible.

It's important to me to show people I love them in small ways.

Doing what you say you'll do is important to me.

Coaching Tip

The responses above may lead us to two or three core values—maybe something about showing love in the little things, accessibility, and integrity. It will usually take another step (like coaching the person around what they wrote, or combining this with the Word Choice exercise) for the person to get from these ruminations to actual values.

Values Clarification

10.5

A fun way to flesh out your values is simply to talk them through with a close friend. Having to describe what you value out loud clarifies thinking and makes it easier to put those values down on paper later. For this exercise, you'll need a good friend, family member or spouse who is willing to dialogue with you for a half hour or so on values.

Simply share your values one at a time, and then try to unpack each phrase and explain what it means. Ask your friend to mirror back to you what he or she hears, to make it is clear. Then discuss back and forth a bit. Give the person the questions below so they can draw you out and coach you a little on your values. And make sure if you say a great line to jot it down!

- "What does the phrase ____ mean?"
- "Why is that important to you?"
- "What's the part of this that makes you different than every other Christian?"
- "Can you give an example of how that value influences your choices?"
- "What's one way you already live that out now?"
- "In all that you just said, what are the two most important phrases?"

Coaching Tip

This is a great exercise for extroverts (who think out loud) or clients who aren't into journaling. Once they've talked the thing through, the act of writing becomes much easier.

Reflection is looking inside—the introvert's natural strength. Extroverts focus on the external rather than internal world, so they tend to find written, reflective exercises more difficult. Making the exercise into a conversation almost always helps—every extrovert loves to talk! Another option is for the person to dictate into a hand-held recorder or speech-to-text program instead of writing. Be alert if your extroverted clients start laboring with all this reflection, and give them some relational options to make it easier and more fun.

10.6 Writing Value Statements

Converting values reflections into statements gives you a memorable, concise summary of your values you can carry around in your head. The more accessible your values, the more useful they are!

Step 1: Review Definitions

Take a moment first and review the *Value Statement Examples* (10.7) and *Values Characteristics* (10.1) to get your objective in mind.

Step 2: Create Statements

Next, take each theme and create a phrase or one–sentence statement for that area. Start by jotting out the key words or phrases you want to include, then try different combinations until you get a statement you like. Most people experiment with several versions before they settle on one. The most important thing is that your values capture what **you** truly value.

Step 3: Create Statement Titles

Create a one-word (or *brief* phrase) "title" for each statement as a memory device.

Key Value Words and Phrases

Money for time.
Freedom: my paycheck is from God, and that's enough.
All the provision I'll ever need.
A tool for a purpose.

Trial Versions

God is enough for me, so I can sacrifice money for time.
Because my paycheck is from God, I'm free to trade money for time.
I will always trade money for time. I work for God.
I will always trade money for time, because God is all the provision I'll ever need.
I always trade money for time; God is all the provision I'll ever need.
God is all the provision I'll ever need, so I can trade money for time.

Title: *Money for Time*

Final Statement: *God is all the provision I'll ever need, so I can trade money for time.*

> ***Coaching Tip***
> *Value statements can always change as you get more in touch with who you really are. If the client is getting hung up in trying to make it just right, sometimes it will get them unstuck to suggest that they take their best shot, live with it a while, and then come back to reword it later.*

Value Statement Examples

Below are some representative examples of short value statements, plus three common values problems with examples of how to troubleshoot them.

Example Statements

- *"I believe in respect for the dignity of the individual."*
- *"I value meeting God everywhere: in nature, in circumstances, in people. It's about relationship, not rules."*
- *"People before projects."*
- *"The transparency that meets God as healer and not just protector."*
- *"Integrity: your word is who you are."*
- *"I value living in oneness in marriage—intimacy in conversation, unity in decision-making and sharing in calling."*
- *"Sacrificing to attain excellence inspires others and honors God."*

Problem #1: Rambling

"I value helping and empowering people to be their best and live their best lives, resourcing them to discover who they were made to be, and walking with them to fulfill that potential, because people are created by God and are of ultimate worth."

Problem: All the "ands" and redundancy will make this a killer to remember. Your values should be something concise you can carry with you.

Better: "*I value seeing people as God created them, of ultimate worth, and helping them fulfill that potential.*"

Problem #2: Goal-Oriented

"I will spend my life empowering people to reach their human potential, and strive to become a great resource that helps them fully walk out their destiny."

Problem: This also sounds more like a mission statement (an ultimate task) than a value (why you do what you do). Values describe your motivations, not what you will do in the future.

Better: "*Human potential and helping people fully attain it.*"

Statement #3: Not Unique

"Being a godly husband and loving my wife as Christ loved the church."

Problem: This statement is vague and not very personal. What are you uniquely passionate about in marriage? How can you make this personal instead of theological?

Better: "*The little acts of love and service that make every moment a romance.*"

10.8 Leadership Values

Organizational leaders greatly benefit from creating a separate set of values for how they lead.

Step 1: Brain Dump

Start by doing a brain dump on the questions below.

- *"What are the four or five most important values that guide the way you lead?"*
- *"What are your non-negotiables as a leader?"*
- *"What are the guiding principles that form the basis for your leadership decisions?"*

Step 2: Check the List

Pick out just the items in this list that strike you as most important for the way you lead, and jot down words and phrases that describe your values in those areas.

1. The place of Scripture
2. Single vs. multiple leadership, teamwork, feedback
3. Decision-making process
4. Interfacing with the culture
5. Relationships and their value
6. Leadership style: empowering, directing, collaborating, etc.
7. Gifting and leadership
8. The poor, the outcast, the less-fortunate
9. Evangelism/missions/community involvement
10. Discipleship/spiritual growth/maturity
11. Authority
12. Training, leadership development
13. A leader's lifestyle
14. Servanthood
15. Roles: of lay people, women
16. Creativity, innovation, change
17. Unity, restoration, reconciliation, diversity
18. Truth, integrity
19. Excellence
20. Authenticity, openness

Step 3: Create Values

Use exercises 10.5 and 10.6 to turn your values notes into final statements.[21]

21 *Values-Driven Leadership* by Aubrey Malphurs is a great resource for leadership values.

Question 4: What Has Life Prepared Me For? (Preparation)

"I will prepare, and someday my chance will come."

Abraham Lincoln

When Moses fled into the desert with his tail between his legs, he thought his life purpose was finished. After identifying with his people and their plight, he immediately attempted to use his power position to seek their welfare. Wasn't he a son of Pharaoh's household, uniquely prepared as a man of destiny on their behalf? Alone of the Hebrews, he was born to rule instead of to slavery. He knew the palace customs, had access to Pharaoh, and knew the movers and the shakers in Egyptian society. Who else was better qualified to lead?

Moses probably had the finest education that Egypt could give, in everything from history and politics to generalship and personal combat. He was accustomed to power, and he leveraged what he knew. Moses almost immediately resorted to force to reach his goal. But when Pharaoh found out about his rebellion, Moses was forced to flee into exile with just the clothes on his back. What a come-down it must have been when the golden child realized the limitations of his personal power and natural abilities!

It's not clear what Moses' strategy for deliverance was, other than that it involved killing. Growing up amidst the palace intrigues, one might naturally assume than an armed revolt and overthrow of the Egyptian government (with Moses ending up in

Pharaoh's throne?) may have been on his mind. But God had other plans, and sent him to an apprenticeship in the desert.

It would have been easy for Moses to assume that those were aimless, wasted years. He knew there was something in his heart about delivering the Hebrews. But if that was the goal, what was happening to him made no sense. As an exile that had lost his palace position, favor and access, everything that looked like it might make his destiny possible was gone. Then to trudge through the wilderness as a total nobody for 40 years, to be stripped bare of everything he thought he was and thought he could accomplish—was there still anything left for Moses but to herd sheep? You can see how beaten down he was at the burning bush. God returned and said, "Now is the time! Fulfill your destiny!" Moses didn't seem to have any trouble talking to God—in fact, I get the impression he was used to divine conversation. But Moses didn't believe in his destiny or himself. "I can't do this!" He wailed, citing excuse after excuse. "I'm a nobody! Who am I to stand before Pharaoh? The people will never believe that you are with me. I'm not a good speaker. Send someone else!" The man that God spent 40 years preparing as his chosen deliverer felt totally unprepared.

There is more going on here than just Moses being humbled, although that was important—it took God 40 years to make him "the meekest man who ever lived" before he was ready for his task. The problem was that *Moses did not see the connection between his preparation and his destiny.* Moses was experiencing a common but little-understood pattern in calling development: preparation in a role outside your area of call.

Very often, God trains us in the skills and character our destiny requires in a place that seems totally disconnected from what we think we're supposed to do.[22] Moses' struggle was intensified because his character preparation required *removing* him from a position very much like his ultimate role, and demoting him into a much smaller sphere of influence. Because Moses did not really understand what his destiny would require of him, or the ways of God in preparing leadership character, he did not recognize God's preparation for what it was.

Consider for a moment a few of the things Moses learned herding Jethro's sheep. Because he was destined to lead a group of slaves who'd lived along the Nile for 400 years, he was the only one of the Hebrews who knew:

- How to survive in the desert.
- Where the roads were and how to navigate through the trackless wastes.
- Where the springs and the oases were.
- Where the best grazing for the cattle was at different times of year.
- What desert plants could be eaten by people and animals.
- The wild animals found in the desert, and how to handle them.

22 For example, many stay-at-home moms are meticulously prepared for convergent ministry or marketplace roles through the process of childrearing. We often don't perceive the value of this preparation because so much of it involves *inward character* instead of *outward skills.*

- What the local customs were.
- Where the forts and guarded places were.

Somebody needed to have a desert survival skill-set if all those slaves were going to navigate that unfamiliar environment, and God chose Moses as that someone. Moses learned basic leadership and cultural skills first, in Egypt. He learned his practical desert skills at the same time as he was learning character—humility and utter dependence on God. In fact, everything in Moses' life, from the circumstances of his birth to his upbringing to his years tending sheep fed into his calling. *Moses' whole life prepared him for what he was born to do.*

Moses' whole life prepared him for what he was born to do.

What is Preparation?

Preparation is one of the four key areas on the life purpose diagram. It's the sum total of the experiences you have had in life that make you ready for your destiny. Since God is actively preparing you *for* something, your significant experiences are also predictive of your life purpose. Studying what God has taken you through reveals themes and connections that point toward your call.

For instance, a common preparation episode involves experiencing the lifestyle or the sufferings of those you are called to serve. When Christ came in human form He experienced every temptation we humans have to endure—that is why we can approach Him with confidence when we face difficulty. He knows what it is like to be human.

In the same way, if you are called to serve those who have struggled in their marriages or who are on the fringes of society, expect that God will take you through your own experiences of marital conflict or being friendless and rejected. That common experience of suffering is what allows those you are called to serve to approach *you* with confidence.

When you fully enter into a convergent role in your area of call, you'll see how everything you've ever experienced and learned is being leveraged into your life purpose. Part of the great satisfaction of that season of life is realizing that all of your life makes sense, even when you didn't understand it at the time. Early in life, experiences of suffering and adversity are often a mystery. It is only later, after we have learned to trust God in things we don't understand, that we begin to perceive how He has intricately woven His purposes for us throughout every experience in life. Coaching preparation is about helping people make sense of life experience in terms of their call.

Nurturing Your Nature

While the area of Design is about discovering your *nature*, Preparation inventories your *nurture*. It includes learned skills, qualifications and credentials, the network and the favor you've developed, and your best accomplishments (as well as your failures). Your Preparation is what enables you to fully function in your Design. Without the character building Preparation of life experience, your Design won't accomplish much of lasting value.

Preparation is what enables you to fully function in your Design.

Here's an analogy. I used to be a woodcarver. Experienced carvers have a large suite of knives, each with a different curvature or "sweep" and a different width. Unlike a pocketknife or bread knife, carving tools have the sharpened part of the blade on the end, like a chisel. Since each blade is differently curved, and it is tough to sharpen a curved surface, sharpening skills are a big part of carving. Some of the best tools actually come from the manufacturer without a finished edge—you have to hone them to a razor-sharp edge yourself before they'll shape the wood.

Your Design is that unsharpened tool from the factory. To make the most of your natural gifts, you have to hone them with learned skills, experience, credentials and more. Preparation takes the rough blade of your innate talents and grinds it to the precision edge needed to move you into an extraordinary level of effectiveness. Only when design is sharpened by preparation and energized by passion does one's calling come to fruition.

Coaching the Connections

Understanding how your life prepares you for your call is in some ways very accessible to clients and in others a total mystery. Because your life story tells the tale of your preparation, all the basic information about what God has done to move you toward your destiny is already in your memories. Most people can easily rattle off their key accomplishments, credentials or important learned skills they've attained.

But understanding how suffering, failure or adversity fits into the picture is more problematic. Often it takes a coach walking alongside to help you see the connections. Would Joseph the favorite son ever have guessed that his preparation for ruling a country would be running an Egyptian prison? Would David have foreseen that fleeing from Saul and refusing to take vengeance on him would make him ready to be a king?

While this section provides exercises for inventorying how you've been prepared, the key coaching task is to help people make connections between experience and destiny. One great approach is through *Destiny Events* (12.1). These special events when we feel like we are hitting on all cylinders and doing what we were made to do can yield incredible clues to one's destiny.

We'll also cover how to inventory learned skills, life experiences and credentials and connect them with the coachee's life purpose. The vague sense of connectedness most people have between purpose and preparation can be greatly strengthened by doing a formal *Preparation Resume* (11.2). Tools are also provided to look at negative preparation (what you have learned you *aren't* supposed to do).

Creating a Preparation Baseline

As usual, we'll start the Preparation section with a baseline assessment. This area is a bit harder to size up. It is important to ask the client not to just make up something on the spot to answer the questions: while that could be done, what we are trying to measure is to what degree the person is already consciously aware of being prepared. Following the example exercise is a page of evaluation criteria.

1.1c Preparation Baseline Assessment

These questions will help us create a customized life purpose discovery plan for you. Take five to eight minutes to complete the assessment. If you don't know what to say on a question, or would have to dream up an answer on the spot, leave it blank. This isn't a test where you get points for having an answer. Instead, we're trying to determine what you know for sure about your purpose so we understand where to start the discovery process.

1. List two character qualities you'll need in your destiny role that life has taught you along the way, and say how they connect with your destiny?

   Standing up for what is right (not being passive) in conflict situations—I'll be working with high-powered people and can't be a wallflower.
   How to overcome discouragement and keep pressing forward—?

2. What are three skills that you've picked up along the way in life that will be vital to fulfilling your call?

   Networking—knowing how to serve people by connecting them.
   Managing my time and my schedule according to priorities.
   Leading a team through creating and implementing a strategic plan.

3. Give me an example of a difficult experience you've gone through in the last few years that you are consciously aware has specifically prepared you for your destiny.

   I've gone through some tough times but I don't see how they have prepared me for my purpose.

4. Name a past event where you felt you were doing what you were born to do, and two things that event tells you about your life purpose.

   Running the annual blood donor campaign. Two things: I love working with community leaders and businesspeople to better our community. I'm really good at schmoozing and recruiting people, and it's a blast, too.

Evaluating the Preparation Baseline Assessment

The first question on the preparation baseline looks at character development. Most people can list some character qualities they've learned in life—the real question is if they can connect those qualities to their destiny. Ask the person about the connection: "Why is this quality vital to your destiny role? What would happen if you didn't have it?"

The second question relates to the *Preparation Resume* (11.2). We're looking to see if the person can link learned skills with destiny. The more significant the connections, the farther along they probably are in understanding what they were born to do. When the person can't make these connections, you may choose to probe a bit, or simply use the *Preparation Inventories* to begin bringing those connections to light.

The third question explores making sense of suffering and difficulty in life. This can be a tough question—if the person draws a blank, the *Negative Preparation* inventory (11.5) can be an important area to work on together.

Question four looks for *Destiny Events* (12.1). Here again, we're most interested in the connections between the event and the person's understanding of their life purpose. In this example, the client is able to identify several things he loves doing from his destiny experience. Sometimes clients will be able to name destiny events but won't know what they mean. Occasionally you'll get someone who can't identify any times in life where they felt like they were hitting on all cylinders. Usually dialoging together can help break the logjam and identify these moments.

Obviously, coachees who don't feel like they have any clue what their life purpose is will struggle with the assessment. Often these people know more than they think they know, but there is some obstacle that keeps them from believing in their own discernment. If that becomes an objection to the exercise ("How can I do this if I don't know what my purpose is?"), often a response like, "Just take your best shot and don't worry about getting it perfect" will get them off dead center.

Once you've reviewed the assessment, it's time for the coachee and coach to create a plan for exploring the area of Preparation. Usually you'll want to at least do the two *Preparation Resumes* (11.2 and 11.4) and the *Destiny Events* (12.1) exercises. You may go on to look at *Negative Preparation* and *Outside Preparation* (exercises 11.5 and 11.3) if the person has a tough time making the connections.

The *Destiny Events* exercise is particularly valuable for people who feel they've lived much of life off-course (or recently became a Christian). Because it bypasses the person's existing conclusions about life and goes back to the raw data of the experiences, it gives the coach the ammunition to get someone who is drawing a blank about their purpose moving again. *Outside Preparation* can also be used here—have the person inventory the abilities they developed before Christ and then help them make the destiny connections.

Chapter 11: Preparation/Life Experience

"We all have dreams. But in order to make dreams into reality, it takes an awful lot of determination, dedication, self-discipline, and effort."

Jesse Owens, Olympian

An in-depth look at Preparation is most valuable for those whose preparation is taking place *outside* of their area of call. When a farmer who's lived in the same town all his life feels called to the mission field, a stay-at-home mom returns to the working world, or a businesswoman feels an urge to move into ministry, they struggle to feel adequate for what their hearts yearn to do.

The classic biblical example of Outside Preparation is Joseph. After a whirlwind shower, a good shave (maybe the first in years), and cleaning the dirt out from under his nails, he was hustled out of the dungeon to stand in front of the King of Egypt. If you'd looked only at his job experience to that point, he would have seemed totally unprepared for that moment. But his character and wisdom were so evident that Pharaoh instantly trusted him and gave him the reins of the Egyptian economy.

How did Joseph gain the confidence and security to move directly from the gutter of society into his call as a national leader? The secret is that preparation is more about inward growth than acquiring skills and credentials. Most of Joseph's outward preparation (learning the language, becoming a good manager, mastering Egyptian customs) happened in Potipher's house. The incident with Potipher's wife that sent him to prison marked his graduation from an initial season of outward preparation, and the beginning of an intensive season of inward work. Outwardly, he was demoted (just like Moses) to a much lower position than he had before. Inwardly, he was right on course, and grew by leaps and bounds in humility, trust and dependence on God. Confidently functioning in your call is ultimately more about dependence on God to come through in the clutch than it is about your own credentials and contacts.

Leaders like Joseph who have large callings go through major shaking and stripping experiences early in life. Being falsely accused, working under an abusive leader or suddenly finding oneself leading in the midst of an organizational meltdown often indicate that God has tapped that person for great influence. That counter-intuitive insight can be a life saver for a young leader in crisis!

So how do you help everyday people make those Joseph-connections between preparation and purpose? Here's an example of coaching a stay-at-home mom through understanding her preparation.

"Going back and getting a masters—that's an exciting dream, Bonnie! I think that would be a great fit for you now that the kids are off to college. But I'm hearing some hesitancy in your voice—is there something there you want to talk about?"

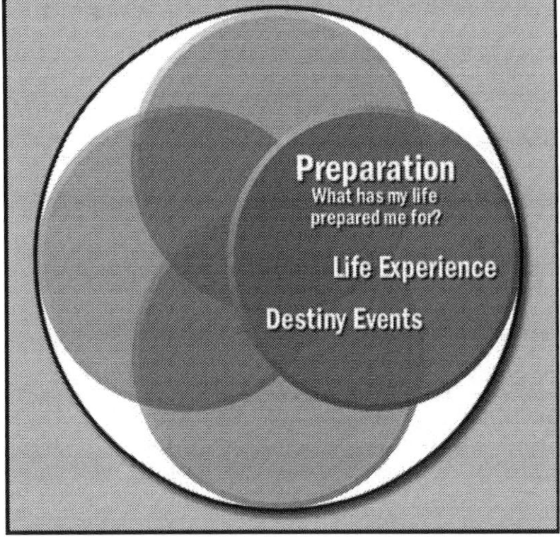

"Um... it just seems kind of scary. I mean, I've been at home for the better part of 20 years, and going back into psychology—there's so much I've missed, there's so much I've forgotten. I feel like I've been on another planet for two decades. I know how to raise kids, but going back to school again..."

"OK. I can see why you'd feel that way. Let's take that apart. What kind of tasks or situations in school do you feel unprepared for?"

"Well, studying for one. I haven't done that in ages. I guess I'm afraid I'll have forgotten so much from undergrad that I'll be embarrassed in class. And then there's actually going out and getting a job. Will anyone want me? Will I have anything to offer? I have this 20-year hole in my resume with no relevant experience, and I'm afraid that is going to sink me."

"So let's see if we can get an objective look at how prepared you are. Take the studying thing first. Imagine the Bonnie of today and the Bonnie of 20-some years ago both coming home from the first week of classes. You have about five hours of reading and a one-page summary to post over the weekend. Talk about how the younger Bonnie would approach that."

"Gosh, that takes me back. When I was in college... well, Friday was date night. Howard and I were almost always out late. Saturday I'd sleep in, bum around in the

morning, maybe do my chores and get in a bit of studying in the afternoon, then hang out some with friends. Sunday night I'd finally crack down and finish the stuff for Monday. Ah, to have no responsibilities again!"

"And how would you approach that work now?"

"Well, we usually go out for supper around 6:30 on Fridays, so I'd probably try to get in an hour or so before that, relax in the evening and be in bed at a decent hour. Saturday morning would be the study time—afternoon is for shopping and errands. I'd want to be done on Saturday, maybe even by noon, so I can take a real Sabbath on Sunday."

"Now imagine you are the professor. Which of those two students do you think would do a better job on the homework?"

"The current me sounds a lot more disciplined and responsible. I got things done back then, but I don't do my best work late the night before. I guess I was kind of a procrastinator."

"So what makes you into a more disciplined student today?"

"Being a mom. There is a lot to do, and if you don't do it, it won't get done. So you just learn to tackle stuff; that taking initiative makes you feel better than sitting on the couch watching Oprah and avoiding it. After 20 years of doing the laundry and the dishes, you're a more disciplined person."

"So being a mom would really help you in school."

"At least in getting my homework done!"

"You also talked about getting a job after you graduation. Put yourself in a manager's shoes for a minute. You are interviewing to hire a new psychologist for your company, and on your desk are the resumes of two Psych Masters. One is you as a fresh-faced, 24-year-old grad student with no experience in the working world, and one is Bonnie at 50, with similar educational credentials, plus having raised three great kids, serving on several boards and community projects, and being a leader in her church. Which one would you hire?"

"Me? I'd hire me at 50."

"How come?"

"Because... well, I just know so much more about real life. Just out of college, I had all kinds of energy and ambition, and a lot of book learning, but I really didn't understand people. I'd just apply the theories I'd read to people and think that they would change. People are a lot more complicated than that. I mean, just with my kids, I've learned so much about motivating different personalities and how to adjust my style to communicate with them. I didn't know that at 24."

"So those 20 years of child-rearing and small group leading really did prepare you?"

"I guess so—I never thought of it that way before."

In this dialog, the coach helps Bonnie shake off a self-defeating belief by helping her make connections between her Preparation and her goal. Bonnie comes to the dialog comparing herself to "others" and feels she is lacking, without really examining what those others bring to the table. To get beyond this false comparison, the coach uses the device of having her compare herself now to what she was like at an earlier age. This takes Bonnie out of the realm of imagination and into reality, because she can remember what she was really like at that age. Once she looks realistically at what her experience gives her in a real situation (studying), she recognizes the value

of her life experience. The coach uses a similar tactic with finding a job. Putting Bonnie into the role of a manager got her in touch with the value of her experience in the working world.

The essential coaching questions for connecting experience with destiny are:

1. *"What have you **experienced**?"*
2. *"How are those experiences **valuable**?"*
3. *"How do those experiences give you practical **skills** for what you are called to do?"*
4. *"How have those experiences given you the **character** you need to reach your destiny?"*

The final question of the four is especially important if preparation is outside one's area of call. Bonnie is not as prepared in practical educational knowledge as other students who are fresh out of an undergrad program. But in inner strengths (like self-management, responsibility and real-world ability to relate to different personalities) her 20 years of preparation shines through.

Preparation and Character

Calling is about serving Christ for the good of others. Preparation to serve others is not just a function of skills: you also have to become the kind of person people in your target audience will look to. You can have all the right answers and the best educational credentials, but if no one is listening, you won't have any influence.

Another way of putting this truth is that *skills channel character.* The eternal content of what people receive when you serve them is the Christ that is in you—the act of service is just the channel for it. The true power of service is not that you fixed my roof when I was in the hospital (although that is certainly valuable!) It's that someone actually cared enough about me to love me in a practical way. And so I receive the heart of Christ through the service.

Much of a leader's preparation focuses on character development, not just skills.

The better your outward skills, the more people are impacted by the heart behind them. So if you have great leadership skills but you are primarily motivated by a deep need for approval and an ambition to be famous, the lasting impact of even the "good" things you do will be the damage and disappointment caused by your mixed motives. Some leaders will stand before Jesus on the last day and say, "Lord, didn't we build great ministries in your name, and give lots of money to your cause, and help many people?" And Jesus will reply, "That was really all about you. I didn't have anything to do with it."

Ministry takes the Christ incarnate in you and channels that embodiment through your skills, strengths and abilities to others. Ministry is something you are that comes out through what you do. Because the heart is such an important part of representing Christ to the world, much of a leader's Preparation involves embodying Him in character qualities like dependence, trust, humility, love, and grace. But since most people think of Preparation almost exclusively in terms of skills, credentials and work experience, reframing life experience around character preparation can lead to huge breakthroughs.

Coaching Preparation

So what should a Preparation discovery plan look like? A good first step is to inventory what clients have experienced in the *Preparation Resume* (11.2). This is a straightforward reflection exercise that doesn't require a lot of preamble—most people can list educational credentials or relevant experience without much help. When a person is being prepared inside their area of call, the preparation experiences make much more sense at the time, so the connections to destiny are easy to make.

The *Internal Preparation Resume* (11.4) is a bit more difficult. Discussing the place of character in Preparation first (see above) can help. Once the inventories are done, spend some time discussing them:

- *"Where do you feel confident in your resume? Where don't you?"*
- *"Where are the holes in your resume? Are there any blank areas? Where do you feel a need for further development?"*
- *"What patterns of skill and character development are apparent? What does that say about what God is preparing you for?"*
- *"Do your life experiences make sense to you as specific preparation for your purpose?"*

For the preparation resume, the next step is often to create practical strategies for filling the holes in the person's resume—*Outside Preparation* (11.3) can easily be adapted to this chore. To take internal preparation a step further, the *Life Messages* exercise (14.1) puts those character qualities in terms of messages God has planted in an individual through their experiences. *Negative Preparation* (11.5—see below) supplements the resume for people who have trouble seeing failures and reverses as part of Preparation.

Remember, for the coachee to make the connection between Preparation and destiny, they have to have some sense of what that destiny *is*. That means that the area of Preparation *is* generally not the best place to start the life purpose discovery process. Do some work with Design and Passion before you tackle this area.

Negative Preparation Experiences

In our example dialog, Bonnie had a set of positive experiences as a mom that she needed to connect with her life purpose. We can do exactly the same thing with negative experiences. Negative Preparation is when failure, suffering or difficulty bring us unexpected gifts that launch us toward our destinies. This is where the coach's perspective is vital—we get so wrapped up in our circumstances that it is hard for us to step back and see the larger story of what God is doing. And God does things His own way—sometimes it is almost impossible to understand what He's doing with our lives until all the pieces finally fall into place. He must like surprises, or just the

joy of seeing us say, "Wow!" when a wonderful part of our passion arises out of what looked at first like a mistake.

For example, my basic calling statement is "building leadership character and creating systems that build leadership character." A vital part of my preparation happened outside my area of call, while working as a custom furniture designer. We were understaffed and overworked most of the time. Some of it was my own doing—I built our sales up to the point where I could barely handle the workload. There were times I hated the pressure cooker. Because so much had to be done, I became a master of minimalism. I sold $15,000 jobs from a ten-minute sketch on a piece of graph paper. I cut the average time to price a custom piece from an hour to less than five minutes. Still, I was inevitably weeks behind schedule. Always delivering later than I hoped and repeatedly disappointing the customers and craftsmen, I often felt like a failure.

At the time, I was just trying to do my job. I didn't see any connection between what I was going through and where I wanted to be (in ministry). All I knew was that God put me in that job and He hadn't given me the freedom to leave—not that I didn't ask Him every year to let me go! Toward the end of that season of life, I began to wonder if I would ever get to do what I was called to. Like Moses, right at about the time when God was finishing up the preparation was when I felt most stuck and abandoned by God.

What I needed and didn't have was a coach to reframe the situation and say, "It seems like God is giving you lots of experiences of working under pressure. Why is He doing that at this point in your life? How is it connected to your ultimate purpose?" Because I couldn't see the purpose of my struggle, *I assumed it had no purpose.* I needed a coach to radically believe with me that every circumstance I was going through was part of God's larger plan.

It was only years later that I realized the incredible gift of that job: I learned to be highly creative and relentlessly productive whether I felt like it or not. A lot of authors struggle with writer's block, or feel like they have to have the right mood hit them before they can write. After 15 years of being forced to produce under pressure, that rarely bothers me. I know how to sit down and write, I know how to work to an achievable standard, and I know when to stop tweaking and say, "It's done." God used my job as a furniture designer to shape me for my call when I didn't even realize He was doing it.

Coaching Negative Preparation

It is actually most common to coach negative preparation when you aren't working on destiny at all. In this life every client will have trouble. Reframing difficult experiences as destiny preparation is a powerful tool that helps clients engage adverse circumstances as part of God's plan instead of as punishment or random evil.

Coaching negative preparation is about perspective adjustment. When times are tough, it is easy to lose sight of how God causes all things to work together for good[23]

---

23 The word "good" in Romans 8:28 means "inward goodness" or "good character." Certainly, everything that happens in the Christian life doesn't work to make you healthier, wealthier or

to those who are called according to His purpose (meaning, *everything* in life works to prepare us for God's calling). Help your clients regain perspective by inviting them to consider God's purposes in the situation:

- *"What if God is in this? How does this situation prepare you for your destiny role?"*
- *"How does God want to meet you and transform you in the midst of this?"*
- *"Let's say that God sent this situation because it was exactly what you needed to prepare you for your destiny. If that were true, what would He be doing?"*
- *"Why is God sending you this kind of experience at this time in your life? How can it prepare you for your calling?"*

Keys for Coaching Negative Preparation

1. Believe that the circumstance is part of God's destiny preparation.
2. Create an invitation that allows the client to reframe around that idea.

Sometimes, juxtaposing the person's calling task or audience with their circumstances can help people see the connection:

- *"So your extended illness has you feeling left-out and overlooked. But I also know your desire is to reach people that are on the fringes of society, who feel unloved. Is there a connection there? Why is God putting you in the same boat as the people you want to reach?"*

In the question above, I've taken the Preparation principle that God will allow you to share the experience of those you serve (11.1) and used it as a question. When coachees start to consider what an asset it will be to share the experience of those they are called to, their attitude about that experience quickly changes.

Often you can just state a growth principle that might apply to the person's situation, and invite them to decide whether or not it has application. For instance:

- *"If you are going to work in a hospital, you are going to be around sick people. That was Jesus' take on ministry. How might that apply to your situation?"*
- *"Usually at some point in a leader's development, God will place her in an unjust situation or have her function under unhealthy authority. What do you think is God's purpose in having you here right now?"*

---

more secure. But it can make you more like Jesus if you frame it in terms of God's purposes for your character and meet Him there.

Preparation Principles

11.1

The best perspective questions come out of an understanding the principles of how God develops leaders. Below are a few examples of preparation principles that occur often in the lives of developing leaders:

- God will take you through experiences that help you identify with those you are called to serve. For instance, if you are called to minister to the grieving, your own grief will prepare you for that task.
- Many of your experiences build the faith and fortitude muscles you'll need to succeed in your calling. Dealing with the annoying people in your office builds the skills and character to deal with human needs on a larger scale.
- Failure is as good a preparation as success. If your calling involves revitalizing dying organizations, what better preparation than to be part of an organization that dies—or better yet, to lead one?
- Often God has to excise a lesser love in your life to make room for you to embrace His greater purpose. Having your company go belly up is an excellent way to become detached from pursuing material things.
- When God deals with a leader, everyone who serves under that person also gets dealt with. This adversity may be primarily about someone else's preparation. Are you willing to pay a price for their destiny?
- Your place of power in ministry is where God has most deeply dealt with your character—because that's where Christ is most fully incarnate in you. For instance, if you are called to teach leadership skills, expect God to put your own leadership under a microscope and hold you to an unfairly high standard compared to others.
- God often gives leaders a glimpse of their call early in life, but then there is a long season of inward preparation in relative obscurity before they emerge into that call. For a 30-something client who feels stuck in that middle season, it always helps to look at the time lines of Abraham, David, Joseph, Paul, or even Jesus.
- God will not allow you to enter your call from a place of security, where all your needs are met. Your destiny will require faith for God's provision.
- Big leadership challenges early in life can be an indicator of a large sphere calling.
- Graduating successfully from a certain stage of your Preparation is usually marked by removal from that sphere or facing a larger challenge. Endings don't mean you've failed. God wouldn't give it to you if He didn't think you were ready for it.
- A wilderness season is a mark of special affection from God. He leads us into the desert to draw us into deeper intimacy with Him (Hos. 2:14-16).

11.2 Preparation Resume

In this exercise, we're going to create a resume of the outward qualifications you've accumulated that prepare you for your life purpose. At this point, don't worry too much about connecting a specific qualification with your purpose—just list everything that falls under each category and your coach will help you sort it out.

1. Credentials

Degrees, certifications, education, awards and other recognized qualifications.

2. Accomplishments

What are your best accomplishments at work, in volunteer roles and at home?

Coaching Tip
You may need to prompt the person to include experiences or accomplishments outside work here as valuable parts of their Preparation Resume.

3. Work/Life Experience

What major things have you experienced in life? What roles have you filled? What does your experience equip you to do, understand or communicate to others?

4. Network/Favor

Who knows you, and where do you have favor or opportunity through your relationships?

5. Skills

What skills have you acquired along the way? Where do you have expertise?

Coaching Tip
Remember, this is learned skills, *not natural abilities—those are part of Design, not Preparation.*

It is much easier to see how you've grown toward your call when that preparation happens within your area of calling. If you are a stay-at-home mom reentering the working world or a businessman transitioning to ministry, figuring out how your prior experience benefits you is tougher. This exercise helps you inventory the skills you've mastered outside your area of call and apply them to your destiny role.

Step 1: Inventory Learnings

Take each of the eight *Life Wheel Categories* (Work, Money, Living Environment, Personal Growth, Health and Recreation, Community, Family, God—see 8.2) and list the major life skills, competencies and character qualities you've developed in life. What have you mastered? What skills have you picked up by working outside your area of call? What do you know that you didn't before? Put down any significant life skills, even if they seems unrelated to your destiny.

Step 2: Generalize into Competencies

The key to this exercise is identifying *general competencies,* not context-specific skills. The underlying general competencies in what you've done apply to anything—the context-specific part only happens in the particular role you were in.

> ***Example:*** *As a mom, you learned how to shop efficiently for groceries, keep to a monthly budget, do meal planning, and get the food on the table by 6:00 every night. Picking which brand of tuna to buy or finding the store with the best price on Pampers™ are context-specific skills—they go with the mom role. The general competencies are more interesting: you know how to manage time, stay within a budget, and maximize the efficiency of a task. Those skills have many applications!*

Step 3: Translate to Your Destiny Role

Now you're going to translate your generalized skills into your area of call. With a coach or a friend who works in your calling area, apply your general competencies to your destiny role. Where would you be doing similar things? How do the skills you've acquired give you a ready-made foundation to build on? What do you still need to learn to succeed in the new role?

> ***Example:*** *If you translate our mom's skills into business-speak, she's run a project on-time and on budget, met her deliverables and maximized the return on investment. She might need to learn to function this way on a larger scale, or in different areas, or gain some specific technical knowledge, but the foundational project management skills are already in place.*

> ***Coaching Tip***
> *When we move between worlds (like business and ministry or family and work) we often feel unqualified. But the most important qualification for success is character: skills training or acquiring knowledge is relatively easy compared to developing a great work ethic or working well with people. Often preparation outside of call is mostly in the character realm.*

11.4 Internal Preparation Resume

Character isn't something you are born with—it is built through life experience. Every circumstance you face has the potential to prepare you for your destiny. In this exercise, we'll inventory the character-building experiences you've had and how they have shaped you.

1. Childhood

What character qualities were deeply instilled in you by your parents? Early lessons on things like truthfulness, hard work, sharing and respect can last a lifetime.

2. Roles

Reflect on different roles you've filled. What were the character lessons in those roles?

3. Failures

What are the significant failures in your life? How have they shaped who you are?

4. Successes

Where have you applied yourself to do something with excellence? What character qualities were built in you through the pursuit of that goal?

5. Patterns

What patterns do you see in the way God is preparing you? In what areas has He worked on you repeatedly or held you to a higher standard? How do these patterns link to your destiny?

> ***Coaching Tip***
>
> *Many coachees have trouble at first with separating character from task and being from doing. So you may see things on their internal preparation list like "Top Boy Scout in my hometown" under Successes, or "Lots of experience in working with difficult people" under Patterns. When you see items that aren't character qualities, just ask, "How did that shape who you are?" or "What did that experience instill in you?" If the person has recorded a significant experience, there is probably a character issue inside it.*

Negative Preparation

11.5

This exercise helps you understand how God is preparing you through the negative experiences in life.

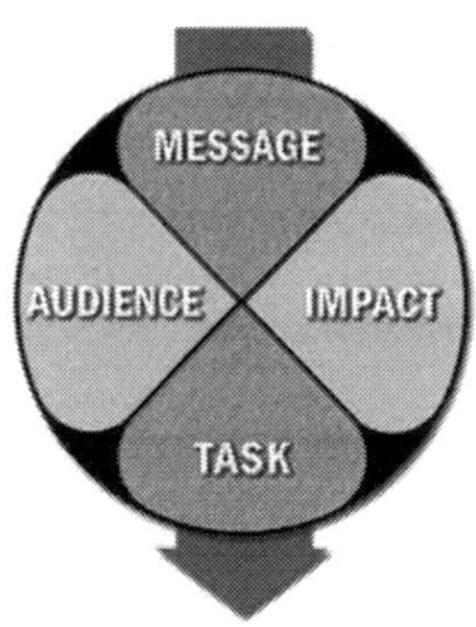

Step 1: Life Purpose Review

Jot down a quick statement of your life purpose as you best understand it.

Step 2: Inventory

What are the major difficulties, failures or experiences of suffering you've gone through in life? Jot them down in the **left** column. Then note potential connections between those experiences and your destiny on the **right** using these questions:

1. **Audience:** How did this experience draw me toward the needs of those I am called to? How might it give me opportunities to reach or serve them?
2. **Task:** What does this experience make me passionate about doing for others? What do I want to change or save others from because I went through it?
3. **Message:** How did this shape my identity? What message for others is implanted in the story of my life from going through this experience?
4. **Impact:** How will this experience make me more effective in my call?

Experience	Connection

Coaching Tip
Explaining how God uses adversity in preparation and providing some examples may be necessary for the client to engage this exercise well. Some important thoughts:

1. *A big part of preparation is developing the character to support your calling. Character building experiences tend to involve adversity (you don't build character when it's easy!)*
2. *Preparation is as much about burning the negatives and obstacles out of your life as it is building positive skills. Difficult situations surface our obstacles and brokenness so they can be dealt with.*
3. *This is how God prepares leaders—for example, Joseph, David and Moses all faced major adversity in their preparation.*

Chapter 12: Preparation/ Destiny Events

"It is with the heart that one sees rightly; what is essential is invisible to the eye."

Antoine de Saint-Exupery

Since you need to know something about your life purpose to connect your preparation experiences to your destiny, how do you work with people who know nothing about their purpose? As an added challenge, those who can't articulate a life purpose often have internal obstacles that prevent them from doing so. For instance, some Christians so spiritualize their picture of calling that anything short of an audible voice doesn't qualify. Sometimes you need a way to bypass coachees' internal roadblocks in order to help them see the calling clues God has already planted in their lives. The *Destiny Events* exercise (12.1) is just such a tool.

A Destiny Event is a brief experience where we sense we are doing the kind of thing we were born to do. Coachees may describe it as a time when they were "firing on all cylinders" or "doing something that brought out my best." These experiences are generally associated with:

1. A sense of **fulfillment**, significance and deep satisfaction.
2. Heightened **effectiveness** or exceptional impact.
3. Strong **affirmation** from others that this is you.

What we do is find the places where the client's own discernment tells them they are living their purpose, tease out the details of those experiences, and generalize (extrapolate) those details to into a picture of the person's destiny.

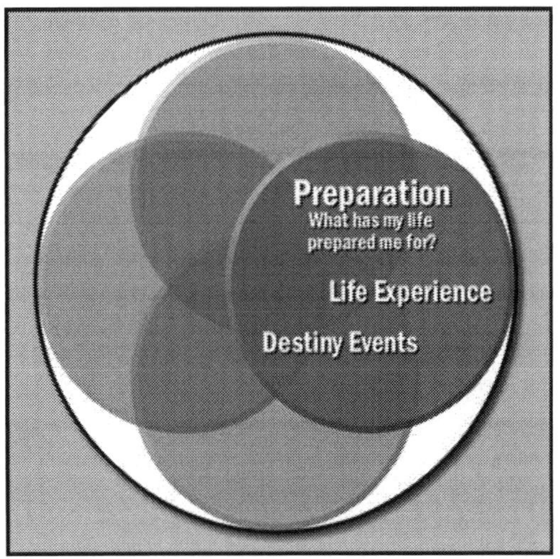

It is easiest to draw out the insights when the experience is a short, discrete event—a weekend workshop, a single conversation, a short-term project, or one business trip. When people talk about a sense of destiny around a role or longer project, they start to generalize and summarize, and that's not what we want. With Destiny Events, the insight comes from examining *specific details.* With access to this original raw data, we can bypass the person's pre-existing conclusions about who they are and get a fresh picture of their destiny.

Randy was pretty locked up when he came to the coaching process. Watch how the *Destiny Events* tool takes him past his obstacle and opens up new possibilities.

"So, Randy—what I'm hearing is that you don't see any clues to your destiny in your past."

"Well, yeah. I mean, I didn't get saved until two years ago. Before that I pretty much wasted my life. When I wasn't partying, I was either sleeping off a hangover or just trying to make it through to the next weekend. I've got my life turned around now, but you won't find my call in my past—it's just a waste."

The client discounts his B.C. (Before Christ) experiences as not related to his purpose.

"OK. Let's try this: think of a time in your life when you were really clicking; when you were doing a project or task that came naturally and you felt you could really excel at."

"Nothing really comes to mind. I mean, I put together some major wild parties, but that's not the kind of thing that would be very useful now."

Step 1: the coach asks for a destiny event without connecting it to purpose, but Randy's obstacle still blocks him.

"Just bear with me here, Randy, and see where this goes—you can tell me if there is anything to it at the end. What was the biggest, most successful or most creative party you ever put together?"

"Well… there was the time I got most of the junior class together for a bash. There were 250 people there before the cops came."

The coach takes something Randy discounted and asks permission to draw out that story.

"All right—tell me about that. Did you set it up?"

"Pretty much. I got all excited and talked a couple of my buds

into helping. I put Brady in charge of posting it on FaceBook and letting everybody know. Deshawn got the beer from his Dad—he drives a Budweiser truck—and Reg held down the door and took people's money. He was the only one of us that could have a wad of cash in his pocket and not just blow it."

"What else did you do?"

"It was around Halloween, so we promoted it as a haunted house. What made it work was recruiting the captain of the basketball team to be the front man. If the parents knew it was my idea they'd have banned their kids from coming. Everything was going great until the neighbors got ticked off about the cars and the noise and called 911."

"Tell me more about the house."

"It was pretty cool—we got skeletons and flashing lights and all kinds of wild stuff. One girl actually fainted on the way through. Paul and I 'borrowed' some black lights from the art wing, and we did a lot with that. I found some girls from art class that were into painting weird animals and corpses and stuff—they were a little whacked out—and they made quite a show of it."

"So why did you go to all the work of doing a bash instead of just hanging out with your friends?"

"I guess I like including people—the more the merrier. I've always run with different crowds, and it seemed like a neat idea to try to get everyone to come. Hanging out in Reg's basement is no challenge—we could do that any time. I guess I wanted to make a mark."

"Great. Now, what I'm going to do is feed back to you what I heard that might connect with your life purpose, and you tell me if it is on target or not. First, you seem to be a natural leader and visionary. I would guess that your destiny involves rallying people around a big dream, recruiting a team like you did here, delegating tasks and catalyzing something big. You don't think small—you wanted the whole class to get together, and you managed to pull it off. Does that sound like you?"

"Well, I've never really looked at it that way. I guess it fits. I've always gotten other people involved in my schemes—got them in trouble as often as not. But yeah, I'm pretty good at organizing, recruiting and delegating."

"I also think it is significant that you understood where the favor was—with the basketball captain—and you were able to use it to allay the parent's concern. You seem to have a natural ability to size up the politics of a situation and plan accordingly. It is also interesting that you recruited a person of influence. You seem to have been a black sheep in your school days, but you didn't just hang out with the Goths, either. Another good guess

Step 2: The coach starts drawing out specific details.

The more details the better!

Drawing out details about inner motives…

Step 3: The coach generalizes the details into life purpose statements.

Step 4: Ask for the client to evaluation what you propose and tell you what of it is on target.

The coach generalizes a second set of details into purpose statements.

would be that your destiny will involve building bridges across cultural divides. I've seen you do that several times since we started meeting. So—what do you think, Randy? What of all that bears witness with you?"

"I guess a lot of it does. People sort of gravitate to me, and I've been able to get in with the fringe kids as well as the parents and the authority figures to do stuff with the youth group. It comes so natural I never really thought of it as something special."

"You are exceptionally gifted in some of these areas."

"So what you are saying is that I learned how to be a visionary while I was still in the world, and now God is going to use that experience for His Kingdom?"

"Randy, the same natural strengths and abilities you used to organize parties are the ones you'll use for God. He's not about giving you a personality transplant—He's redeeming your life. All of it."

"Wow. That's amazing."

The client begins to make the missing connections between these experiences and his calling and design.

Randy had lived on the wild side before he gave himself to Christ. Because he saw his life before Christ as "wasted," identifying the destiny clues in his life story wasn't part of Randy's paradigm. To bypass this obstacle, the coach employed the *Destiny Events* technique (12.1).[24]

Notice that Randy brought up organizing a party as a Destiny Event, but then immediately discounted it as useless. That's the obstacle talking. However, his coach understood that the important thing for discovering Randy's destiny wasn't what he did back then, *but how he did it.* Randy never wants to host another kegger, but the fact that he successfully organized a large scale project and included lots of diverse people tells you something about his talents, his passions, and what he's good at.

One of the most surprising things about Destiny Events is how accurate the minor details are in revealing the person's passions, abilities and call. Because we've asked for experiences that closely align with the person's destiny, the details matter.

Coaching Destiny Events

The four steps to coaching the *Destiny Events* tool are:

1. **Identify stories**
   Find one or more of these "best-fit" events where the person felt very on-purpose and in the zone.
2. **Draw out details**
   Use open, probing questions to bring out specific details about the event.
3. **Generalize details into purpose statements**

24 The Destiny Events concept adapts an idea originally utilized by Doug Fike under the name "Mini-Convergences."

Treat the details as if they were one of many similar examples of that person's life purpose in action, and suggest life purpose insights based on them.

4. **Ask for evaluation**
   Ask the client to evaluate your statements and decide what they mean.

Examples of coaching questions for each step are provided in the exercise. If you've asked the client to share several stories, look for themes that appear in all of them and point them out. If you are evaluating a single Destiny Experience, take the most significant details, generalize them into life purpose statements and ask the client to comment on them.

For instance, if the story was about going on a trip to help the poor rebuild after a hurricane, you might offer, "It sounds like part of your destiny is to help the less fortunate in crisis situations." Or if the person talked a high-ranking military officer into providing government resources to set up a homeless shelter, you might say, "It seems like you have an ability to gain favor and funding for faith-based initiatives from people in authority."

The step of making generalized purpose statements always feels risky. Essentially, you are taking a single piece of data and extrapolating it to the person's entire life! What makes the technique work is that you've asked clients to sort through literally thousands of experiences and pick the ones that most closely align with their destiny role. Because you've sorted so precisely for best-fit experiences, those seemingly-random details become exceptionally significant. Believe that there is meaning in the details, and you'll be amazed at the connections that pop out.

If you know the person well, it is often easy to suggest meaningful connections from a single story. If you aren't as familiar with that individual's life, you may choose instead to talk through several Destiny Events and look for themes that run through them.

Since you as the coach are offering perspective on a person's life purpose, make sure you allow the individual to discern what you are saying and decide what of it is meaningful. In a coaching relationship, the client always has the final say on what things mean.

Work through at least one destiny event together before you turn the coachee loose to continue working on his or her own. Since perspective is such an important part of this process, you may want to discuss several more experiences in your next session. I encourage the coachee to involve a friend or spouse in the process to get added input.

Destiny Events Technique

1. Identify destiny events
2. Draw out details
3. Generalize details into life purpose statements
4. Ask for evaluation

Encourage clients to think of stories from different times in their lives, different roles they've filled, and from different spheres of influence (like church, work, home, or community). When the experiences they process are from widely different parts of life, the common themes in them are even more striking.

Destiny Events

Recruit a spouse, friend or coach to help you do this exercise.

Step 1: Identify Destiny Events

Destiny Events are experiences where you felt totally in the zone: fulfilled, effective, and aligned with your call. Identify three of these experiences where you felt you were doing what you were born to do, doing it well, and having a great impact. Think of *specific, discrete events:* something that happened in a day or a week, NOT a role you filled or a longer season in life.

Step 2: Draw Out the Details

Take 10 to 15 minutes to identify as many specific details as you can remember about each experience. If possible, recruit a good friend or your spouse to ask questions like the ones below. Jot down possible connections between those details and your destiny as you see them.

- "Exactly what happened? Walk me through the experience, step by step."
- "Who did you serve? What impact did you have on others?"
- "What kind of task were you doing? How did you do it? What was accomplished?"
- "What else can you remember?"

Step 3: Generalize/Look for Themes

Compare your three stories using the following questions. Since we sorted out stories with a high sense of destiny, the details can give an amazingly accurate picture of your life purpose (especially when they pop up in more than one story). If you generalized these repeated themes into statements about your life purpose, what would they say?

- "What's a common element in all these stories? What does that tell you?"
- "Is there a message you have for others that comes up repeatedly in these experiences?"
- "What do the people you served in these three stories have in common?"
- "What strengths or gifts are you drawing on in all these events?"
- "It was interesting to me that ____ [cite a detail that caught your attention]. How might that connect to your life purpose?"

Question 5: Where is the Master Sending Me? (Calling)

"...Nevertheless, not my will but yours be done."
Jesus

Although God did not intend for Israel to have a king, when they asked for one He honored their request. God spoke to Samuel the prophet: "...and you shall anoint him [Saul] to be prince over my people Israel; and he will deliver my people from the hand of the Philistines. For I have regarded my people, because their cry has come to me" (I Sam. 9:16). Saul's calling task was to lead God's people and save them from their enemies (I Sam. 10:1).

When the Bible lists Saul's qualifications, the focus seems to be on outward appearances. He was the tallest and most handsome of all—the rock-star method of leadership selection. The task was delivering the people from a foreign oppressor, and Saul seemed suited for it. The people were very taken with their physically-imposing king—whom they then discovered hiding in the baggage to escape his call! Apparently what was on the inside was less important to them than looking the part. The Design was there, but the Preparation was lacking. You get the sense that God was saying, "It wasn't *my* idea for you to have a king, but since you asked for one, here's a man that fits *your* criteria."

The calling of David has a completely different flavor: "...The Lord has sought out for Himself a man after his own heart, and the Lord has appointed him as ruler over his people…" (I Sam. 13:14). In the process of recognizing this king, Samuel got an impromptu lesson on the leadership qualities God prefers. When Samuel set eyes on tall, handsome, first-born Eliab, God warned, "Do not look at his appearance or the height of his stature, because I have rejected him; for God sees not as man sees; for man looks on the outward appearance, but the Lord looks at the heart" (I Sam. 16:7).

These two different emphases explain why Saul's kingship was a failure. Even though he largely accomplished his calling task of delivering Israel from their oppressors (I Sam. 14:48), Saul never embodied the heart of his call—modeling God as King to the people. He was the people's King, but never God's. In the end, his accomplishments were a hollow shell: successful on the outside, empty on the inside. And that failure to become the man he was called to be eventually cost him the people's hearts, the throne, and his life.

David, by contrast, was a great success in the fundamental message of his life—being "a man after God's own heart." David's story and his Psalms preserve a record of his victories and failures, his rejoicing and repentance, and his wrestling with God. We even get a window into David's lifelong struggle with vengeance, from the heights of refusing to raise his hand against Saul to the depths of telling Solomon on his death bed to be sure and take care of old enemies.

David was never a perfect man. The message of his life is not about doing it right, but about bringing all of the human heart—passion, desire, emotion, identity, self-image, failure, success—to God. David was a man after God's own heart because everything in his heart was brought to God. The center of David's surpassing, world-class excellence was his relentless engagement of God at the deepest level. *That* was the heart of David's call—and he fulfilled it.

The External Commission

We've defined calling as "an external commission I accept in order to serve a greater good." What distinguishes Calling from Passion and Design is that it comes from outside one's self. You can answer a call to serve your country, your tribe, your family, or a cause. Christians look for that commission from God, and believe a divine call supersedes a one from any other human institution. So as believers, we might say that:

*"A **calling** is an external commission from God for others."*

When the source of your call is something external, it lifts you beyond merely pursuing your own desires. If David's life purpose had been only about fulfilling his Passions and Design, he would have killed Saul when he had the chance. That was the clear path to his kingly destiny, and it would have been easy for him to justify taking the life of a man who stole his wife and tried to murder him. Although getting rid of Saul made complete sense to his compatriots, David had his eyes on a bigger prize. The primary objective was ***not*** to begin his life task of ascending to the throne, but to be a man after the heart of his Lord. David chose to become the heart of his call instead of grasping after his destiny role.

If the source of calling is God (not your passions); the object of a call is serving others (not self). If you are called to be an intercessor, for example, that doesn't mean you spend three hours a day praying for your own needs! The very word means to stand in the gap for others. If you are called to build a business, that call is not ultimately about increasing your net worth or early retirement—it is about embodying something of Christ to those you do business with. Service is at the heart of every call

And, ironically, it is living for others that makes your own life feel satisfying and significant. In his book, *Reclaiming the Fire,* Dr. Stephen Berglas talks about his experiences working with high achievers who actually attain the personal passions they've built their lives around. When the deed is done, the goal is reached or the medal is won, instead of feeling that their sacrifices have all been worthwhile, intense disappointment sets in. When the thing they've given their lives to fails to satisfy, they ask "Is this all there is?"

The source of calling is God, not your own desires. The object of calling is serving others, not self.

Athletes even have a term for this: Post-Olympic Depression. It's the disillusionment of reaching what you thought was the penultimate objective, only to see the contentment and significance you sought slip through your fingers. If you make your objective finding personal fulfillment, nothing on this earth can ever satiate that hunger. But when you let go of self to serve others, the joy of every accomplishment multiplied by the gratitude of those you serve finds you, even though you never sought it. That's what Jesus meant by saying, "He who has found his life will lose it; and he who has lost his life for my sake will find it" (Mt. 10:39).

The Four Facets of Call

David's life is an excellent example of the being/doing tension in calling. One way to understand how all this fits together is to examine four facets of Calling:

Calling is...
A **message** you embody
To a specific **audience**
For an ultimate **impact**
Through a unique **task.**

You have a **message** that impacts others as you do your life task. The message is Christ embodied in you in some particular way for the world. It's the unique way Jesus shines through you because of how He has shaped your identify. Here's an example. Years ago some good friends discovered their unborn child had a heart deformity and almost certainly wouldn't survive. Instead of getting an abortion, they prayed fervently through the full term, went through the birth, and then watched their child die a few days later. It was a heart-wrenching experience putting that tiny coffin in the ground on a lifeless winter day.

Calling is...
*A **message** you embody*
*To a specific **audience***
*For an ultimate **impact***
*Through a unique **task**.*

That couple went through the pain with Jesus and came out whole on the other side. If I ever run into someone who's enduring the death of a baby, that's where I'd send them. Because they met Jesus and allowed him to make a home in that part of their hearts, they can embody him to others who are in the same valley of death.

Life messages are powerful in coaching because they explain areas that tools like strengths and type completely miss. The message of your life is rooted in the places God has deeply dealt with you, not in your natural strengths or what comes easily. Opening yourself to allow Christ to engrave his message on your heart is the heart of your call. It's not the outward task that accomplishes God's purpose, but the impartation that comes *through* the task—like the message of David's heart that shines through every time we read the Psalms. Our good deeds are only truly good as the Christ-in-us shines through them.

Your life message is designed to resonate with certain people—your **audience**. Those you are called to serve need exactly what God has put into your heart. Your preparation uniquely qualifies you to speak to them, and makes you the kind of person they'll listen to. Identifying the specific audience or need you are made to serve is a key part of understanding your call.

The reason for all this is to create an **impact** on those lives. Your legacy is the ultimate impact of your life message on your target audience. It's your lasting contribution to society and the Kingdom of God. The true goal is never to build an organization or accomplish a mission—it is to serve real people through the organization or mission.

But the **task** your message flows through is also crucial. You have a unique life mission/calling task (or series of tasks) that is the most effective conduit for your message. That task is what puts hands and feet to the Christ-in-you and connects Him to your audience. And there is a certain kind of role that fits your design and best enables you to express it. The task without a message is empty; but a message that is not channeled through the right kind of tasks and roles is limited and ineffective.

Using the Calling Section

Together, these four facets make up the guts of your call. We'll explore them in the next few chapters. This is the longest section, since few models for calling as an external commission have been presented in other coaching literature.

We'll start by exploring *Revelation*. Since a call comes from an external source, it is something you hear by revelation instead of discovering by looking inward (like with Passion or Design). The *Revelation* chapter has exercises and handles to help clients identify what God has revealed about their call. We'll also examine common obstacles clients have around hearing God and the word "calling," and how to coach them. One key obstacle is the "road map" paradigm of life purpose (which often becomes a road*block*)—we'll compare it to the dynamic, progressive unfolding of Abraham's call.

The *Life Message* chapter fills in the details of the incarnation that forms the heart of your call. Since these messages develop in areas where God has deeply processed us, they are often connected to transition, adversity or failure. So we'll spend some time looking at common calling patterns related to suffering.

The *Audience/Task/Impact* chapter helps people translate their life purpose insights into a specific audience they called to serve, a tangible impact they are shooting for, and the task that best channels that message.

Finally, I've also included a chapter on *Convergent Roles* that is targeted toward mature leaders. This material uses concepts like influence style and sphere of influence to flesh out what a destiny role might look like. We'll start with a baseline assessment and go from there!

Calling Baseline Assessment

1.1d

These questions will give us a baseline for creating a customized calling discovery plan. Take 10 to 15 minutes to complete the assessment. If you don't know what to say on a question, or would have to dream up an answer, leave it blank. This isn't a test: we're just trying to determine what you know for sure about your calling so we know where to start the discovery process.

1. What has God revealed to you about your calling in life?

   I think I am called to build future leaders in finance at the university—it's not the teaching classes so much but the opportunities to touch students' lives that got me into that. I feel drawn to influence them to live lives of character and integrity instead of just going into it for the money.

   When I was a kid I always played the counselor. Everyone came to me with their problems, and that's an area where God has always used me.

2. To what degree do you feel you are on-course with what God has called you to? How do you know that?

   I feel like I must have missed it somewhere—nothing is happening. After college I had an offer to go on a mission's team and I chose to go to grad school instead. Sometimes I wonder if that was a wrong choice.

3. Describe one of your life messages: a message for the world God has uniquely incarnated in you in a place He has deeply dealt with you.

   I guess He's dealt with me a lot on personal finances: integrity with money, getting out of debt and living within my means. Is that a message?

4. Describe specifically the people you are called to serve or the need you are called to meet.

   See number one above. More specifically, students who have an idealism that I can fan into flame.

5. What is your life mission? (The task(s) you must complete in life.) What role will you ultimately be in, and how does it fit your design and help you fulfill that mission?

   I guess the mission is building future leaders in finance and the role is being a professor. My role puts me in touch with young leaders every day, which is great. I like the classroom part, but the committee work and grading papers and stuff is for the birds. Not sure that does anything to help my mission.

Evaluating the Baseline Assessment

The first question on the baseline asks directly about revelation. Look for whether people can give answers that actually sound like revelation and not just rambling. Are they willing to state what God has revealed without equivocation, or are they uncertain? Do they cite more than just one method of revelation? This client has some inner knowing and childhood dreams about call, but nothing in the way of specific guidance experiences, key Scriptures or words from the Lord. Helping him become aware of other ways God has spoken to him using the *Revelations Journal* (13.2) or *Lost in Translation* exercises (13.4) might create a big win.

I'm also looking for the being/doing tension in calling. Is the person's description of the call solely in task terms, or do you see some evidence that he or she also understands calling as incarnation or being? The *Lost in Translation* (13.4) and *Life Messages* exercises (14.1) are good resources here.

Question two touches one of the great bugaboos of calling: many people feel they are off course or have missed it. For mature leaders at the stage where they should be functioning in their call, these feelings may be God's prompting to realign their work in convergent roles. These situations lend themselves to a practical approach, often one of aligning the leader's responsibilities with their Design (strengths and type).

For younger leaders (like in this example), feeling off course is often due to thinking within the MapQuest paradigm (see pg. 219). The Bible studies of Jesus' and Abraham's lives (on-line at www.ALeadersLifePurpose.com) are excellent tools for surfacing and processing what it means to be on course.

Question three looks at life messages. This is unfamiliar territory for most people, so don't be surprised if you get an "I don't know." Look for whether clients can connect God's dealings with them with the places where they lead with exceptional impact. The client in our example seems to have identified an area of God's dealings, but has not connected it to incarnation or message, which means there is probably more to be discovered here. *Life Messages* (see 14.1 and 14.2) are consistently one of the highest-payoff areas to explore with more mature leaders. The *Message of Your Life* (14.4) is a key statement describing the being portion of an individual's call.

Question four touches on audience (it's hard to know your impact if you don't know your audience!) How specific is the group the person names? Does the description include a variety of audience characteristics (see box in exercise 15.2)? *Who Do You Love* (15.1) and *An Audience for My Message* (15.2) can help flesh this out. Leaders who understand their audience can name multiple characteristics of it and give examples of real people who exemplify it.

The last question touches on life mission and convergent roles. While this is most important for leaders in the second half of life, younger leaders can benefit from doing some work here, too. Can the person state a clear destiny role and task, and describe how they fit together? The Message > Audience > Impact > Task framework might help this individual gain more clarity about his call, particularly its Message and Impact. There are some things about his role that fit and some that don't—I'd want to explore the match with exercises like the *80/20 Job Description* (16.4) and *Influence Styles* (16.2), and see if there are other job options or changes he could make to his current role to make it work better for his design.

Chapter 13: Calling/ Revelation

"Go forth from your country, and from your relatives and from your father's house, to the land which I will show you; and I will make you a great nation... in you all the families of the earth will be blessed."

Genesis 12:1-3

When I was 22 one of the leadership books I regularly devoured grabbed my attention. The author's thesis was that for the first five years after the early church began the only people who led anything were the 12 apostles, because "you've got to get sanctified before you can lead." Whatever you think of that idea (I have my questions now), at the time I took it very seriously. I began praying daily: "Lord, take the next five years of my life and just sanctify me!"

My prayer was based on how I understood calling and leadership development. God called you to do something (I knew I was called to ministry), you entered into a period of intensive training (which I was clearly in), and then you moved directly into that vocation. The more dedicated and radical you were the faster and higher you would be promoted. The scope of your call was not a function of what you'd been given, but of your devotion. Waiting until you were 40 or 50 before you really entered into your life mission was for wimps.

When I prayed for five years of sanctification, I thought I was asking God to take *longer* than normal (!) to prepare me, so that I could really function in power when I was released. I was already leading a cell group, traveling the country doing worship renewal in a band, producing songs, and discipling young men. In five years I saw myself teaching big crowds, traveling the country, and being a big-time minister. In my mind, sanctification was a smooth, upward on-ramp to glory.

However, God had other plans.

Three Misconceptions about Call

The biggest obstacles to coaching calling discovery are often the images Christians have of what receiving a call looks like. The classic picture is a young man, kneeling in a grove to pray for direction for his life. Suddenly, a light flashes around him (or an almost-audible voice speaks) and God gives that young man an unmistakable call to the ministry. Or a girl sits listening on a Sunday night to a missionary's videos of destitute villages in Africa. Something stirs in her heart, she goes to the altar and receives a call to serve the less fortunate on the mission field.

Unfortunately, this picture is infected with three big misconceptions you'll often face when you coach calling. First, most people think of calling as a special, dramatic, one-time *event* where God gives a person a specific lifetime assignment. We're so locked into looking for these calling events that Christians who can't identify that one distinct moment feel like second-class citizens. When you ask about their call, they mumble and stumble, embarrassed to admit that they've not received a call. And yet for most of us, calling is actually revealed *progressively* over time instead of through a single event. In fact, few leaders fully understand and function in their call until their 50's and 60's. When you expect God to speak to you through a dramatic special event and He doesn't, it can be very disconcerting.

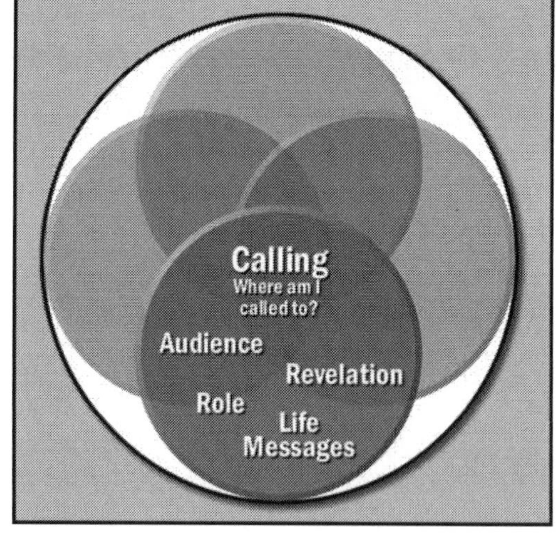

A second misconception is that a calling is to a task. I was on the phone yesterday with a young pastor in a self-described "leadership funk." He was not accomplishing what he hoped to, and felt bogged down, guilty and frustrated about his lack of progress. After a little probing, I began reframing the situation with some "What ifs." What if God is in the fact that you aren't getting much done right now? What if God *is* answering your prayers, but the road to changing your church begins by changing the inside of you? What if overcoming your leaders' reticence to step out is God working on your own fear of failure? The lights started to come on when he began thinking in terms of inner growth instead of merely getting tasks done.

While we have each been given a mission to do in life, our call is first and foremost something we become, that is then channeled through what we do to impact others. When we think of calling solely in task terms we get all tied up in knots about doing the right thing and finding God's will. When the focus is on embodying our call, much of that performance anxiety disappears.

A third misconception is that when you find your calling, you are supposed to just start doing it. If I am called to run an organic farm or to help foster kids as a social worker, I need to find a position in those fields right away and get started. Even when we realize that some preparation is required, our assumption is that it will happen within our field of calling. Either way, once I know my call, any time I spend doing something else is wasted. The reality is much different. Preparation usually takes decades, not just years, and it is just as common for God to do most of that preparatory work in an unrelated field as it is for you to be that social worker or farm owner all your life. Remember that Jesus was prepared for his ministry call by doing manual labor as a carpenter.

Misconceptions about Call

1. A call is one special moment when God gives me a life assignment.
2. My calling is to a task.
3. Once I figure out my calling, I'm supposed to just start doing it.

Those three misconceptions about killed me when God started answering my youthful prayers for sanctification. What actually happened was everything I was doing for God came to an end. I was the lead male vocalist and guitarist in the band—then another guy joined who was better at both, and I was relegated to running sound. Then we cut an album, the sound engineer got saved and he joined us, and I got demoted again to gopher. Then one day my small group started talking about how things were going, and they all decided to disband because "they weren't having a good small group experience."

That was a blow. I couldn't understand what God was doing. If my life was on track, I should have been moving into *more* ministry and influence, not less! Failure and demotion were not part of my preparation paradigm. The only possible conclusion within my view of destiny was that I was doing something wrong.

Up until then, I had been Mr. Discipline. I had my yearly goals, my monthly goals, my budget and financial records, and my Bible study plan. I fasted twice a week, I prayed an hour a day, I met with a friend for prayer three times a week, I took monthly retreats—I was doing it all. In reality, my spiritual disciplines were an idol I depended on to feel right with God.

Then God pulled the plug on my disciplined life. I got to the point where I couldn't even pray for five minutes. The feelings of guilt and failure I'd beaten down before exploded into a crushing burden. If I couldn't even do the basics disciplines of the Christian life, how was I ever going to become the leader I yearned to be?

The image I have of those years is sliding down a greased rope in the dark. By then I was barely clinging to the knot at the rope's end. That knot was trying to make the Christian life work. There was no way of knowing how far I'd fall if I quit striving and let go of the rope.

After a year of misery, I finally gave up. I remember telling God, "My life is over.

I'm no good to you or the Kingdom. If you can save me, you do it, but I can't live the Christian life." Amazingly, I began to hear God speaking to me for the first time in a long while—about how much He loved me! It was months before I could accept that, before it finally dawned on me that God loved *me*, and not what I did for him.

That shaping experience has become the foundation of my calling. But it arrived in a way I never could have anticipated, violating my conception of faith and tearing down and rebuilding my whole identity.

God built three great messages into my heart in that time. First, I understood grace. Before I had been graceless with myself and others. Now, it was much easier to relax and let God take care of things. Second, I learned that God uses our circumstances to deal with our hearts. One of the central themes of my coaching and writing is helping leaders discover God's purposes in adversity and engage Him there from the heart. And third, I learned to think of the Christian walk as a developmental process of God reshaping our identity, instead of like a walk through a minefield of right-and-wrong choices, where one misstep could blow a leg off. Understanding the ways of God in building leadership character is at the core of my calling.

Calling and Revelation

Without revelation, and God's sovereign action to redirect my life, I never would have reached my life call. Calling is an *external commission* from God for others—meaning to find it, we must look outward to God for revelation instead of only looking inward. The greatest distinctive of Christian life purpose coaching is that challenge to receive a revealed commission from God instead of simply identifying and following one's own desires.

However, the word revelation carries some baggage with it. The common image of revelation is something mind-blowing and dramatic: an audible voice (Paul), a burning bush (Moses), or an angel coming to inform you of your destiny (Mary). Are these the model for the average Joe-Christian, or is it something else?

One of the challenges of figuring out what's "normal" with calling is that the dramatic stories are the ones that get remembered and retold. Scripture includes examples from two thousand years of Hebrew history—do they represent what's normal or are they unusual examples from unusual life stories?

One objective way to find the norm is to look at the callings of a group of people instead of cherry-picked examples. The 12 disciples had very different experiences. Peter, James and John were amazed at the great catch of fish, and in that supernatural moment Jesus asked them to follow (in another version, they are called while sitting on the beach mending nets). In Matthew's case, Jesus just happened along the road one day and invited him to become a follower—not very dramatic.

Andrew (Peter's brother and John the Baptist's disciple) went after Jesus when John pointed him out as the Lamb of God. He was a referral disciple. They met again while Peter and Andrew were fishing on the seashore, and Jesus told them to follow. I don't think that would qualify as the kind of stereotypically supernatural event many people expect.

Jesus "found" Phillip one day and said to him, "Follow me." Apparently that was enough for Phillip—again, not too dramatic. Phillip then went and recruited his brother Nathaniel to come along—and Jesus named his inner identity and shared a vision of him under a fig tree. That supernatural insight so impressed Nathaniel that he was ready to call Jesus "the Son of God" on a first meeting.

We only have stories of half of the 12. Of those, roughly half are dramatic and half less so. I would guess that the stories that got in the Bible would tend toward the more dramatic rather than the everyday ones. For instance, from Jesus' early life we have one dramatic story of Him amazing the temple priests with His insights, but none of His everyday work as a carpenter. So for probably half to three fourths of the 12 disciples, the call came through everyday conversations and circumstances instead of miraculous events. If that was true for Jesus' own disciples, I'd say it's a pretty safe bet that for the majority of us, the call will not be attended by outward manifestations like angelic visitations, audible voices or miracles.

Revelation Methods

Revelation can come through dramatic events, everyday circumstances, or it can be an insight that develops progressively over a lifetime. When we use the word "revelation" as coaches, we are referring to all three. We simply mean that God has shown us something we wouldn't have known on our own. Two general categories of revelation are *Calling Events* (specific experiences we've been called through), which can be dramatic or everyday happenings; and *Progressive Revelation* of call, where we gradually come to understand our destiny over a period of years. For instance, Abraham received a series of calling events over a period of 25 years that when put together progressively revealed his calling.

> *Progressive Revelation is when God gradually unfolds your call to you over a period of years.*

Worksheet 13.1 shows 12 common ways people report receiving a call (take a minute and scan it). The *Revelation Journal* (13.2) allows clients to record insights in many of these areas, either on their own or as you coach them through each one. You'll usually begin to coach the area of calling here.

Inheritance, Community and Calling

One calling method that we often don't examine is inheritance and communal calls. While it is common in some eastern cultures to understand calling in the context of community or inheritance, western cultures ignore it in their emphasis on the unique, individual. But since a call from God is only a part of a much larger plan, often it *is* entwined with the larger story of one's family or community. For instance, many families have a heritage of generations of involvement in pastoral ministry, the military, a family business or a family farm. That family story and history can exert a strong influence on children. Or a family may have deeply held values (like higher education or community service) that influence the next generations' sense of what is significant vocationally. Some individuals, like Abraham's descendants, find their personal destiny in being part of a family calling that spans generations.

Knowing the calling of your parents can be very revealing. A few years back I was talking to my mother (in her 70's) about her sense of call. She had grown up in a conservative Mennonite community that frowned on higher education, especially for women—but her father had been a teacher and she felt called to the same thing. So she went off to college and spent most of her vocational life in elementary education.

There wasn't much of a connection for me when we talked about her calling tasks and roles. I never wanted to be a schoolteacher. But then I asked, "What was unique about the way you taught? What message did you want to communicate through that role to your students?" She began to talk about her desire to engage them creatively, as individuals, and to go beyond rote learning to find ways for them to grasp the principles experientially. She felt her call was really about creating learning environments where people could grow and change.

I was amazed! That same message is an integral part of my own call. I am passionate about using adult learning principles to connect learning experientially with people's hearts instead of just with their heads. I had never realized how my own sense of mission was intimately linked to that of my parents.

Tapping into family and community heritage can be a crucial part of calling discovery, especially for those from Asian backgrounds. We've included an inheritance section in the *Revelation Journal,* plus a *Family Calling Interview* exercise (13.3) to help clients explore their family's sense of call.

Confirming, Naming and Calling Out

Coaches can also be actively involved in the revelation process by *Confirming, Naming* or *Calling Out* what they see in their clients. Because you are walking closely with them, you are well-positioned to affirm what they see, call attention to things they don't see, and challenge them to rise to their true capacity.

Terrell had a big idea for a training program that would help apply transformational principles to parenting teens. It was the kind of thing his whole life prepared him to do, but still he held back. That's when his coach gave him the

Naming Examples

- *"You are very good at solving complex problems—that's one of your natural strengths."*
- *"As an "ENTP," you are an idea person. "ENTP's" are constant streams of creativity and new ideas for how to make life better."*
- *"As you tell your story, I see a pattern of preparation for a certain calling. God has repeatedly placed you in situations where things have been broken through sin or character failure and you have been the agent of restoration."*
- *"Whenever you talk about hands-on service, like with Habitat for Humanity, you get more animated and speak with real conviction. You have a passion for serving in practical ways."*
- *"You exude a deep passion for generosity. Whenever we talk about how you do business, I can see Jesus in your heart blessing everyone you do business with."*

challenge to step up.

"You've been talking about writing this program since last July, but every time you start, something seems to get in the way. What's up?"

"Yeah, it's dragging. Maybe I'm looking for a distraction—I sit down to write and I get antsy, and then the phone rings, and it's easy to just dive into something else. I'm having a hard time staying with it."

After six false starts, the coach knows there is more here than just managing the phone.

"So what do you believe about yourself as a writer and a trainer? Who are you?"

"Well, I guess I have a lot of experience, from my own parenting to teaching to the research I've done. I think I can help people."

"I agree—you have a wealth of experience in this area. Push that out: who are you? Are you the person to do this?"

The coach *Confirms* (agrees with) the client's insight to express belief.

"That's where I'm not sure. In my best moments, I want to take this to the whole world. When I am sitting alone in my office, getting all tied up in knots trying to put what's in my heart in words, I start to wonder. Will anyone really want to read this stuff?"

"I've heard you tell lots of great stories of the impact this material has had on others. Look—this is a new field. You've done some of the basic research here, and there's probably no-one in the world that knows this material like you. Do you realize that you are the expert *on this?"*

The coach *Names* who the client is—you are "the expert."

"Sometimes I believe that. Other times, I get discouraged."

"Here's what I see in you. Your whole life has prepared you for this moment—you have the education, the track record, the passion, the ability and the professional network to make this happen. The only thing that stands in your way is that you don't believe you can do it. I believe in you. The people you've trained believe in you. God clearly does, too—he keeps on encouraging you to do this! You can keep shrinking back to this place of fear or you can decide to be the man you already are—what's it going to be?"

Here the coach shares his own perspective, *Naming* who Terrell is and *Calling him Out* to be that person instead of shrinking back.

Terrell has everything he needs to move into his destiny except self-confidence. The first technique the coach uses is to *Confirm* what Terrell sees. Simply adding, "Yes, I see that, too," to a client's insight can increase self-assurance. Confirmation is especially relevant with Calling. While I can take an objective personality assessment that affirms my design, Calling comes down to believing I've heard God's voice. It's a matter of faith; and in matters of faith, it always helps to have others stand with you.

Naming goes beyond confirmation to bring to light new insights that the client doesn't see. Here, the coach names Terrell's expertise and invites him to rethink how he sees himself. Notice that naming is a declaration: "*This* is who you are." You observe something of the client's design, passion or identity, and reflect it back in statement form. (You can pose these insights as questions, but you lose a lot of the force of the technique.) Some examples are given in the box on page 214.

Notice that the impact of the statements increases as you move down through this list. While the first few examples highlight skills and strengths, the last several strike closer to the heart, at the client's passions, calling and core identity. The closer you get to the core, the greater the power of the affirmation.

A third coaching skill that goes with revelation is *Calling Out*. Here, you take a quality you are Naming (that God is in effect revealing through your feedback) and mate it with a challenge for a coachee to rise up and lay hold of what he or she has been given:

- *"You have a unique ability to articulate a plan for that. When are you going to act on it?"*
- *"You don't need any more credentials to be ready for this—the message of authentic transformation is built into your life, and it comes out of you in all that you do. You are ready because you already are the message. This is who you are. Rise up and live it out!"*

It takes great faith, courage and sacrifice to do what you were born to do. Sometimes you need a friend or coach to spur you on to do the things you aren't sure you are really capable of accomplishing.

Lost in Translation

Another challenge in hearing God's voice is that He speaks to us in the spirit. But to understand and communicate a spiritual experience, we have to translate it through our minds into words and images. Almost inevitably, something important gets lost in translation. Pinpointing the difference between the words and images we pick to describe our call and the spiritual reality of the call itself can be a powerful tool.

For example, a young man at 23 feels called to the ministry. At his age, he'll tend to visualize himself working with people who are his peers or younger—that's what he knows. So the container he chooses to describe his calling is "youth pastor." That image serves him well as he moves through Bible school and takes his first ministry position. But the more he grows as a leader, the more constraining it becomes. He was called to be a minister. He assumed that meant ministry to young people. The container he's used to describe his call no longer fits the true revelation. But because he believes those human words and images *are* the revelation itself, it is very difficult to change them, and he feels stuck. The real call is lost in translation.

The Call is God speaking in the spirit realm. The words and images we use to understand it come from us.

Here's what a coaching dialogue around this kind of issue sounds like. Watch for how the coach helps Phil discover new options through what was lost in translation:

"So—great to see you today, Phil. Have you heard anything back from the University yet?"

"Unfortunately, yes. They hired someone else. The committee felt I 'was lacking the qualifications and experience to provide the needed leadership.' After two months of going in circles with all their policies and politics, I'm not sure it would have worked anyway. So I guess that's that."

"So how is that outcome impacting you?"

"Well… I guess I'd have to say I'm pretty down. I feel like I stepped out on what God told me to do and nothing happened. Did I miss it somewhere? Do I just settle for what I'm already doing? I don't know where to go with it."

"What would you like from me as a coach today?"

"I need some help sorting this all out. I can deal with being turned down for a job, but it is a lot harder to feel like the thing God has prepared you to do with your life fell through."

"OK. One place to start might be back at the beginning. You've mentioned several times that God called you to this. Talk about your sense of call—how did that come about?"

"Well, I guess the main thing was about four years ago. I was at our annual conference, in a breakout where we were talking about our leadership shortage—we are barely training enough leaders, and the proportion of people who burnout and leave in the first three years is way too high. Anyway, I'm sitting there watching us wrestle with the leadership shortage, and I just felt God saying that this is where he wanted me to give my life. That's about the clearest sense of a call from God I've ever had, and now it's cratered. That's what's got me shook."

"Let's unpack that a little further. Go back to exactly what you heard at that moment. What were the words, or the impression? What was your inner witness saying?"

"Let me think for a minute… well, I remember us talking about the problem, and all of a sudden I had this impression—like, 'You can change this. This is your job. This is what I made you for.' We had faced a similar situation in the international division a few years before, and I was thinking about that and realized that I had the tools to make a real difference here."

"So what's the connection between that calling event and this position?"

"Well, the problem was leadership training—we didn't have a curriculum or a learning process that matched the need. It was the same thing I'd faced a few years before in Southeast Asia. And God said it was my job to fix it. So when this job opened up, I thought God was opening the door."

"So you felt the problem was leadership training, leadership training is mostly done at the university, and therefore taking a position there was what it would take to affect change."

"That's pretty much it."

"When you had that sense of 'this is your job'—did God give you any specifics at the time about what that position was?"

"Well, the job was to fix the problem, not so much to take a certain position. The position isn't the job; it's the platform to get the job done."

"Did God specifically say that you should work through the university?"

"Well, not exactly... I mean—God didn't say, 'Go work at Chandler U.' He said it was my job to fix this problem. So I guess I just assumed..."

"Assumed what?"

"Assumed that I was supposed to take a job there."

"So if God didn't specifically say to tackle this through a university position, is there another way to do it that would fit what He said?"

"Hmm... You know, what we actually did in Thailand was, instead of trying to redo the academic training on the front end, we first installed a bunch of on-the-job adult learning programs that filled in the holes. Eventually we went back and reintegrated that into the original training program, but by then we were just rearranging the stuff we had already created."

"So is that kind of approach an alternative here?"

"I never really thought about it but—that might work! We'd bypass all the existing systems, so I wouldn't have to spend two-thirds of my time placating the late adopters—just from the interview process, I saw what a huge burden that would be at Chandler. And I could design toward the need instead of backward toward the existing structure. If I built an organization to do this, I'd be free to function out of my 'D' on the DiSC™ and we could use best practices out of business as well as academia... Wow! This has real possibilities!"

In order to wrap his mind around his calling, Phil translated it into a mental image of working at the university—and that assumption later trapped him into seeing only one way to fulfill his call. To help clients like Phil get unstuck, we go back to the original revelation to see what was lost in translation. First, have them recount the calling event as accurately as possible. Then we compare: "Is there anything specific you are expecting that God didn't specifically say?" By removing the container and refocusing on the calling, you open up new options for fulfilling it.

The *Lost in Translation* exercise (13.4) can also be used immediately after a calling event—writing down exactly what you heard is one of the best defenses against the misinterpretations that creep in over time.

Coaching Around Hearing God

Revelation is about hearing God, and hearing God is a matter of faith. God rarely speaks so clearly that there is no possibility of doubt—to do so would compromise our free will. We see through a glass dimly because to see God in His fullness would completely overwhelm us. God has designed the world to work on the basis of faith because that's the only way we can relate to an omnipotent God as free agents.

However, since God doesn't eliminate the possibility of doubt, doubt arises. You see it in clients who seem to spend forever "seeking the Lord" before they take a single step, because they doubt that they have heard accurately, or those who know which way to go but pursue it hesitantly, afraid of failing or missing the mark. Sometimes the word "calling" is freighted with such spiritualized expectations that nothing God says can meet our standard of proof.

Remember: the vast majority of the time, *the problem is not hearing something, but having confidence that you heard.* Given that, simply believing in the doubting client is

often the biggest service you can give. I like to approach these situations by assuming that God has already been speaking, and constructing my questions accordingly. Here are some of my favorites:

- *"So what **have** you heard so far?"*
- *"Take your best shot: what is God saying here?"*
- *"What do you think you might have heard?"*
- *"What's the clearest thing you have heard from God on this, even if it seems fuzzy?"*
- *"Have you had any experiences where you thought it might be God's call, but then later you discounted it?"*

Many times, just recounting what they thought they heard and being taken seriously provides enough confidence for them to move forward in what they've heard. Another tack is having them talk about what they *might* have heard, or heard and doubted. Sometimes the box they have for "God's voice" is too small. Verbalizing those expectations can reveal when the issue has been over-spiritualized. So I might ask, "If God had spoken to you about your call, what would that have looked like?"

For those who still don't believe they've heard anything, try reviewing the 12 *Revelation Methods* (see 13.1) together, and ask for examples of how God might have spoken through each one. Or, inquire into what the client gains by hanging onto their unrealistic picture of calling. "Why is it important to you to hear a call in this particular way? What does that give you?"

The MapQuest Paradigm

Even when you know your calling, there is still the question of how to walk it out. Some people see following the call as akin to tiptoeing through a minefield. One false step and it is over—you've missed your call. I call this way of thinking the MapQuest Paradigm. It sees pursuing a call as following a list of turn-by-turn directions like you'd get off of MapQuest.com. If you haven't used MapQuest yet, you go to the web site, type in the starting point and the destination, and it gives you back a complete list of each turn you need to make to get there.

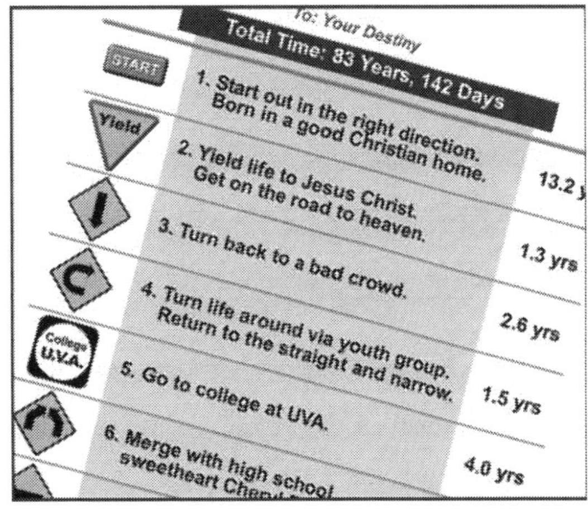

The thing I hate about MapQuest is, without an actual map, if you miss a turn you are *totally lost.* (That's why I always print out the map, too.) A simple turn list doesn't help you visualize the twists and turns of the road, or show which compass direction you should be heading toward, or give you any landmarks en route. It's a sick feeling to figure out that you missed a turn somewhere 20 miles back (especially at night) and you have no idea where you are or how to get back on course.

That's how many Christians operate. Each decision in life is a turn, and to get to the right destination you have to follow the directions exactly and get every turn right. If at some point in life you have taken a major wrong turn (say, bankruptcy, divorce or coming to Christ later in life), your calling is lost. In the MapQuest paradigm, there is no way to get back on the highway once you miss a turn—the call has passed you by, and you've missed God.

I've worked with several individuals who had a sense of call early in life, and for various reasons chose to go in another direction. When that fact resurfaces in their 40's and 50's, the question is, "What do I do? Have I completely missed my calling?" How do you coach someone who believes they have taken that big wrong turn?

MapQuest vs. Map

The answer is to switch paradigms. If you have an actual map you travel by instead of just a list of turns, you can find many ways to get to the same destination. You can even make a wrong turn or change your mind along the way and re-plan your route based on your current location. There may be one way that is faster or more direct than the others, but the scenic route will get you there, too.

I think the map image gives a much more accurate picture of calling, because a map lets you base your route on principles (interstates are faster than county roads) rather than just blind adherence to a pre-determined plan. In other words, following your call is as much about knowing the ways of God (the principles) as it is knowing exactly where to be, when (the turns).

The MapQuest paradigm is rooted in a worldview that says that life is a series of right and wrong choices—if you make the right ones you are blessed, and if you make the wrong ones, you lose. It's a pre-Christ worldview: grace and redemption are not part of the picture. In the reality of God's grace, there is always a future and a hope. No matter where you are starting from, *today* (and each day) God will take your life and make something great of it.

Coaching the MapQuest Paradigm

- *"What are some other courses of action that would take you to the same destination?"*
- *"What if there were many different routes to take that would fulfill your call? How would that change things?"*
- *"It sounds like you are thinking of your call as a set of directions you have to follow to the letter or you'll miss it. Stop and evaluate that: does that sound like the God you know?"*
- *"What do you think God might do to bring glory out of that failure?"*

When you are coaching this legalistic worldview, techniques that bring grace into the picture can be very helpful. For instance, you might ask, "Since Jesus was all about redeeming us from our failures, how does that principle fit with your understanding of following your call?" Another method (which I am stealing from Jesus) is to compare the situation with parenting. "If you gave your son a set of step-by-step directions for cleaning the garage and he messed up a step, how would you handle it? Would you say, 'That's it—you are never going to amount to anything?' Or would you correct him, do a reset, and have him start again?" Sometimes I'll simply describe both the Map and MapQuest paradigms, and then ask which approach describes the way they are thinking.

Learning through Failure

The biggest practical shortcoming of the MapQuest model is that it doesn't acknowledge how God grows us into our calling through failure as well as success. Years ago I finally left my long-time professional role and moved across the country to make a new start. The last few months in the old role felt like being squeezed out of a toothpaste tube. My right-hand man at work left and I had to take over most of his responsibilities, train his successor and train mine all at the same time. In the midst of that, I also lost my secretarial support. Meanwhile, the house was up for sale (which meant constant extra chores to keep it show-able) and things had gotten very frustrating at church. I basically lost it attitude-wise for about three months. I grumbled, I stewed, I let myself get angry, and I was on the point of refusing a farewell banquet from the church until my sister got in my face about it. Not my finest hour.

Two months after we finally moved, I was taking a walk one day when suddenly God showed me how I had handled those three months. I was mortified at how poorly I'd responded. After repenting and dealing with it, it occurred to me that I had still learned the lesson about attitude that Jesus wanted to teach me—I had just done it the hard way!

The lesson I took away from that experience was that if God is trying to teach you something, you can get the lesson whether you initially respond poorly or well. You can fail and still get to where God wants you to be, because where you are supposed to be is more about who you are becoming than being in the right place doing the right thing at the right time.

If the primary thing God calls you to is to embody a certain quality of Christ, there are myriad ways to express that incarnation. In fact, when you become like Jesus, the message of your life comes out in *everything* you do, whether you are functioning in your calling task or not. So not only are there many ways to get to the destination, but no matter how you get there, *your calling can be expressed through your being along the way.*

One challenge I often give is to create "A Call for All Seasons" (see box): to express one's call in a way that no change in external circumstances can hinder. That action step forces us to remove the external trappings of a role or project and get down to the guts of the message we are trying to communicate.

Another way to address the "I made a mistake and therefore I missed it" obstacle is to compare it to the stories of biblical characters. You feel called to eradicate human trafficking but you ended up in business for the last 20 years instead? Maybe you and Moses ought to have a heart-to-heart—you've got a lot in common. Had an affair with a friend's wife and destroyed your ministry along with your friendship? David repented, dealt with God and became a better man for it—why can't you?

Ashamed of how much you did in your pre-Christian years to turn people away from God? Maybe you and Paul should compare stories. If these leaders can walk through catastrophic failures and still go on to fulfill their destinies, what does that mean for you? God is in the redemption business.

The One True Destination

A final trap for clients is thinking that there is one right *destination* as well as one right route to get to it. There is only one place I must go that will suffice, one right role to fill, or one particular task to complete to fulfill my life call. It's pretty obvious how that kind of thinking gets people tied up in knots. I've worked with several individuals who felt God had shown them the one right person they were called to marry—and then that person went off and hitched up with someone else! What do you do with that?

> **A Call for All Seasons**
>
> Can you state your call in a way that is completely independent of external circumstances or what modes of expression are available to you? This means putting it in "being" terms. Can you pose your call in a way that you could fulfill it even if you were…?
>
> - Debilitated
> - Laid off
> - Imprisoned
> - Become seriously ill
> - You must become a primary caregiver for a relative

Is there just one certain role in a particular town with a certain organization doing exactly the thing that represents your call? In short, no. Calling is not primarily a destination—it is an incarnation. The call is to embody something of Christ. The task is the channel. While there is a mission that best channels your call, it can come in many different flavors.

But it goes even further. At any moment, God takes whatever you are and works with you to make the most of it. If you choose course "A," He will take whatever that makes of your life, roll it into your call and work to help you maximize it. If you choose the opposite thing, He will take what that makes you and partner with you to make the most of it. *Calling is not a static, predetermined destination, but a dynamic, adaptive journey.* God actively recalibrates our calling after each choice, to take into account what He has to work with. We actually partner with God in our life purpose and our choices shape the plan and the destination—and yet all was foreknown by a God who stands outside of time and sees all days as one.

From a human perspective, God continuously adapts our call to our choices. From a divine one, He foresees every choice and His plan accounts for it. The mystery of receiving a call from a God who is outside of time is complicated.[25] However, the

25 I'm using the idea of human and divine perspectives to keep us from getting hung up on free will versus pre-destination. God dwells outside of the river time, in the timeless; so from His perspective, every moment happens in front of the same spot on the riverbank. We flow by in time, but He stands still and sees all. For the great I AM, there is no past or future—everything

practical application is simple: we do the best we can to follow the best we know of our call, assured that God is working with us to make things turn out the way He desires. Nothing we do wrong or that's done wrong to us can thwart that.

Coaching Calling Failure

Here are some coaching questions (or personal reflection questions for use as an action step) for the client who feels s/he has failed or been unfaithful to a call:

- *"If God redeemed your call like He redeemed your life, what would that mean?"*
- *"God doesn't wipe away all the consequences of our failures. Let's say you have to deal with some lasting fallout from this. How might God weave that suffering into your call?"*
- *"What life message might come from this failure that would embody Christ to the world?"*
- *"If you started fresh now, and didn't worry about what was behind but focused on what lies ahead, what could you accomplish with your life?"*

Abraham's life is a good example of this principle of God dynamically recalibrating a call based on a person's choices. When God called Abraham to "go… to the land which I will show you" (Gen. 12:1), the promise was to "this land." After Abraham separated from Lot, and chose to hold his inheritance lightly instead of trying to make it happen, God appeared to him again, and told him that all the land in sight to the north, south east and west would be his. Then, after Abraham rescued Lot from the warring kings and refused to take the spoils of Sodom (another good choice), God appeared to him again and promised him the land "from the River of Egypt to the great river, the River Euphrates" (Gen. 15:18)—and then named nine additional tribes that his descendants would dispossess.

See the pattern here? As Abraham obeyed and grew in character, the revelation and scope of his call grew with it. God adjusted Abraham's call on the fly based on his choices (again, keeping in mind that we are describing this from a human perspective). Obedience expands your destiny.

Coaching the Obstacle

Coaching around the One True Destination obstacle is a matter of perspective. For instance, we might ask, "Which do you think is more accurate: that God designed life as a series of right and wrong choices, and if you blow one you'll never reach your destiny; or that wherever you are at and whatever you've done in the past, God wants to take your life and make something great of it?" Or we can reframe using the comparison-with-parenting technique again: "If your child set out to become a doctor and couldn't get into med school, how would you treat the situation?" Then ask them

---

is now. But from a human perspective, in each moment is new and unforeseen. We make choices about how the direction of our lives will flow, and our future is the product of those choices. That's how free will and predestination coexist without conflict—it's a matter of your frame of reference.

how their response as a parent is similar to the Father's heart for them.

That still leaves the underlying fear of missing it, which is a much larger issue. This is a golden opportunity to take the conversation to a deeper level and grapple with the person's fundamental picture of God. "For fear has to do with punishment, and he who fears is not perfected in love" (I Jn. 4:18; RSV). When we think God will punish us for a wrong choice, we are naturally afraid. I might ask, "Where in your life does this fear of punishment come from? What experiences feed into it?" Or even, "Let's take a moment and pray. What would God say to you right now about those fearful memories?" Fear is most powerful when it lives in darkness, unexamined and unchecked. Just bringing it to light in a coaching conversation robs it of some of its power.

Repentance is another tool for conquering fear. If you've made choices to not follow God's call, have you talked that out with God? If not, you'll probably be afraid of going to that place in your life.

Repentance is warranted on questions that involve obedience. If you dreamed of taking a balloon ride some day and never did, that's a simply your choice. But if God specifically directed you to do something and you never carried it out, that's an obedience issue. You won't be free from the fear of being judged for it until you stand before the judge and fess up. But if the king of the universe pronounces you forgiven, what else do you have to fear?

- *"How have you talked with God about this fear of missing it?"*
- *"Now that you are on the other side of what happened, is there anything that is still affecting your relationship with God that you need to talk through?"*
- *"Is this an honest mistake or an obedience issue? In other words, is there anything here you need to confess and repent of?"*

We don't often talk about the place of repentance in a coaching relationship. But it's amazing how often mature believers forget to take this simple step. One tip: if you are going to ask your client about confession and repentance, you'll be far more effective if you do it regularly in your own life. When you are comfortable with your failings before God, others will be comfortable talking about their failings with you!

Twelve Revelation Methods

13.1

Here are 12 common ways people experience hearing a call from God.

1. **Drawing to a Need**
   I see a person, group, or need my heart is drawn to serve, and through that feel a larger sense of calling to meet those needs long-term (Moses).
2. **Personal Suffering**
   My call grows out of a personal experience of suffering and what is birthed in my heart through it (Job).
3. **Personal Success**
   God speaks to me through my success or overcoming something with a realization of what I can do on behalf of others (David, with Goliath).
4. **Demonstration of Gifting**
   My calling is demonstrated (and often recognized by others) through unusual or early manifestations of gifting or ability (Joseph).
5. **Childhood Dreams**
   God implants significant insights about the future in the hearts of children (Samuel).
6. **Holy Discontent**
   I can't stand something that is going on, and in the process of working against that injustice I discover my calling (Nehemiah).
7. **Inheritance/Community**
   My call comes through being part of my family, tribe or community, and embracing that group's sense of collective call (Isaac, Jacob, or Ruth).
8. **Affirmation/Confirmation**
   God uses others to name, confirm, or prophetically reveal my calling to me (David).
9. **Scripture**
   God reveals my call through a Scripture that is brought to life for me (Josiah).
10. **Circumstances**
    I find myself in a place of destiny where circumstances force me to respond (Esther).
11. **Direct Revelation**
    God speaks directly through an inner witness, dreams, visions or other supernatural means (Paul, Mary).
12. **Progressive Revelation**
    God uses many events, circumstances and insights to progressively unfold my call over a period of years (Abraham).

13.2 Revelation Journal

Record here what God has revealed to you about your call throughout your life. Keeping a running revelation journal is a great habit to develop!

Eureka Moments

Ever had an experience where everything came together and you felt you were doing what you were born to do? That's an inner witness that you are in your area of call. Jot down these experiences and what you think they tell you about your calling. (Look back at your responses in *Destiny Events* (12.1) if you completed that exercise.)

Direct Revelation

What has God directly spoken to you about your call, through His inner voice, words, dreams, or visions? What do you have an inner witness to pertaining to your call? Be bold about what you think you've heard. Even if you aren't certain, write it down here as something to look at.

Affirmation/Confirmation

What has God spoken to you through the people around you? If you've received strong affirmation in a gift or skill, someone you respect has named who you are, or you've received an important word or Scripture from someone, put it down here.

Key Scriptures

What key verses has God given you concerning your destiny? Is there a passage you are repeatedly drawn to because it expresses the essence of who you are and what's in your heart? Record those verses and the purpose insights that go with them here. Check your margin notes in your Bible or old journals if you need ideas.

Childhood Dreams

Sometimes God speaks clearly to children about their future, even when they don't know it is Him. What did you want to be as a kid? What did you want to do when you grew up? Who did you want to be like? Jot those items below, and if you can, identify what attracted you to that role. Don't get hung up on the outward role or the image ("I want to be a fireman"). Instead, look for what in that role that attracted you.

Design, Passion and Preparation

Take some time to go back and review the exercises you've done in the areas of Design, Passion and Preparation. Are there things you wrote down that are more than personal insights—that you sense are direction from God? Jot them down here.

Inheritance/Community

Think about your family, community and other groups you strongly identify with. What part of your call has been passed down to you (i.e. a family business, farm or lineage in a certain profession)? What strong values and traditions from your community or family influence your sense of call? How does your heritage make you part of a larger calling? (Exercise 13.3 can help you flesh this out.)

Revelation Summary

Once you've finished each category, step back and look it over. What are the common themes? What jumps out at you? Summarize what revelation tells you about your destiny.

13.3 Family Calling Interview

This exercise identifies aspects of call that are passed down through generations in your family. Interview your parents or grandparents about your family heritage, using the questions below (they use terms like "story" and "vocation" that most people are comfortable with instead of "calling"). If an interview isn't possible, simply answer the questions yourself from what you know of your family history.

Family Vocation

- *"What professions did your parents, grandparents and great grandparents enter?"*
- *"What did your family most value vocationally?"*
- *"Does our family have a history of entering a certain profession? What's behind that?"*

Family Story

- *"What's our family story? What have we contributed to society through the generations?"*
- *"Is there one particular patriarch or matriarch whose story has defined our family heritage? What is that story?"*

Family Values

- *"What are you most proud of in our family history?"*
- *"What part of your heritage do you most value? What parts do others in the family value?"*
- *"What do you think your parents felt was most important to pass on to you? What was most important to you to pass on to your children?"*

Your Vocation

- *"How do you feel God has led you in what you've chosen to do with your life?"*
- *"What have you done vocationally that most felt like what you were made to do?"*

Your Message

- *"What is the message you most wanted to come through your life to others?"*
- *"What was unique about the way you did your job? How did you express who you were through it?"*

Part II: Interview Learnings

- *"What were the most important insights into your heritage you got from this interview?"*
- *"How have your family's vocational choices and values impacted your sense of call?"*
- *"How is your family calling expressed in your own sense of call?"*

Lost in Translation

13.4

A call is revealed by God to our spirits but is interpreted through our minds—and sometimes things get lost in translation. This exercise will help you record a calling experience or separate the substance of a calling event (exactly what God said) from the image you used at the time to understand or remember what was revealed.

Step 1: Record Current Understanding of Call

Sketch out the call you received in this calling event as you currently understand it. Is there an image or analogy you've used to describe it? Is there a certain task or role that seems to be "it?" Record your current images and expectations to whatever degree of clarity you have.

I am called to use music and the arts to communicate intimacy with God. I picture myself traveling with a band, writing, performing and recording songs that come out of my own intimacy with God.

Step 2: Go Back to the Beginning

Next, try to write down *exactly the words or impressions you received from God* during the actual calling event. Try not to add anything—what *exactly* did God say to you, and how did He say it? What was the impression? What words did you hear or images did you see? Recapture as much as you can of that original moment.

There were several events. The key one was (I guess) a destiny event, where I was up on stage singing "Holy is Thy Name" and felt like I was really in the zone. My heart was connecting with the audience's hearts on a deep level. We went into a holy place and felt the peace of God there. At that moment I felt like, 'This is what I was born to do—connect hearts with God at this intimate level.'

Step 3: Fact Check

Compare the two versions of your call. Some changes may be due to additional progressive revelation since you received it—that's OK. We're looking for any assumptions you made about the original that might differ from what was revealed or no longer fit.

I guess when I look back, the call came in a musical context but God didn't specifically say anything about me being in music. It was all about intimate relationship with God.

Step 4: Evaluate

If you found some differences, step back and brainstorm with your coach. What other scenarios could fit what God said? How has your human interpretation of God's call limited your options? Is the image or container you've placed around your call still a good fit?

Interesting. Are there ways other than music I could make that kind of connection?

Chapter 14: Calling/Life Messages

"The will is transformed by experience, not information."

Dallas Willard

David and Jeroboam were both prepared by God to be kings in amazingly similar ways. Both were secretly chosen and anointed as king early in life by a prominent prophet. Both received the promise of having an enduring dynasty. David went through long wilderness years away from power between his anointing and when he actually became king—as did Jeroboam. Both were valiant warriors whose natural abilities and successful leadership brought them to the attention of their predecessors. They both served in national-level leadership positions while still young men. Both evidenced the presence of a divine destiny.

As Saul became jealous of David's ambitions and tried to kill him, so Solomon saw Jeroboam as a potential rival and tried to kill him. Both men fled into exile in a foreign land until the death of the king who preceded them. Both were called back home by the nation they were anointed to lead, and asked to assume the kingship in a time of national crisis. Both assumed power in one half of a divided nation. Both faced the specter of civil war.

But that's where the parallels end. David was faithful all his life to worship only Yahweh, while one of Jeroboam's first major acts as king was to set up two golden calves as idols for his people to worship. David reunited the kingdom under godly leadership, while Jeroboam left it divided both politically and religiously. David left a legacy in his life story that millions of people have drawn from for 3000 years, while Jeroboam is a virtual unknown, his life history mainly cited as an object lesson in how to miss the mark.

God took these two leaders through *virtually identical circumstances* in order to prepare them for their destiny roles. Yet one fulfilled his destiny, and the other failed. The difference was not in the situations they faced, but how they handled them. David opened his heart deeply in every circumstance, and consistently gave God permission to shape him at the identity level. David let God have his heart, but Jeroboam kept his heart to himself. And without his heart, God was unable to bring him to the fulfillment of his call.

The core of calling is incarnation—Christ becoming a message embodied in your heart. The word incarnation means to "enflesh"—to make something inward or invisible visible through your life. In the life purpose arena, I call this embodiment a *Message* because it is the underlying meaning that impacts others through what you do.

A while back I was teaching at a conference on this subject and asked the group for examples of events that had deeply shaped them. One older woman spoke up, and said, "The death of my husband." Certainly, that's a major shaping event. So I asked, "If you wouldn't mind sharing, how did you meet Jesus through that experience of suffering?" Without hesitation, she replied, "He became my husband. I learned to depend on Him totally, for everything. My Jesus became so precious to me through that time." Wow. Imagine the impact of this woman, who has walked through that place, ministering to others who have lost a loved one (which is what God has her doing). That's the kind of message that can transform lives.

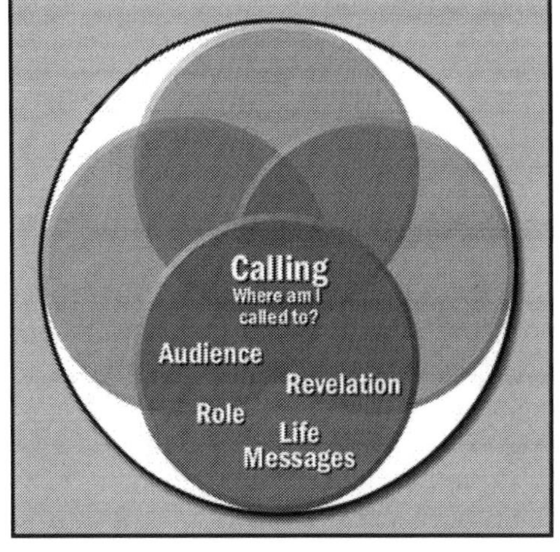

Life Messages become part of us—they are permanently seared into our souls through significant experiences where we meet God and are transformed. For instance, one of Martin Luther's life messages was grace. He was deeply convicted and morbidly guilty as a young man. Priests reportedly fled from the confessional booth when they saw Luther approaching, because he was in the habit of confessing every sin he'd ever committed from childhood, keeping his confessor there for four or five hours at a time!

When the message of grace in Romans (he got it from Paul, who also had a life message of grace) finally penetrated to Luther's heart, it turned his inner world upside down. *The power of the Protestant Reformation grew directly out of the depth of God's work in Luther's heart.* Luther engaged God profoundly, to the depths of his soul, and the profundity of that encounter is directly proportional to the force of his message. That's the most common life message pattern. Luther was deeply broken and needy in the area of grace. God met him powerfully. Luther was so transformed that that same grace was powerfully embodied for others.

St. Francis of Assisi had a life message of renouncing all to have all of Christ. When he left his rich upbringing for the life of a monk, he actually stripped himself of all his expensive clothing, left it with his father and walked out naked into his new life. The impact of his life message down through the ages grows directly out of being ripped free from his encumbrance to the world, and the depth to which he embraced utter dependence on God.

These are all good pictures of life messages. When we encounter a shaping event, do the hard work of meeting God in it, and allow the character of Christ to be truly embodied there, we've created a place of power in our lives. Whatever we speak or do out of that part of our heart has exceptional impact on others.

Can you think of some additional examples from the lives of leaders you've studied? How about one or two from your own life? Take a minute and find your own examples.

Coaching Incarnation

Since incarnation is Christ worked deeply into our character, it is developed in the character-building situations we often wish we could avoid: practicing discipline, suffering, failure, challenging circumstances, or iron sharpening iron in relationships. What that means for you as a coach is that the places where you'll find life messages are where the person has gone through unusual adversity or protracted struggle. So we start by identifying significant shaping events where God has dealt with the client's heart. And if you see a person going through unusual struggle or adversity now, that's potential life message material. Those are the moments you win your destiny! So as a coach, I want to seize them by challenging my clients to rise up and engage difficulty as an opportunity to develop a world-changing life message.

The *Life Messages* exercise (14.1) is designed to seize these moments in a person's life story. We identify key turning points or shaping events in life, and then ask the question, "How did that shape your identity? Who did you become through that experience? What was the message God implanted in you for the world through that?"

Coaching Life Messages

1. Identify a significant shaping event.
2. Discuss its impact on who you are.
3. Find how the person met God in it.
4. Distill into a message.

You can also coach life messages in your sessions. Since most people aren't familiar with the term, the first step is describing the concept and giving some examples. I like to coach the person through identifying at least one life message before I turn them loose on the reflection exercise. Here's how to do it.

First, identify a significant shaping experience:

- *"What's a significant experience in life that shaped who you are?"*
- *"What difficulties have you faced that had a deep impact on you?"*
- *"Where in life has God deeply dealt with you?"*

Second, talk about the impact of that experience on the person's core being. The key here is to go beyond a principle that was learned or an outward change the person made ("I'll never do that again!") to how this experience shaped one's identify. Since life messages are embodied in our heart, you have to get the conversation down to the heart level to find them.

- *"How did that experience fundamentally change you?"*
- *"What effect did this have on you as a person? Your core beliefs about life?"*
- *"It sounds like you learned some important things on the practical level. But let's go deeper—how did this touch your heart? How did it change who you are?"*

Third, we want to find how the person met God in the experience. You can have a deep experience that doesn't become a life message. For instance, if the way your older brothers treated you really beat you down and you've never been able to get over it, that's a scar, not a message. It only becomes a life message when you meet God within a significant event in a powerful way. So your questions need to help the person connect the dots:

- *"How did you meet God in that experience? How was Christ formed in you in it?"*
- *"At the point where you felt you touched God's heart (or God touched yours), what changed about you?"*
- *"How was this redeemed? How did you meet your redeemer in the process?"*

Finally, take that insight and help the client distill what they've embodied into a message:

- *"What is the unique message God has formed in your life for others through this?"*
- *"What does this qualify you to do and say for others? What's the message?"*
- *"If you summed it up in a sentence, what is uniquely embodied in your life through this experience?"*

An alternate way to look for life messages is to start with how they impact your client's life now, as opposed to going back to the shaping events that spawned them. The *Life Messages in Action* exercise (14.2) provides a way to work backward from the effects of the message in the person's life to the actual message.

One area this exercise looks at is our *Soapbox Issues.* The soapbox image comes from the old practice of standing on a soapbox at a street corner and shouting your ideas to everyone who passes by. Soapbox issues are ones we constantly talk about, or weave into all we do. Anyone who's been around you for a while has heard your soapbox issues. For instance, one of my life messages is meeting God in difficult circumstances. Can you tell? Whenever I write or speak or coach, that theme invariably comes up.

Another indicator of a life message is the unusual impact or authority that comes with it. Life messages are your places of power in ministry and service, because they are the places Christ is most deeply in you. So another way to find life messages is to look at where you communicate or serve with the greatest impact, or where others consistently seek you out for input.

A third area is qualification—the idea that your life experience qualifies you to speak into situations that others can't. For instance, in the example of the woman whose husband died, she has a unique qualification to speak into the lives of others who are grieving a loss. She's qualified to stand beside the casket and weep with you because she's been there, she knows your pain and she met Jesus in it. Because Jesus experienced everything we deal with, we have a high priest we can approach with confidence. He knows what it is like. Where are those places in your life?

The fourth area is drawing. The people who could benefit from your life messages are naturally drawn to you. It's amazing how they somehow sense that you're the right person to meet them at their point of need. So another tool for identifying life messages is to find the people you are drawn to serve, and who are drawn to you, and then ask, "What is the message or impartation they come to receive from me?"

Life Message Indicators

1. **Soapbox Issues:** The ideals and issues you always talk about.
2. **Places of Power:** Where you have unusual authority and impact.
3. **Qualification:** What you've been through makes people listen to you.
4. **Drawing:** Where you are drawn to others and they're drawn to you.

The way to verify a life message is the same as with a value: ask for some examples of how it is lived out. A true life message will manifest itself in some way in almost everything you do. A *Confirming Life Messages* exercise (14.3) is included for clients who want some extra assurance or feedback on their life messages.

The Message of My Life

There's a special life message that's a summary of your story—the place where your various life messages join together in one theme. What one message does Jesus speak most clearly through your story? What is the central impartation that animates everything you do for others? That one-of-a-kind message is the heart of your call. It's your life purpose in being terms; what you must embody to fulfill your destiny.

For instance, some of my life messages are authenticity, dealing with God, meeting God in suffering and adversity, transformational change, Sabbath rest, and grace instead of rules. The central theme (as best I understand it) that's the message of my life is, "You can meet God at the heart level in every circumstance, especially suffering and adversity, and be transformed." That explains this book's emphasis. I didn't write an encouraging, follow-your-bliss book about the adventure of living your destiny, because *that's not the message of my life.* I have the greatest impact for God on others when I am imparting my core message.

The message of Abraham's life was justification through faith, not works. The Bible calls Abraham a "father of faith" because he was the first person to figure out that if he believed God and walked in that faith, that was what God was really after (as opposed to simple rule-following righteousness). Faith as the foundation of one's relationship with God is Abraham's great legacy.

The message of David's life is being "a man after God's own heart." David's life story still communicates centuries later the full range of what it means to be human. We watch him seeking God with his entire being whether in victory or defeat, success or failure. David was a man after God's heart because he was quick to allow God to deal with him at the heart level—and that's his primary legacy to us today.

Job's message might be summed up as, "Though he slay me, yet will I trust him" (Job 13:15; KJV). Can you see how his life story both produced that message and gives it incredible power?

The primary message of your life always comes through progressive revelation, because it is progressively built into your heart over years of life experience. Even in the instances where God revealed this message from the beginning (as with David and Abraham), it was not until much later in life that they understood what it meant, let alone embodied and lived it. So don't worry if you aren't quite sure what the message of your life is—God knows, and He is working every detail of your life to bring it to fullness in you.

However, for those who are mature believers in the releasing and fulfillment stages of calling,[26] identifying and aligning around the message of your life should be on the agenda. Grasping the message of your life is a touchstone that keeps you focused and on course.

There are several potential paths to uncovering the message of the client's life. One way is to start with the desired ultimate impact (the result of the message—see pg. 254) and work backward. If the person knows their calling task or role, look underneath it and ask what that task is supposed to accomplish:

- *"Why do you want to do this task? What is the purpose of doing it?"*
- *"Why is this important? Why does God care about this?"*
- *"What part of Christ's heart is this task meant to convey to your audience?"*
- *"If the total of your impact was that people 'got' something that Christ built into your life, what would you most want that something to be?"*
- *"If you strip away all the externals—the actual acts of service, the organization, the planning, the finances—and all that was left was the message you want to convey, what would it be in one sentence?"*

---

26 For more on the stages of calling, see *The Calling Journey* by Tony Stoltzfus

Another avenue is to look at the convergence of the person's individual life messages. Sometimes one message is dominant, or all the messages point in a similar direction. *The Message of Your Life* exercise (14.4) puts some structure to the process of identifying this theme.

Calling Patterns Involving Suffering

Paul, one of my first coaching clients, engaged me to help him discover a sense of purpose in his life. He had been very successful in business but was in the midst of a mid-life reevaluation. Several months into the relationship, his teenage son was tragically killed in a car accident. That event completely changed Paul's focus and his sense of what was meaningful in life. Over the next year, we talked about issues like transparency, grieving, how to allow others to support you, who your real friends are, and much more.

When Paul was finally ready to reengage the life purpose question, nothing seemed to really motivate him. We looked at several different business or ministry tracks he could have gone down, but nothing clicked—until he hit on the idea of setting up memorial funds to help young families with the financial burden of adoption. The idea was to help the family that lost a life find new life by investing in another.

He mentioned the idea in passing in one session, so I didn't think much about it. But two weeks later he had already put together a plan, set up a web site, hired his first staffer, and the thing was well underway. I was amazed at his energy! He had found a genuine passion that re-energized his entrepreneurial side. That passion came not through the fun and fulfilling things of life, but in helping others navigate the kind of devastating loss he had suffered.

Most life purpose discovery tools look for destiny in the things that energize you and give you joy. That's a legitimate approach (we've looked at it in the section on Passion). But what is often overlooked is how many individuals find their sense of call is birthed through suffering. Obviously, this is an important insight for life coaches. For someone like Paul, suffering can lead to a passion that energizes and gives meaning to life. However, it's a different kind of energy than what comes from feelings of joy and fulfillment, and you have to go down different roads to find it.

Common Patterns

Six common calling patterns associated with suffering are:

- Confronting injustice you and I now suffer.
- Preventing you from suffering what I have suffered.
- Being drawn by compassion to alleviate others' suffering.
- Earning a platform through suffering (qualification).
- Overcoming difficult circumstances.
- Adapting to or accepting adversity with grace.

Let's take a quick look at each. Martin Luther King Jr. (see chapter eight for part of his famous "I Have a Dream" speech) is a good example of the first pattern: fighting a present injustice that you also experience. King channeled his Passion for justice through his Design (gifts of eloquence and leadership) and his unique Preparation as an influential, highly educated pastor into a Calling—working non-violently for equal rights for African Americans. Individuals with this calling pattern are partners in suffering the injustice they fight; but what makes it into a calling is that they channel the energy of that pain into finding justice for others (remember, a calling is from God, for *others*).

Six Calling Patterns from Suffering

1. **Confronting.** I stand up to the injustice we suffer now to bring a better future for all.
2. **Prevention.** I work to prevent others from suffering what I went through in the past.
3. **Compassion.** I take up the cause of others whom I see suffering.
4. **Qualification.** Suffering qualifies me to speak to or serve a certain audience.
5. **Overcoming.** I win through to conquer adversity and help others to overcome it.
6. **Acceptance.** Through suffering I've acquired special grace to be fully at peace with my condition.

The word "for" in our definition of calling takes on special meaning here. Just to suffer injustice and get mad about it doesn't mean you have a calling. We are not called to work primarily *against* injustice, but *for* justice. *Any identity or call grounded in the negative departs from the way of Christ.* A person focused on the hope of God's future becomes more and more like heaven; while the person focused on anger over injustice becomes more and more a child of hell. Those like Martin Luther King who are called to fight injustice are motivated by a vision of God's ideal future that helps them transcend simply agitating for their own rights, seeing others as enemies or hitting back using force. A coaching challenge for this kind of calling is to help clients stay focused on what they are called *to* as they work to end suffering. Samson is a good example of someone who found a calling in fighting injustice, but never seemed to figure out what he was *for*. The result was that his personal life didn't line up well at all with his message.

The second of these four calling patterns is saving others from what you have suffered in the past. Lance Armstrong's "Live Strong" campaign (a cancer survivor working against cancer) is a well-known example. This pattern is very common among people who have experienced the worst that life can offer. Those who've survived painful divorces may find meaning in life through helping divorcees. Men who have been unfaithful or struggled with pornography end up helping other men escape the same bondages. Children of alcoholism strive to give their own kids the kind of home life they wish they'd had. Past pain translates into present passion to eliminate that suffering for others.

A third pattern is being drawn to the sufferings of others and taking up their cause, even if you personally have not suffered in that way. That's compassion.

Mother Teresa is a classic example of this pattern. She entered a culture where the poor were at times left to die because that was their karma, and discovered a call to help every dying person pass away with dignity and love. Moses is another example of a leader whose heart was drawn to suffering that he had not personally experienced, and that call led him out of a life of ease to a life of significance.

Many who go on short-term mission trips find their hearts broken by the needs they see, and feel commissioned to devote their lives to alleviating that suffering. Even an image in a book or on the news can grip someone's heart in a way that compels them to respond. Part of the reason so many people experience a call this way is that responding out of compassion deeply reflects God's compassionate heart. He is for the poor and the needy.

A fourth pattern is when individuals find a platform to minister or address issues through what they've suffered. Charles Colson's incarceration gave him a platform to speak to the issues faced by those in prison (they never would have listened if he hadn't been there). Paul's experiences of suffering on behalf of the gospel (even his refusal to take money from the churches he served) gave him a strong platform to stand up for preserving the heart of it. The coaching question here is, "Who will pay attention to your message—that would never have listened otherwise—because you went through this experience?"

The fifth pattern is overcoming. This one is more familiar. What adversity have you conquered that you want to help others conquer? What have you learned through difficulty to do well, that you can help others succeed at?

A sixth way calling is connected to suffering is through successfully adapting to difficult circumstances. The proper response to adversity is not always to try to change the world. Sometimes we need to make our peace with what is and move on. Joni Erickson Tada is an example of someone who faced disability and made something great out of it—and the way she lives her life is a message of hope. Job inspires us because he lost everything he had in a way that made no sense to him at all—yet he refused to "curse God and die." We admire people who have the internal fortitude to overcome challenging circumstances. And through doing so, they gain a life message and a platform to share it.

The *Calling Through Suffering* exercise (14.5) can be used as a reflection or a set of coaching questions to help people get in touch with a call that came to them in one of these ways. Sometimes individuals who do not have anything to say on the Revelation exercises can find their life purpose here.

Calling Lifestyles

A final aspect of incarnation has to do with lifestyle. There is a life pattern—including things like your standard of living, the things you choose to own and the schedule you keep—that maximizes your ability to be who you are and do what you are called to do. Your lifestyle can also be a great hindrance to the message God has placed in you for others. Let's listen in to a coach helping a client grappling with his calling lifestyle. This individual is struggling to make ends meet and trying to understand why things are becoming so difficult for him.

"I can't understand why this isn't working, and neither can my business mentor. These deals come right up to the edge of closing, or we even have a verbal agreement, and then something weird happens and it falls apart. He says he's never seen so many strange circumstances in so many separate projects as I'm having. It makes me wonder if I'm in the right place, because this just isn't working, and I don't know why."

"Tom, you mentioned earlier that the reason you came back from the mission field and started a business was to live what you teach. That intrigued me. Can you say more about that?"

Since the client is asking directional questions, the coach goes back to the original call for answers.

"Well, these bi-vocational pastors I am mentoring and teaching are out there struggling to make a living while they are planting a church, and it's tough. You really want to give yourself fully to the ministry, but you also have to provide for your family. So your attention is divided: you never really give the business what it needs to succeed, your ministry suffers and so does your family. It just seemed like there had to be a way for these guys to be more successful in business to remove the financial and family stress they were under. And I felt like, if I'm going to teach them how to do bi-vocational ministry, I need to have walked that walk, too. So here's where I ended up."

The coach sees dissonance between Tom's sense of call and his lifestyle expectations.

"OK. So what I'm hearing is that you got into this business to understand their walk and the pressures they face, and to be able to speak to them out of having lived there."

"Right."

"And how were you expecting things to turn out when you launched this business? What did you think it would look like?"

Asking about expectations brings the dissonance out in the open.

"Well, clearly the Lord led me here and confirmed it multiple times. I guess I just expected that this would work out—that I'd be making money and the deals would go through. I thought making it work would give me something to take back to people."

"So let's compare your objective with your expectations. If you went into business to identify with the bi-vocational pastors you work with, how well would you really understand them and have walked their walk if your business took off, and a year into it you were making a six-figure income?"

Juxtaposing two dissonant goals—calling and expectations.

"Oh... I guess not very well. I never thought of it that way."

"So what would you expect your life to look like if God **were** *answering those prayers and you were meeting that objective?"*

This question helps realign expectations with the call.

"Wow, that's a new thought. Maybe pretty much what it looks like now. If everything came easy for me, and I went back and told them that's how it should work for them, I'd be totally irrelevant."

This dialogue reframed the conversation using the concept of a calling lifestyle.

There is a unique lifestyle that fully supports your calling, and living it daily is an important calling discipline. If you are true to your call, your life will not look like everyone else's. If you are called to offer hospitality in your home and reach professional people, your calling lifestyle may include an exquisitely decorated house in which to do that. Another's call may mean buying whatever house is closest to a college campus and taking in students as boarders, or finding a dilapidated crack house and renovating it while you reach the unwed mothers in a poor neighborhood. For all of these situations, only one particular kind of house will do—any of the others would be an obstacle to fulfilling your call.

In the example dialog, Tom's calling was to minister to bi-vocational ministers. Therefore, the lifestyle of his call likely involved living like them. However, Tom's expectations for financial success pointed him in the opposite direction from his life mission—in this case, *struggling financially actually furthered Tom's call.* Immediate financial success would have increased the gap between him and his target audience. The coach simply invited Tom to come back to the central mission of his life and refocus his lifestyle expectations around that objective.

The Lifestyle of Your Calling

- **Step 1:** Identify the client's destiny objective.
- **Step 2:** Assume that God is using the current circumstances as preparation.
- **Step 3:** Paint a picture of what it would look like if God were rearranging the client's lifestyle around his or her calling.

Jesus clearly understood that He had a lifestyle that fit his call. For example:

- "The foxes have holes and the birds of the air have nests, but the Son of Man has nowhere to lay His head" (Mt. 8:20).
- "The son of man did not come to be served, but to serve, and give his life as a ransom for many" (Mt. 20:28).
- "...though He was rich, yet for your sake He became poor, so that you through His poverty might become rich" (II Cor. 8:9).
- "Why do we and the Pharisees fast, but your disciples do not fast?" And Jesus said to them, "The attendants of the bridegroom cannot mourn as long as the bridegroom is with them, can they?" (Mt. 9:14-15).
- "The Son of Man has come eating and drinking, and you say, 'Behold, a gluttonous man and a drunkard, a friend of tax collectors and sinners!'" (Luke 7:34).
- "... they were amazed that He had been speaking with a woman, yet no one said, 'What do you seek?' or, 'Why do you speak with her?'" (John 4:27)

If Jesus had preferred to stay in the villas of the upper crust of society instead of with the working class, or had owned slaves on a big estate in the hills of Galilee, or even lived the ascetic life of a Pharisee, His lifestyle would have undermined His message. The son of man came to seek and save the lost—and that mission required Him to live among them, as one of them. That's why He chose to go to their parties, to hang out with people who drank, to break the gender and culture barriers and talk to a Samaritan woman, and to be surrounded by people who were ritually unclean. All His lifestyle choices—from money to social customs to the circles He ran in—reinforced His message.

Finding Your Lifestyle

So how do you help a client align with the lifestyle of their call? Our sample dialog illustrates a step-by-step process. First, the coach revisited Tom's call. Next, he assumed that the current life circumstances weren't an obstacle to that call, but were exactly what was needed to fulfill it. Finally, the coach juxtaposed Tom's expectations for his lifestyle with what might be expected if God were arranging it in a way that was consistent with Tom's call. Instead of wondering why he wasn't living the lifestyle he expected, this conversation helped Tom ground those expectations within his life purpose.

The key to this technique is the assumption that all of life flows toward one's destiny, and that God sovereignly leverages every circumstance to that end. That's a powerful combination for reframing: "If you are called, and your circumstances are intentionally moving you toward that call, then what does the fact that you are here now mean?"

What alerts the coach to the need to reframe is the dissonance between Tom's stated objective (to walk the walk of leaders who are struggling financially) and his expectations (that he would quickly enjoy financial success). Tom thought he would help his leaders best by succeeding and showing them how to succeed. The coach offered another potential perspective: a straighter road to his objective might be

Lifestyle of Your Call: Practice

Want a little practice wrapping your mind around this concept? Take the following callings, and then apply the questions at the bottom to each of them.

Calling I: to political leaders, with a life message that true joy and legacy in life comes from serving the least of these.

Calling II: to the surfing subculture, with a message that with Christ you can live to the full in every moment and have a real future, too.

- Where would you live?
- What standard of living would best support your message?
- What would you own, and not own?
- Who would you hang around with?
- What would you wear?
- Would you have a tattoo or body piercing?
- What kind of job would you have?
- What would make you real in that world, and what would make you a hypocrite?

entering into their struggles.

Usually you'll have to introduce the concept of a calling lifestyle into the coaching dialogue and help clients wrap their minds around it before you start talking about realignment. Once they've got the general idea, there are several key questions to ask. **Location** and **Identification** are important considerations. If you are called to reach this certain group of people, where do you live? What lifestyle would put you among them? And what lifestyle would give you insight into their struggles and issues? What would help them identify with you?

Another great area for reflection is **qualification**. What kind of life experience would make you credible to your target audience? What kind of life would demonstrate your message, so that your lifestyle would communicate it even if you didn't say a word? Conversely, what kind of life would undermine your message, so if people knew how you lived they would discount the message because of it?

Standard of living is an important question, too. How much time and energy would be wisely spent on possessions and income given your call? Where do money and things become a distraction? And is there any thing you've acquired that is a plain old distraction from your mission?

The impact of lifestyle on calling can be a rich area for developing action steps that create better alignment. Exercise 14.6 offers a formal process for discovering the lifestyle of your call.

Life Messages  14.1

Take half an hour in a quiet place and reflect back on your life story. We're going to identify the major shaping events in your life and what they mean for your destiny.

Step 1: Identify Shaping Events

In the left hand column, record major transitions, difficult experiences, important relational influences—the experiences in life that most deeply shaped who you are. Times you met God in tough circumstances and were transformed are particularly likely to produce life messages.

Step 2: Discover Life Messages from Events

Take each experience in turn, and reflect and journal on it using these questions:

- How did this experience shape who I am? How am I a different person because I went through it?
- How did I meet God in this? How did God use it to shape my heart and my character?
- What is the message this experience built into me for others? Where am I drawn to others, qualified to speak to them, and have a deep impact because of this experience?

Shaping Event	Life Message
Getting dumped by my high school sweetheart	*God is the keeper of my heart*
Mentoring relationship with the pastor's wife	*God is looking out for me! (and you!)*
Two miscarriages in a row	*God is the keeper of my heart (again)* *Dreams are only safe in God's hands*
Finally having the baby after three yrs	*I know that my redeemer lives*
Husband laid off; no job or income for almost six months	*Life is more than having it all*

14.2 Life Messages in Action

An alternate way to discover life messages is to find the places where they operate in your life now, and then work backwards to discover where they came from.

Step 1: Examine Your Life

Take a look at the following four areas to try to identify your life messages in action. Jot down your responses to the questions on a blank sheet of paper.

- **Themes**: What are your Soapbox Issues: the themes you come back to over and over when you are helping or serving others? What are you always talking passionately about? What do you most yearn to impart to people?
- **Impact**: Where are your places of greatest impact? What do you seem to impart to other people there? What messages do they consistently learn or draw from you?
- **Qualification:** Are there situations you can speak into because of what you've been through, where others can't? Where have you met God in suffering in a way that opens the door to other's hearts? What is the message you have for people in that situation?
- **Drawing:** What people are you most drawn to help? Who is drawn to you? What are they looking for, and what do you most want them to receive from you?

Step 2: What Messages Stand Out?

When you've been through all the questions, step back and look over what you jotted down. What messages come out the strongest? Are there themes that are repeated over several of your entries? These themes are your life message candidates.

Step 3: Where Did it Come from?

Take a few moments and trace back each potential message to where it came from. How was this idea implanted in you? Was there a certain experience or relationship that imprinted this message on your heart? True life messages always have a component of meeting God in a significant way in their origin, because the message is something God plants in your heart.

Step 4: Name and Record

If you haven't done so already, name your message. A single word, a pithy phrase or a fragment of Scripture can be perfect—make it something memorable that sticks with you. And write down the story of how that message developed in your life! These stories are some of your most powerful tools for impacting others—so don't let the memory fade.

Confirming Life Messages

14.3

If something is a true life message, the people who are close to you will know it (probably because they've heard you talk about it or seen it in your life repeatedly). For confirmation, find a friend, fellow leader or family member, and ask for some honest feedback on your tentative life message list. Describe the self-discovery process you are going through and explain what life messages are before you start. Here are some life message symptoms:

- Jesus is readily apparent in your life here.
- You paid a price for that incarnation.
- It's a theme you return to repeatedly.
- You have unusual impact on others in this area.
- Others are drawn to you for help and solace here.

For Feedback

If you want feedback on a list of possible life messages that you've already developed, try this approach:

- "I've tentatively identified ____ as a life message—an area where there's a God-implanted message in my heart to pass on to others. What do you think? Do you see that in me? Are the life message symptoms apparent here?"
- "Which of the items on this list do you most see as my life messages?"
- "Help me understand what makes you say that. What specific examples in my life lead you to that conclusion?"

For Input

If you've had a hard time identifying life messages on your own and you'd like some input from those around you, use the following questions.

- "What do you think my life messages might be?"
- "Where do you see me operate with unusual impact? What is the heart of that impact?"
- "When I am serving, when do I most connect with others at the heart level? What is the message I communicate in those times?"
- "Can you help me understand what makes you say that? What specific examples in my life story make you believe that?"

You may also want to show your friend the *Life Messages in Action* exercise (14.2) and talk through some of the questions there together.

14.4 The Message of Your Life

The *Message of Your Life* is the heart of your call—the key way the heart of Christ touches the people you love and serve. Here are several ways to get at that central message. This is an exercise that you'll come back to repeatedly as God unfolds more and more of his purpose to you. So do it in pencil, and don't worry about getting it perfect the first time. You can use any one or all of the approaches below.

Option 1: Start with Life Messages

Look over the list of your life messages from exercise 14.1. Use the questions below or work with your coach to identify a dominant message or a theme in your messages:

- Is there one dominant message?
- If the people you serve really "got" only one message, which would you want it to be?
- Where do all your messages point? Is there a theme they converge around?

Option 2: Start from Your Life Mission

Take your *Life Mission* (15.4) and explore why you want to do it:

- What does doing this communicate or give to people that is vitally important to you?
- Why does God care about you doing this? How does it reveal His heart?
- What's the central message God wants to touch people with through your task?

Option 3: Revisit Your Passions

Go back to the work you did on your Passions (see chapters 7-10), and examine it for clues to your message:

- What have your life experiences made you most passionate about communicating or giving to others?
- Which of your passions are closest to the *Passion Bull's Eye* (7.1)? What value is most important to you? What's the message in it?
- If your legacy was that five people fully caught your passion and carried it on after you were gone, what would you most want them to catch from you?

Part II: Create a Statement

Once you've looked at the options above, take your message and distill it down to a sentence. You may need several tries or to let it stew for a while before you come up with something you really like. Don't worry—that's normal.

Calling through Suffering

14.5

This exercise offers a series of questions to help you uncover life messages or callings that are connected somehow with suffering. Take some time to meditate on each question, or (especially if you are an extrovert!) talk it through with a good friend or spouse. What surfaces as you ponder these questions? What do these experiences have to say about what you may be called to do?

- What are your most significant experiences of suffering?
- What does this make you passionate about changing?

Confrontation

- What injustice makes you want to rise up and fight for the good of all?
- What's the injustice you see, where you also have a compelling vision of the better future that could be?

Prevention

- Where do you have a deep desire to save others from what you've suffered?
- What experiences sensitized you to that particular area?

Compassion

- What kinds of images or situations consistently cause compassion to rise up in you?
- Where do you identify with the weak or the needy? Who are the people your heart is drawn to, and why?

Qualification

- What difficult experiences give you a platform to speak to others in that same area?
- Who will listen to you because of what you've been through, that would never listen otherwise? What do you want to impart to them?

Overcoming

- Where have you overcome significant difficulty in your life?
- What have you done well that you are motivated to share with others?

Acceptance

- Where have you learned to walk in great peace in the midst of suffering or injustice?
- Where has God given you special grace to accept as a gift something others might see as a curse?

14.6 The Lifestyle of Your Calling

We all have a lifestyle that fits what we were created to do and be. What you own, how you spend your money and your time, where you live—all these things have implications for your destiny. Start with the picture you created in the *Ideal Lifestyle* exercise (8.3). Then add lifestyle elements that directly support fulfilling your God-given call using the questions below.

Identification

Jesus became one of us so that we could approach God through His life. How must you identify with the audience you are called to serve (live their lifestyle) so you can understand them and they can approach you?

Qualification

What life experience will qualify you to speak to your target group? What kind of track record, life story or lifestyle would open the doors to their hearts? What life would make you "real" to them, and what would make you look like a hypocrite?

Standard of Living

What standard of living are you called to? (It should be determined by the needs of your calling, not by rising to meet whatever income you can generate!) What possessions are needed for your call and what would be a distraction or distance you from your audience? What kind of home, wardrobe, income, hobbies, etc. would fit best with your life mission?

Location

Where do you need to live or spend your time to walk in your call? What lifestyle would get you into the lives of your target audience and support you best as you pursue your mission?

Fellowship

Who do you need to be with to fulfill your destiny? What kind of lifestyle will put you in the relationships and the teams you need around you? What community will best support you in what you are called to do and be?

Coaching Questions

- *"How does this lifestyle help or hinder you in accomplishing your life mission?"*
- *"What does this lifestyle eliminate that would get in the way of your mission?"*
- *"Who does your lifestyle say that you are? Does your walk match your talk?"*
- *"What one lifestyle change could you make now to better align it with your call?"*

Chapter 15: Calling/ Audience, Task and Impact

"The end point of our best desires is not selfish, not the having *of love and belonging, but the* giving *of it."*

Peter Temes, in *The Power of Purpose*

"So, Nate—give me some specific examples. What kind of people are you most drawn to help?"

"I guess it would be other parents, people with teenagers—that sort of thing."

"What draws you to them?"

"Well, we had so much of a struggle with Jennifer that I guess we feel for them. And when Jeremy came along, it was a whole different set of issues. So we look around at church and in the neighborhood, and when we see the kids acting out or the parents yelling across the street at them in frustration, we want to do something."

"Let's get a bit more specific here. If you could name one person or couple who exemplify the kind of parents you want to reach, who would it be?"

"Hmm… Maybe Jeff and Emily down the street? They've got two in junior high and one in high school."

"Tell me more—why them?"

"We talk every so often when I see him jogging. I can tell they're hurting. The middle one, Brendan, barely talks to them. They just don't know how to bridge the gap."

"What else?"

"Part of the reason I picked them is because we have some natural contact—I run into

them and I see their kids around, so I have some idea of what's going on. But mostly I see the little things they don't know how to do that would make all the difference. Like going to their soccer games—Jeff is always too busy, but he doesn't even connect his absence with what's going on with his kids."

"So I heard four things that draw you to Jeff and Emily: kids in their teens, people in proximity to you that you see in your daily routine; the little parenting skills that they are missing, and the hurt you see in them over the communication gap. Anything else?"

"Well... Jeff's a professional guy like me, so we have something in common. And Emily and Charlene seem to hit it off. That's something important. We like to do this as a couple, so it is important that Charlene connects with the wife as well as me with the husband."

"Good. Anything about the kids other than being teenagers?"

"Well, obviously that they are troubled to a certain extent. I'm not really drawn to situations where the kids are doing fine—they don't need me—and kids with drug problems or abuse issues seem a bit out of my league. So probably your basic American parents who just don't quite know how to cope with their teenagers."

"That's a great description. Last time we were working on the message of your life—how does this target audience tie in with your message?"

"Oh—that connects the dots! My message is, 'There is a unique way for you in your situation, and God will show it to you if you make it job one to find it.' Even better would be, 'Every kid is unique, there is a unique way for a parent to touch that kid's heart, and you need to find that way.' These are the people I see every day who can't find their way—and that's who I want to help."

Calling is an external commission from God *for others.* That "for others" phrase has great significance for life purpose discovery. If your life purpose is for others, you're going to have to figure out who those "others" are, how you are going to serve them, and how you want to impact them. Those three things are your *Audience, Task* and *Impact.* The goal of this chapter is to identify them.

> **Calling is...**
> *A **message** you embody*
> *To a specific **audience***
> *For an ultimate **impact***
> *Through a unique **task.***

The **Audience** of your calling is the people or need you are called to. Your service may be targeted at whole nations, a few individuals you know by name, or about anything in between. Or the call may focus on meeting a need in a way that impacts certain people. In this example, Nate felt called to reach certain people (couples with troubled teens) with specific needs (a parent's heart, which was Nate's life message) that were in a certain place (in proximity to his life). The coach brought out these details by using an *exemplar*—a real individual who personifies the qualities of Nate's target audience. Exemplars (see exercise 15.2) are a useful tactic when coachees have trouble naming specific details of the audience they are called to.

There are many types of audiences. Some of the different categories are:

- **Specific Individuals**
  Your audience may be particular, named individuals. For instance, a mother

called to raising her children, or the coach who takes in a boy and treats him like a son.

- **A Group**
  A calling can be directed to a group; for instance, all those in a certain profession, a people group (like the homeless), a community or all employees in a certain business.
- **A Point of Contact**
  The call can be to touch those you come into contact with in some area of life. For example, it could be whoever I meet in my job as a realtor—customers, brokers, home inspectors, and sellers; or those in my neighborhood or visiting my church.
- **People with a Certain Need**
  Examples might be kids with Down syndrome, villages in Sudan that need a well or elderly people in your community who need assistance with home maintenance.
- **A Societal Need**
  Here the impact on people is indirect—it is on society at large. For instance, I am a researcher creating better drugs to fight cancer, or a forest ranger who cares for a national park. We work to create a better world for everyone.

Finding Your Audience

So how do coaches help people find their Audience? The most direct approach is simply to ask—often people already know at least some characteristics of their target group. The question is simple: "Who are you called to serve?" or "What need do you want to meet for what group of people?"

Another avenue is to start with *Life Messages* (14.1 and 14.4) and think about the recipients that need that message:

- *"Who is this message for? Who needs to hear it?"*
- *"With what kind of people would this message have the greatest impact?"*
- *"Who does this message and the experience behind it qualify you to speak to?"*
- *"Who are you drawn to and who is drawn to you because of this message?"*

This approach is especially useful if the client has already done some work on Ultimate Impact—if you know the message and what impact you want it to have, that tells you a lot about who your message could help. The *Audience for My Message* exercise (15.2) uses this approach. If this isn't working, you might try showing them the different categories of audiences, as in the box in exercise 15.2. Sometimes just getting some options out on the table gets the insights flowing.

A third avenue is to look at Passion and Preparation. Who have you served in the past with passion and impact? Who are you prepared or qualified to serve? Who do you dream about serving now? *Destiny Events* (12.1), *Dreams* (8.1) and the *Passion*

Bull's Eye (7.1) are good places to look for Audience clues.

Ultimate Impact

Ultimate Impact is the "why" of your call—the outcome your call produces in others' lives. (Some call this your Legacy or Ultimate Contribution). It's why God commissioned you to do what you do in the first place. Your ultimate contribution is not the doing of the calling task, but how that task and the message that comes through it changes lives.

- *"How will your audience's lives be different because of your contribution?"*
- *"How will they see a picture of Jesus in what you do?"*
- *"Take a person from your target audience—if you can think of someone by name that's perfect—and tell me exactly how this will benefit them."*
- *"If people are eternal and things aren't, tell me how this task will have an eternal impact."*

Defining calling as a Message to an Audience may seem a little restrictive at first glance. Many professions are focused on creating tangible objects of value (like auto workers, artists or chefs) instead of directly helping people. How does that fit this model? What's the message of being a plumber or a truck driver?

Actually, this focus on impact is a key distinctive of Christian coaching. As Christians, we believe in a heaven so incredible that nothing you can have on earth has any value compared to being there. People are eternal and things are not. Therefore, *possessions and things only have eternal value as avenues for impacting people.*

That's the point of the parable of the unrighteous steward: use whatever tangible things you have to invest in people now, so when things pass away those people will be there to welcome you into heaven. Jesus goes even further: "Therefore if you have not been faithful in the use of unrighteous wealth, who will entrust the true riches to you?" (Luke 16:11). In other words, if you *don't* use the tangible things you've been given for their intended purpose (to help people), why would God entrust you with anything truly worthwhile in heaven? Because heaven is real, a Christian's life purpose always focuses on people over things.

The beauty of this is that it isn't the job you have that matters—its how your heart touches people as you do your job. A plumber can channel his own unique message of Christ through his job in the same way that a pastor can, by allowing Christ be in every act of service, every kind word to a customer and every worship song that wafts up from the crawl space where he's working. Even doing a dirty job with excellence and a great attitude is a message. And in a Kingdom where the last shall be first, there will be unknown plumbers who attain higher stature in heaven than well-known preachers.

Although impact is crucial, comparatively few people seem to have formally defined it. I often coach leaders who have worked out their visionary task in intricate detail but have only vague images of how their message will impact people through that vision. Missing this crucial step leaves them vulnerable to the temptation of becoming about the task instead of about the call (see box), which can have devastating results. Here are a few questions to help you draw out the client's Ultimate Impact:

- *"Why are you doing this? What's the ultimate objective?"*
- *"What impact will this have on the people you are serving?"*
- *"Describe specifically how their lives will be different because you did this."*
- *"Visualize a real person who exemplifies your target Audience. How exactly do you want to change that person's life?"*

Why Focusing on Ultimate Impact is Vital

Keeping the focus of call on Impact as opposed to Task completion is crucially important. One of the most subtle temptations for visionary leaders is for "The Work" itself to become the objective, gradually crowding out the benefit we were called to create for others as the goal. Our focus shifts from how *they* are blessed to how we are accomplishing *my* vision. And that breeds all kinds of abusive leadership behaviors.

The classic example is the church that is so driven by the task of ministry that they use up their staff in the process. Good leaders burn out, others feel used and sour on the church, and families are damaged because dad is always at a meeting. The whole apparatus rolls relentlessly forward under the banner of "bringing people to Christ," when they are simultaneously driving their own people away!

When we lose focus on impact, we move from serving Christ by serving people to building big organizations that help people, or creating influential models of how to help people, or to doing visionary projects that help people. The leader's focus becomes *the leadership task itself* (the ability to lead and to "minister") instead of on impacting people. In the worst cases, entire ministries become merely vehicles for the leader to fulfill his personal life vision.

For example, I got a call one day at my bookstore from a young pastor who was looking for discipling resources for his youth. Although he served at a prominent church with a beautiful facility, he couldn't seem to afford any of the options. I finally took pity on him and offered him the materials at cost (65% off). That still wasn't enough. I suggested that group members pay for the books—at that price, it was only a few bucks each. That wouldn't fly either. When I got curious and started asking questions, it came out that every dime they collected went to the church's personality-driven television ministry, and that the youth group was responsible to raise additional money for it beyond what they could give themselves. They were literally bled dry. This young man was reduced to begging in the streets for the tools to help his little sheep grow up in the Lord.

Somehow, the concept of "ministry" at this church has lost touch with it's root meaning: to serve. *Whenever the Task becomes more important than the Impact, leaders use people.*

The *Ultimate Impact* exercise (15.3) can be used as an action step to help the client reflect on these questions.

Finding Your "One Thing?"

Your **Task** is the primary channel the Message of your life goes through in order to Impact your Audience. It's the wineskin of your call—the practical form your message takes on when it is communicated. While the method of fulfilling a call (the task) can change with changing circumstances, the message rooted in our core identity stays much the same.

So is your job your calling task? While many times the words "calling" and "vocation" are used synonymously, I think that is a misnomer. Your vocation (i.e. your job) may well be the primary channel for the unique message of Christ in your life. Or it may be one of a wholes series of channels that together comprise your life task. Or it may be that your profession is not a primary channel of your call at all. Tent-making missionaries, home-school moms, a worker on permanent disability or retirees are all examples of people whose calling task is not synonymous with a job. As a coach, it's important that you give people room to find their call in whatever area of life God chooses, and not confine it to career only.

This leads us to an important insight. An oft-overlooked question is whether the client's call was ever meant to be channeled through only one particular role or task in the first place. The "City Slickers" movies with Billy Crystal are a good example of this concept. The key line in the movie was "you have to find your 'one thing.'" There is one unique role or accomplishment that is your purpose in life, and you must find it and do it.

Some individuals are called in this way. Their purpose is to build a certain organization, take a given leadership position or complete a visionary project. For people like Mother Teresa, Warren Buffet, John the Baptist or Abraham Lincoln, that "one thing" is obvious. Many large-sphere leaders and visionaries fall into this category.

But is that true in all cases? For instance, I once worked with a client who just could not figure out what he was called to do. We looked at different roles he could fill and how his strengths would play out in certain types of projects, all to no avail. His "I don't knows" and "but that just doesn't do it for mes" were starting to get frustrating for both of us.

Then one day we got on the subject of who he wanted to work with. He finally put it together when he said, "To be honest, I don't really care what industry I work in or what my job title is, as long as I get to work in such-and-such a team." A light came on for me that day—for some individuals, the task is simply to serve or relate in certain ways, regardless of what project or profession they are working in. For a client like that, thinking of calling as always being to a single life task can be a big barrier to discovering their call.

I had a similar conversation a few weeks ago with a staff pastor in a large church. He was an engaging, 50's, self-confessed A.D.D. man who seemed very contented and energized by his role. When I asked him what he did, I discovered he was essentially the church's troubleshooter: whenever there was a difficult assignment or something new that needed to be launched, they called on him. And after three to six months of getting that project going, he would move to another role. He loved it: lots of variety, and the ability to get in there, quickly evaluate the situation, get things started and then hand it off to others. His call was not to any particular accomplishment, but to serve in a certain way in a whole series of projects.

That's actually a pretty common pattern in the whole continuum of how people are called. If your call is to demonstrate the father heart of God to kids, you may express it through coaching little league, running for the school board, parenting, or joining the Big Brother program. And at the far end of the spectrum from the "one thing" people are those whose call is simply to be who they are and do what they are good at in whatever opportunity happens to come their way that day. The myriads of faithful people who serve in the background fixing things, setting up chairs, attending to practical needs and keeping the world from falling apart often fit this pattern. To sum up, some individuals (especially leaders) have a "one thing" role, vision or accomplishment that represents fulfillment of their calling task, while others are called to express their message through a whole range of roles and acts of service.

Your Life Task May Be...

1. A **single** project to complete or role to faithfully execute.
2. A whole **series** of projects or roles that all communicate your message.
3. A particular **service** done through many individual acts in many different roles and venues.

As coaches, we've tended to skew the life purpose discovery process toward a "one thing." The fallout is that those who aren't called to a single central task begin to wonder if they are called at all. Here again, understanding calling in being terms is vital. If calling is first about embodying Jesus, everyone is back on equal footing whether they have a "one thing" task or not. With these clients, the question is not, "What one thing are you called to do?" but:

- *"How are you called to serve? What will your acts of service look like?"*
- *"Let's say the central calling question isn't finding the one task you must do, but the* ***way*** *of serving God made you for. If that's true, how would you express your calling?"*
- *"What are some different ways you've expressed this passion? How could you do more things like that?"*
- *"You may be called to one big thing, or to many small things that all express a certain part of God's heart. Which of those pictures fits you best?"*
- *"What if the important thing was communicating your heart for people and the role or project you did it through didn't matter? How would that change your view of your call?"*

This doesn't mean that all tasks are equal. While there may be many tasks where you can embody your calling, some will do it better than others, and some may even create obstacles to your message. Adding the idea of Impact on your Audience will help you distinguish the tasks that fit from those that don't.

Coaching the Task

The first question most clients have about calling is, "What is my Task?" I prefer to start the journey with Message. It puts the focus on being instead of doing, and pulls us toward the real objective (Impact on others) and away from fixating on outward success or personal gratification. It's keeping first things first: discover the God-given Message and what Impact it is meant to have on our Audience first, *then* figure out how to deliver it.

Obviously, this is not a hard and fast rule—many times people have already partially defined the calling task without being clear on the message. It's just my way of helping people avoid the calling as task box.

Big Dreams (8.1) are often the place to start when looking at the calling task. Many leaders already have a big dream in mind that they feel called to pursue. For those who are not natural dreamers ("S's" on the Myers-Briggs), the coach should help them get in touch with past and present roles and tasks that fit the call, then project those tasks into the future. "What roles or tasks have you done in the past that really communicated your message, and how could you do more of that?" is the type of question to ask. "S's" need to ground dreams in the concrete to freely visualize and engage them. Design and Preparation also feed into the person's life mission. The *Life Mission* exercise (15.4) offers a process for reviewing all these areas and translating them into a statement.

An important part of the coaching process for clients who've already envisioned their life tasks is connecting it back to the Message it is supposed to convey and the Impact God meant it to produce. Being explicit about all four elements gives a much more balanced and focused picture of call than the task alone. Going through all four of these steps also makes it easy to create a final life purpose summary statement (see exercise 17.2) based on your Message, Audience, Impact and Task.

Who Do You Love?

15.1

One way to start finding your Audience is to look at the people you've already helped in your life. In the left column, jot down specific individual and groups you've helped in a significant way in the past. Briefly note how you served each one. Once you have the left column filled up, start looking for patterns or common elements. What types of people or needs consistently appear in your list? They may be a certain age, gender, nationality or socio-economic status; people with specific needs or that you bump into in certain places, neighbors, saved or unsaved, etc. What characterizes the people you help?

People & Groups I've Helped	Characteristics/Needs
Young women leaders who need a sounding board	*Women*
People who worry about provision	*Fear/intimidation/worry*
Women with fear or intimidation issues	
Young disciples—discipleship house leader	*People who need discipling*
Church leaders - administrative assistant	
Wives of ministry leaders	*I support up-front leaders*
Leaders thru spiritual direction	*Leaders*
Retreat facilitator	*Depth in relationship with God*
Families that need a meal or babysitting	
Teaching youngsters in Sunday school	*Practical needs (it's more about*
My kids—homeschooling, chores, parenting	*that than it is about children)*
Our family business—bookkeeping	
Church groups—worship team leader	
Neighborhood group chairperson	*Teams that need leadership*
Small group leader	

15.2 An Audience for My Message

This exercise offers three separate options for identifying your Audience.

Option 1: Start with Life Message

Your message points naturally to an audience that needs that message. Start with the *Life Messages* you identified (14.1), and try asking yourself the following questions:

- What kind of people are you drawn to because of this message? Who is drawn to this message in you?
- Who do you notice because of this message that others miss? What needs are you sensitized to?
- Who does this message or the experience behind it qualify you to serve?
- Who needs your message?

Option 2: Check Several Exercises

- What has God revealed about your audience? Review the *Revelation Journal* (13.2).
- Look back at Passion and Preparation. Who have you served with passion and impact? Who are you prepared to serve? Who do you dream about serving? *Destiny Events* (12.1), *Dreams* (8.1) and the *Passion Bull's Eye* (7.1) are great places to look.
- Add any info from the *Who Do You Love?* exercise (15.1).

Your Audience Might Be...

- **Specific, Named Individuals**
  Like your kids or a young man you mentor.
- **A Group**
  People in your profession, the homeless in your community or your employees.
- **A Point of Contact**
  Like individuals you meet in your profession, or those in your neighborhood or church.
- **People with a Certain Need**
  Like Down syndrome kids, villages in Sudan that need a well or shut-ins needing home maintenance help.
- **A Societal Need**
  You help society at large—like a researcher creating cancer drugs, or a forest ranger who cares for a national park.

Option 3: Exemplars

You may find it easiest to describe your audience if you think of a specific person you know. Who do you know that best exemplifies the people you want to touch? Then describe the qualities of that person or their need that make them your example. If you are a practical, down-to-earth thinker, this type of concrete picture of a real person may be the most helpful.

Part II: Name Your Audience

Finally, create a brief description of your audience. It can be a bullet list of qualities and needs, or a specific named group (i.e. Latino businesswomen in Bakersfield). Try to express it as succinctly as possible. Create a profile of what a typical person in your sweet spot would look like—their age, where they live, marital status, needs, what's on their mind, etc.

Your Ultimate Impact

15.3

Your Ultimate Impact is the lasting effect your message has on your audience in the course of your life. You are called to serve for a reason—to create an ultimate impact. How do you want to change the lives of those around you?

Naming the Impact

Take the message you identified (see 14.4 or 14.1) and begin to think through how you see that message touching others. If you are having a hard time visualizing the impact you desire, identify your target Audience first (15.1 and 15.2) and then come back to this exercise.

- How do you want to change their outward circumstances?
- How will your message touch their hearts?
- What suffering will you alleviate, or what blessing will you bring them?
- When the people around you remember you after you are gone, what do you most want them to say about how you impacted them?

Create an Exemplar

The exercise may become more real for you if you find an exemplar: a real person who is a near-perfect example of your audience. Find an exemplar with the *Audience for My Message* exercise (15.2). How would you answer the questions above for this specific person?

> ***Coaching Tip***
> *You have two options for exemplars: use an actual, living person, or create a composite portrait that takes characteristics from several individuals. The exemplar approach is often a better way for people who aren't natural dreamers ("S's" on the Myers-Briggs).*

15.4 Life Mission/Calling Task

This exercise will help you sum up your life mission—the task or role that best channels your Message to your Audience for a certain Impact.

Step 1: Review

Now we're going to roll together all the work you've done so far into a calling task. Take 20 minutes or so to flip through all the work you've done on Passion, Design and Preparation. Make sure and look at big dreams (8.1) plus your Message (14.1 or 14.4), Audience (15.2) and Impact (15.3). As you review, reflect on the following questions and jot down whatever comes to mind:

- What do these insights tell me about the task(s) I am called to do in my life?
- What task(s) or roles am I drawn to that might be great channels for my message?
- What have I done in the past that conveys my message well, and what tasks and roles would let me do more of that?

Step 2: Task or Tasks?

Some individuals accomplish their call through a single role or life task, others through series of tasks that all display their message and still others by simply engaging in acts of kindness wherever life takes them on a given day. Which seems to fit you best? Are you called to one ultimate task, or a certain type of service done in many ways? If your call is to a series of smaller tasks or many acts of kindness, what theme would hold those things together?

Step 3: Create a Statement

Now, take your jottings and distill them down to a one-sentence statement. Simple and memorable is best! You may need to play with several versions or to let it stew for a while before you come up with something you really like.

> ***Coaching Tips***
>
> *The "one thing" life task is a familiar idea—having a series of tasks as your calling is not. If you sense the client may fall into the latter category, explain both options, give some examples (see pg. 256) and ask the client to evaluate which camp he or she falls into.*
>
> *Some people (especially high "I's" on the DiSC™ or "NF's" on the Myers-Briggs) love to create rambling, inclusive statements that allow room for every possible group or opportunity to come under a big tent. However, it is tough to produce a statement with any utility without leaving some things or people out! It can help to explain that this statement isn't setting your **boundaries** (if I don't mention it, I can't do it) but your **focus** (this is the main thing).*

Chapter 16: Calling/ The Convergent Role

"I went into the woods because I wished to live deliberately, to front only the essential facts of life, and see if I could not learn what it had to teach, and not, when I came to die, discover that I had not lived."

Henry David Thoreau

"I've had a good run these last 10 years", Brian stated in our first session, "But now I'm getting a little antsy. I'm 55 years old, and I can see the end of my productive life coming ahead of me. That creates an urgency to maximize my impact for the time I have left, and make sure I leave a legacy behind."

Brian was a secure, mature leader in the fulfillment stage of his calling journey.[27] What he wanted was to craft a role that fit his message, mission and audience—and his Design. Over the next few months, we identified his type and his best strengths. Then we studied his current role. What was he doing that fit him well? What didn't fit, or wasn't a priority? Brian was more of a visionary than an implementer, so we talked about how he could rearrange staff roles to allow him to look at the future while others pushed out the day-to-day program. He found that some tasks he'd assumed would always be in his corner were things he could actually delegate. Others could be minimized by changing his focus or job description.

Understanding his own design opened up a new world of opportunities for his staff, too. As roles on the team were reconfigured, Brian aggressively worked to

27 See *The Calling Journey* for more on stages of calling.

discover their strengths and types, and to create roles that fit them. One key leader was clearly called to something larger and was chafing in his current role. It was hard to let go of his right-hand man, but Brian was able to help him identify what he needed and transition into a better-fitting role elsewhere.

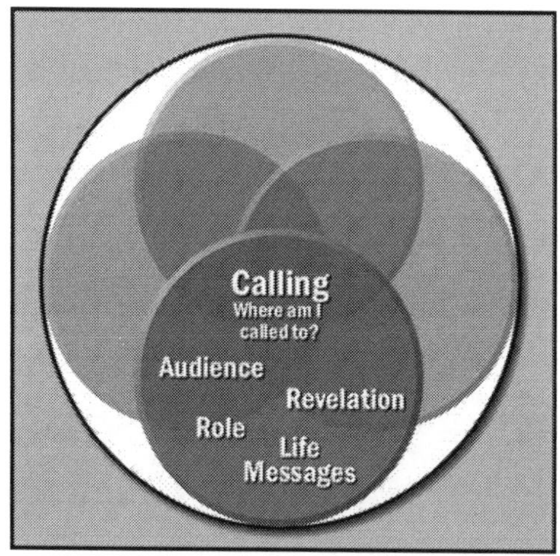

But it still wasn't enough. What began to rise to prominence in Brian was his urge to write, to mentor other leaders and to move into a larger sphere of influence. That put a whole new twist into working with his role. We began to explore other leadership models that would allow him to contribute his best at home but still have time to go on the road—like co-pastoring, moving into an apostolic relationship with his church, or raising up and gradually transitioning to a successor.

We also identified some internal issues that held him back—agonizing over decisions, avoiding certain types of conflicts and carrying on a constant inner dialog that sapped his energy and upset his sleep patterns. The whole process was very energizing for Brian. "This is great! I've been feeling like it's either stay here and be stuck with a bunch of stuff that isn't me and isn't my best, or leave everything and start over. This gives me a whole new way to think about fulfilling my call."

Your call is to embody Christ in certain ways through your life task. Sometimes (particularly for organizational leaders) the venue for that task is a certain convergent role. Remember that some individuals express their calling through multiple tasks and positions instead of one best-fit role. Before you start working on convergent roles, it's important that you look at this distinction (see pg. 256).

A convergent role enables you to accomplish your life task through a role that fits your Design.

The idea of convergent role was laid out by J. Robert Clinton in *The Making of a Leader*. The idea is that in the latter stages of life, when your preparation stages are complete, you move into a convergent leadership role that enables you to accomplish your life task in a way that fits your Design.

Senior leaders who are moving into their life task (often in their late 40's or 50's) frequently come to coaching to create this unique convergent role. At this fulfillment stage of their calling, they have much more of an ability to re-think their roles than they did at age 25. And they have a much better idea of what those roles ought to look like.

In earlier stages, the focus is much more on what leaders are learning along the way than it is on what roles they are in. Therefore, *you coach them according to the calling stage they are in, not to find and enter the perfect convergent role.*

This is a crucial distinction that is often overlooked by life coaches. For leaders in their teens and 20's, it's about accumulating a wide variety of experiences to gain information about their Design and begin the Preparation process. Trying to find the one right role at this point in life is usually counter-productive. In early to mid-life, God often *removes* leaders from what looks like a best-fit role to engage them at the heart level. Just assuming that your job as a coach is to help them find a convergent role is not very helpful when God is moving in the opposite direction! For leaders who are not at the stage of accomplishing their life mission, it's premature to create the convergent role that is made for that season.

*Coach leaders according to the calling stage they are in, **not** just to find and enter the perfect convergent role.*

Influence Style

There are several destiny areas we have yet to cover that are important to developing this convergent role. One is what I call *Influence Style*. It's the method you use to get your message across. Frank's dream was to create an inner healing center where people could come for several-day stays in a retreat setting and receive ministry for inner wounds. He came to me because he was having trouble getting traction on moving the thing forward.

After working at it for a while and not making much progress, I took a different tack. "Frank, let's stop and take a look at your influence style. That's your preferred method of functioning in ministry—the way that you impact people the best. Some people are organization builders: they create structures and teams that accomplish the mission, while they lead the team. Some are trainers who teach others to do the ministry. Some are mentors who invest in a small group of others to carry on their legacy. And some are practitioners—they want to do the hands-on ministry themselves, and not be bothered with leading an organization. Which one of those best fits you?"

Frank quickly identified that he was a practitioner. He felt most productive and in the zone when he was working one-on-one with a person in need of healing. His second preferred influence style was trainer.

The problem was that Frank's dream required him to function in an organization builder style—to envision, fund, build and maintain a retreat center where these people could come. The places his dream was bogging down were the organizational leader issues. So my question was, "How can you do your dream as a practitioner and trainer, without having to be an organizational leader?" The breakthrough came when Frank realized he could take his healing center on the road instead of creating a physical location for it. Scaling down the organizational part of his vision by working through existing retreat centers could allow him to focus on the personal ministry he loved best. He could also do training (his second preferred influence style) through other ministries. The idea of not having any fundraising or management duties immediately lifted a big weight off of his shoulders.

Every leader has a preferred influence style and aligning with that best-fit style is a key part of a convergent role. Organizational leaders usually don't want to be practitioners—they are fine with someone else doing the hands-on work if they can build the team that does it. Leaders with a Second Man style prefer not to be the point person—they flourish best as the right-hand man to another leader. I recently coached one of these types to leave a senior pastorate and take an associate position. It's a counter-intuitive career path, but he is much happier in his new role.

Worksheet 16.1 includes a list of 12 possible styles, along with a description of each one and its lasting legacy. The *Influence Style* exercise (16.2) has a procedure for choosing your style. Below are the kinds of questions you might ask if you are coaching the exercise informally:

- *"What is the vehicle you'll use to impact others? How will you get your message across?"*
- *"What are you doing when you are having the most impact on others?"*
- *"Will the greatest legacy you leave behind be the individuals you directly touch, the organization you build, through a leader or organization you serve, the materials or write, through a few you mentor or empower who touch many others—or what?"*

Sphere of Influence

Another important question is your sphere of influence. What's the scope of your call? In some cases, God chooses to make the leader aware from early on the size of their mission, while others find themselves surprised in the various life transitions as God calls them up to a larger sphere.

I like to break this question down into two parts: your *Immediate Sphere* and your *Ultimate Sphere*. Your immediate sphere is the size group that you like to work with at one time. The coaching question is, "Are you at your best working with large groups, medium-size groups, small groups, or one-on-one?"

I'm a small group and one-on-one guy. I am into personal transformation and reshaping identity, and those things happen much more effectively in smaller settings than in mass meetings. So I choose to work in smaller contexts.

However my ultimate sphere is much larger. I dream of influencing movements and creating models that many others employ. My materials are published in other countries, so even though I never travel internationally to minister (except in Canada), my sphere of influence is international.

Spheres of Influence

- Personal Relationships (a disciple or parent)
- Neighborhood, Church or Workplace
- Your Organization
- City/Locality (local leader)
- Profession (leading figure or influencer in your entire profession)
- Regional
- National
- International

These two sphere questions make for interesting combinations. I have a pretty small immediate sphere but a very large ultimate one. A local pastor with a Trainer/ Teacher influence style would have a large immediate sphere but a local ultimate one—while he preaches to large groups, it's pretty much the same local group every time. So you can have a large immediate sphere and a small ultimate one, or vice versa. None is intrinsically better than any other—the best one is the one God designed you for. Exercise 16.3 helps clients explore both their immediate and ultimate spheres of influence.

One other interesting variation of sphere is with legacy. Legacy is the ongoing impact of your life after you are gone. An interesting example is St. Augustine's mother Monica. She was sainted for her role in praying her son into the Kingdom from an immoral, profligate lifestyle. Her immediate sphere of influence was basically one person; her ultimate sphere of influence was basically one person, but her legacy is computed in the lasting impact of her life through those she touched. Augustine is a giant figure in church history. So although she functioned in a very small sphere all her life, St. Monica created an enormous legacy. You never know what the final impact of your life will be!

Creating the Convergent Role

The coaching process is straightforward. It starts with an in-depth look at the leader's Design. While senior leaders generally have a pretty good feel for their Design, at this stage they often need to take it to a new level of clarity. To craft this special role, leaders must be able to precisely name and describe in-depth who they are instead of just going by feel. This process requires a life coach with genuine expertise and fluency in personality type and strengths.

Values are often important as well. Here again, having a general idea of their values may get leaders to this point, but it isn't enough to create a convergent role. Leaders need to know what their non-negotiables are. Any leader at this stage of life should have a formal ministry or leadership value set.

The energy exercises come into play as well. Often senior leaders are encumbered with certain responsibilities or expectations that are serious energy drains. If they have gotten to this place in life without eliminating them, there is usually an obstacle behind it. Either they are assuming they are the only one who can do that task, or some internal belief keeps them in an unproductive place. Identifying that these are energy drains can open the door to get at the obstacle.

We'll also look at sphere of influence and influence style as well. Here again, the leader probably functions out of their style intuitively, but naming it and defining how it works can be a big aid in reorienting them toward their best.

As leaders gain more clarity on what a best-fit role would look like, they immediately want to put those insights into practice by reworking their roles. Understanding the Design of prominent team members is a key to a successful realignment. This often leads to an expanded coaching engagement where the coach works with the entire team on strengths, type and role realignment. The *My Ideal Team* and *Typing a Team* exercises (6.3 and 6.4) are an important part of this process.

At some point in the information-gathering process, I like to have clients envision their perfect role. What kind of job description would perfectly support doing their life mission? The *80/20 Job Description* (16.4) exercise is a good action step here. I want the starting point to be an absolute best-fit role, not a pragmatic compromise with the person's current circumstances or limitations. Some compromises will of course be necessary, but without aiming high, the leader is sure to settle for less. It's amazing how often identifying the best inspires leaders to find a way to change the unchangeable.

One leader I worked with just assumed that hiring and firing would always be part of his role, even though he hated it. He was a people person, and found it stressful to have to sit down face-to-face with friends and say no to raises or cut someone loose. But when he finally put his true desires down on paper, it occurred to him that circumstances had changed. When he first started out, everything was on him. But now the organization had grown to the point where he had a strong leadership team with the capacity and authority for that type of task. There was no reason he couldn't off-load that function to a team member. He was very excited about the change—and so was his team! They were frustrated with how he avoided or compromised in those situations, and were happy to see someone else take on the responsibility.

Up to this point in life, part of the leader's journey has involved accommodating to roles that don't fit perfectly. That's part of the plan. But now that it is time to really go for the best, sometimes we've gotten so used to accommodating that we've forgotten what we really want! For ministry leaders in particular, it can be a challenge to believe that it's actually OK to desire a role that really works great for them. The step of envisioning the best brings these issues to the surface.

Influence Styles

16.1

Here's a list of eleven common leadership influence styles with the enduring legacies each one produces. Sometimes small spheres of influence can produce enormous legacies!

- **Organization Builder**
  You exert influence through starting and building organizations around a specific vision. Church planters and entrepreneurs fall in this category.
  Lasting Legacy: The impact of that organization both now and after you are gone.
- **Organizational Leader**
  Your gifts are channeled into leadership of existing organizations, and your influence comes through the organization accomplishing its collective mission.
  Lasting Legacy: What is accomplished by the organization through your contributions?
- **Second Man**
  You find your greatest influence in serving as the right hand of a larger-sphere leader. Alone, your influence is small, but together you can operate on a much larger stage.
  Lasting Legacy: Your own impact plus the impact of the leader/ministry you served.
- **Service**
  You influence through practical service or accomplishing tasks for others. You're the person who takes a vision and actually does the grass-roots work to make it happen.
  Lasting Legacy: A part in the influence of everything you served and each life touched through it.
- **Networking**
  Your influence comes through connecting people and opportunities through a peer network. Your impact is through how much more is accomplished by bringing people together than is by them working alone.
  Lasting Legacy: The fruit borne by those connections and opportunities.
- **Ideation**
  Sharing your original ideas is what gives you influence. Your best contribution is thinking and communicating those thoughts to others through writing, speaking or media.
  Lasting Legacy: The impact of those ideas and every person or project they touch.
- **Family**
  Your primary influence and legacy is through your children and what you have invested in them as a parent, discipler and friend.
  Lasting Legacy: Children that surpass you, and whoever is served through them.

- **Mentor/Discipler**
  Your greatest impact is on the people whose lives you have changed by walking with them one-on-one, and their lives are your legacy.
  Lasting Legacy: A cadre of disciples who carry on your message after you are gone.

- **Trainer/Teacher**
  Your best impact comes through imparting skills, wisdom and knowledge to groups using your communication abilities.
  Lasting Legacy: The changed lives of the people you teach and who they touch because of it.

- **Practitioner**
  You want to do hands on-ministry instead of organizing, training or empowering others to do it. Your role must keep you in direct contact with the people you serve.
  Lasting Legacy: The changed lives of the people you help and who they touch because of it.

- **Empowerer**
  Your influence comes by promoting, encouraging and believing in other leaders.
  Lasting Legacy: What those leaders are able to accomplish because of your sponsorship.

Your Influence Style  16.2

Every leader prefers certain methods of exerting influence. Influence styles are particular channels your calling runs through best. Knowing your style is very helpful in crafting a role that fits your Design.

Step 1: Find Your Style

From the list of common leadership influence styles in 16.1, choose the two that best fit you (or make up your own if none really fit).

Step 2: Apply Your Style

Take a role or dream you are pursuing and evaluate it in light of your preferred style:

- What percentage of your time would you get to spend in your preferred influence modes in this role?
- What are the major tasks or responsibilities in this role that would require you to function outside of your best influence styles?
- What are three creative ways you could reconfigure this role to increase the amount of time you spent in your preferred influence style?

Coaching Tip

Often this exercise will call for follow-up around realigning the leader's dream or role to better align with his or her preferred style. It's a good place to just brainstorm:

- *"What would you have to change about this dream to cut in half the amount of time you'd need to function outside of your best style?"*
- *"Observation: it seems that you've configured this dream to put you in a teacher style much of the time, yet that's not a style you prefer. How could you change the dream so it doesn't depend on teaching or someone else handles that function?"*

16.3 Sphere of Influence

On what playing field you are called to exert influence? Your calling may be to thoroughly and deeply mentor six people in your lifetime—or to influence whole organizations, professions or even nations. Bigger spheres are not necessarily better—the best sphere for you is the one God made you for. This exercise looks at two types of spheres:

Part I: Your Immediate Sphere

Your immediate sphere of influence has to do with the size group you feel you are at your best working with at any one time. Do you influence others most effectively one-on-one, in a small group or team (under 20), in medium groups (under 150) or large groups? Remember, this is about influence. Think of a number of situations where you were very effective in exerting a positive influence. Which size sphere works best for you?

Part II: Your Ultimate Sphere

Your ultimate sphere of influence is the sum total of the influence of your lifetime. You may touch thousands of people only once or twice through brief, chance encounters, books or speaking engagements. Or you may spend years with family, neighbors or a few others, and sow very deeply into the lives of only a few. Here are some questions to get you thinking:

- Do you best influence through long-term relationships or one-time encounters?
- Do you prefer to go deep with a few or briefly touch many?
- Is your influence direct and person-to-person, or through indirect means such as ideas, corporate cultures, training others or organizational missions you are a part of?
- What is the ultimate task you want to accomplish in life? On what size of stage will that mission play out?
- What spheres (business or ministry, a certain profession or organization, a certain locale) will your influence ultimately touch?

Coaching Tip
Everybody always seems to think that the bigger the sphere, the better Christian they are. Faithfulness is not a matter of doing the most—it is about being obedient to your unique calling. If your intuition is saying these dreams sound awfully grandiose, it might help to talk about what faithfulness to a call looks like:

- *"How would it look to be faithful to the call, versus just doing as much as you can?"*
- *"What part of this has the Lord specifically instructed you to do?"*
- *"What motivates or drives these dreams? What would you lose if you never reached them?"*

The 80/20 Job Description

The 80/20 rule says you should spend 80% of your time in the area of your gifts and strengths—but that most people spend 80% of their time on things they aren't good at! Thinking through a role that fits is an important part of succeeding as a leader.

Part I: Assessing the Current Role

Think of the kind of tasks and responsibilities your role requires. In the left hand column, jot down the ones you are best at and find energizing. In the right hand column, list tasks or responsibilities that aren't your strengths, you find draining or you'd love to delegate if you could. Review your *Strengths* and *Weaknesses* inventories (7.2 and 7.3), influence style and your personality type report to add to your lists.

What Fits Me	What Doesn't Fit

Part II: The 80/20 Job Description

Now, create a job description for yourself that lets you spend 80% of your time doing what you do best: the things in the left column above. The idea here is to define your absolute best. Let yourself dream freely about where you want to be in three years and push the boundaries of what seems attainable—just bypass any obstacles in your current circumstances. You may find it helpful to look back at jobs you've had in the past and take the parts of each one you really liked to make up your dream job.

- What kind of role would best support me functioning in my life task?
- What's my average day/week look like in this ideal role?
- In what strength areas am I spending 80% of my time? What am I delegating that is not my strength?
- What job description would maximize my ability to do what's in the left column above and minimize the time I spend on the right?

Coaching Tip

Here are several key obstacles clients may hit when working with best-fit roles:

- ***It is unfair to expect to be in a convergent role.***
  Sometimes leaders are afraid to craft roles around their strengths, because they feel that would mean delegating all the dirty work to others. Personality type is a great coaching tool here: there is always somebody out there whose type loves to do the things that you hate. Surfacing this belief and then talking through it from a type perspective is a good way to root out this blockage.
- ***Undervaluing my strengths.***
  Since my strengths are so familiar and come so easily, the leader thinks that everyone must be good at what I'm good at. It may help to offer some feedback from your own life here (if the client's strengths are ones you aren't good at!)
- ***I don't like my strengths.***
  This can happen when the person focuses on the flip-side weaknesses that go with their strengths. I like to draw out the strength/weakness connection, with a question like, "How is this weakness connected with your strengths?" or "If you no longer had this weakness, what would you lose? What important part of who you are would disappear?"

Part III: Realigning Your Role

Once you've defined your ideal, you can begin moving toward it. Compare your ideal to your current role and note the differences. Then choose the three places where you could most easily transition toward your ideal (the quick wins) and work with your coach to create strategies for changing each one.

Chapter 17: Life Purpose Summaries

There is a tide in the affairs of men,
Which taken at the flood, leads on to
fortune; omitted, all the voyage of their life
is bound in shallows and in miseries.
On such a full sea we are now afloat;
And we must take the current when it serves,
or lose our ventures.

William Shakespeare, in *Julius Caesar*

The final step in the life purpose discovery process is bundling all the insights together in a set of brief summary statements. Life purpose statements clarify the core of one's calling and put it in memorable form. There is great utility in having memorized a one-sentence purpose statement you can call up at a moment's notice.

The *Workbook* provides a two-page *Life Purpose Summary* worksheet (17.2) for those key life purpose statements. In this compact format it can be put up on the wall (or you can download an electronic copy at www.ALeadersLifePurpose.com)—a great way for clients to keep their values, vision, mission and message in front of them.

Depending on which areas clients have already worked on, they may be well on their way to having these summary statements already. *Value Statements* (10.6) offer a good summation of the area of Passion. Personality type (from an assessment) provides a brief, memorable statement of one's Design (and is much easier to recall than a list of strengths). Under calling, the *Message of Your Life* and *Life Mission* exercises (14.4) produce being and doing summary statements that can be dropped right into the worksheet.

Those last two also provide a great way to create an overall life purpose statement. Use the Message > Audience > Task > Impact format, and simply fill in all four to create a *Life Purpose Statement* (see exercise 17.2)

Here's an example. I serve on the board of a non-profit that provides leadership coaching to missionaries. Our aim is to help missionaries and mission organizations accomplish their objectives by increasing the health and effectiveness of the individual missionaries we coach. So a calling statement for our organization might look like the first example on worksheet 17.1.

Another approach is to substitute the Convergent Role for the task. This can work well for individuals who find their calling in a certain profession. For instance:

I am called to honor the uniqueness of every student	*Message*
In my classroom	*Audience*
Through my role as a teacher	*Role*
So that they know and believe in their own value.	*Impact*

This step is hard work—it is a challenge to capture what a person is all about in a single sentence! It will probably take more than one session to create a statement, get feedback and revise it to their liking. Some will (still!) freeze up over getting it just right. Encouraging them to do the exercise in pencil can help. Some of my clients have found that scheduling time a year down the road to reevaluate the statements takes off the pressure of trying to get it prefect.

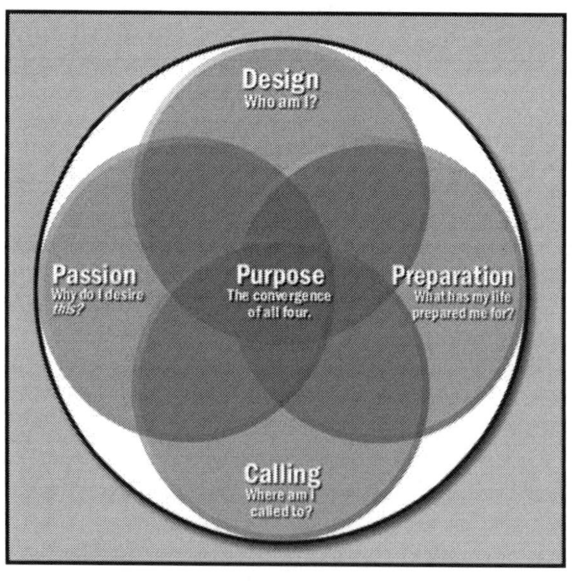

Life Vision

One other important piece of the puzzle is a *Life Vision Statement* (17.2). A vision statement is a visual picture of what it would look like to be fully living out one's call. This summary is around a page in length. The focus is on capturing the feel of that future and connecting with the motivation of seeing one's greatest passion coming to fruition.

Several exercises can feed into this process, depending on what the client has done to this point. The leader can draw on their work with envisioning a fun *Ideal Lifestyle* (8.3), their *Ideal Team* (6.3) and the more serious *Lifestyle of Your Call* (14.6). Insights from the *80/20 Job Description* (16.4) about the convergent role should be fed in as well.

Since this is a vision exercise, it is important to emphasize the idea of visualization. Often you'll get vague details ("I'll work with great people") or summaries ("We'll help financial planners") instead of actual details. What people will you work with? Give me some names or profiles. What's a specific example of the kind of planner you'll target? If you get a generic vision statement, pick one part of it and use probing questions to pull out specific details. That should give the client enough of an idea what a vision should look like to go back and finish on their own. Another helpful device is to have them describe an actual day in that ideal future—every place they go, person they meet or task they work on can be described as an actual, concrete event.

Reminders

Once the life purpose statements are completed, my last request in the discovery process is often for the person to create some kind of reminder system to keep their life purpose work in front of them. The worst thing that can happen at this point is for all this effort to go into a binder sitting on a shelf that is never touched again. A reminder can take many forms—here are a few that clients have come up with over the years:

- Regular reminders in a PDA that pop up with a value or purpose statement.
- Posting purpose summaries up on the wall at home.
- A painting or artwork that represents my purpose—like "The Prodigal Son" by Rembrandt.
- A sign on the wall at work.
- Something I carry around in my wallet or pocket—like an engraved stone.
- A set of cards with values and statements in the car—look at one each day.

The point here is that memorized statements are useful statements. Values that you remember working on way back when but can't quite remember don't accomplish much.

Where You Go from Here

It is finished! The next steps in the coaching process involve creating goals and actions to pursue dreams, align with the call, and engage the stage of the calling development process where God has you. Tools for this part of the coaching process are found in *Leadership Coaching, Coaching Questions* and *The Calling Journey*.

Your legacy as a coach is not just your impact on those you coach—it's also what those leaders do for others because of what you did for them. You may work out of your home with a few people at a time in a one-on-one influence style, but through those you invest in, you can change the world. So go out and create a great legacy for the Kingdom; and God be with you as you do!

17.1 Life Purpose Statement Examples

A Life Purpose Statement sums up your purpose in a single sentence. Here are a few examples. Notice that the order of the phrases (Message, Audience, Task and Impact) can be shuffled to make the statement read more smoothly.

Our purpose is to...

Demonstrate God's heart to empower, resource and care for	Message
Missionaries and mission organizations	Audience
Through providing leadership coaching	Task
In order to help them accomplish the Great Commission.	Impact

I am called to...

Embody the undeserved grace of God	Message
To unwed mothers,	Audience
To bring them into the family of God	Impact
By taking them in, caring for their children and helping them build a life.	Task

The words "embody" and "demonstrate" in the first lines build the being focus explicitly into the statement. This is what makes it a statement of your life purpose (both being and doing) and not just a life mission or task statement.

Here's an example of how to build a purpose statement from the individual exercises. If the *Message of Your Life* (14.4) is, "You can engage God from the heart in every circumstance, especially suffering and adversity, and be transformed"; and your *Life Mission* (15.4) is, "Building leadership character and developing systems that build leadership character"; a final life purpose statement might be:

I am called to...

Embody engaging God in every circumstance	*Message*
To build ministry leaders	*Audience*
Who are transformed to transform others	*Impact*
Through building systems that build leadership character.	*Task*

If you want to get fancy, you can add your *Sphere of Influence* (16.3) and *Influence Style* (16.2):

I embody engaging God in every circumstance	*Message*
To help ministry leaders worldwide	*Audience, Sphere*
Experience transformed character	*Impact*
Through prototyping and multiplying	*Influence Style*
Systems that build leadership character.	*Task*

Life Purpose Summary—Instructions  17.2

Use the worksheet on the following pages to summarize your life purpose. This worksheet was designed for you to copy and put it up on the wall in a place where you see your purpose statements regularly. (The worksheet can also be downloaded as an electronic file from www.ALeadersLifePurpose.com so you can type your statements into it.) Feel free to do this exercise in pencil if you want to allow the freedom to go back and adjust your statements in the future.

The Message of My Life (14.4)

Transfer the statement you developed in exercise 14.4 to this blank.

Life Mission (15.4)

Write your one-sentence *Life Mission/Calling Task* statement (15.4) here.

Personality Type

Enter your personality type, StrengthsFinder© type or spiritual gifts here.

Life Purpose Statement (17.3)

Create a life purpose exercise using exercise 17.3 and insert it here. Put this one in big letters—it's the center of everything!

Life Verse

If you have a life verse, write it here. A life verse has special meaning, speaks about the direction of your life or the core of your being, and is one you return to again and again (you may have recorded it in exercise 13.2, the *Revelation Journal*).

Life Values (10.6)

Copy your one-word or short-phrase value statements from exercise 10.6 here. Values are a key part of making great decisions, so having them in easy reach is a big plus.

Life Vision

A vision statement is a *visual picture* of what it would look like to be fully living out your call.

You can draw on your work from several exercises: with envisioning a fun *Ideal Lifestyle* (8.3), your *Ideal Team* (6.3) and the more serious *Lifestyle of Your Call* (14.6). Insights from the *80/20 Job Description* (16.4) about your convergent role should also be included.

Since this is a vision exercise, it is important to include specific details. Statements like "I'll be living in Texas" or "I'll work with kids" are too vague. Where in Texas? What will your house look like? Your commute? Your neighborhood? If you are having a tough time being specific, walk yourself through an actual, specific day when you are living out your call.

The idea here is capturing the feel of that future, not about getting every detail perfect. So dream, enjoy the process and don't worry too much about whether it will all turn out exactly like this. Shoot for about a page of description.

LIFE MESSAGE

LIFE MISSION

TYPE

LIFE PURPOSE STATEMENT

LIFE VERSE

CORE VALUES

My Life Purpose

LIFE VISION STATEMENT

My Life Vision

17.3 Life Purpose Statement

An easy way to create a calling statement is to start with the Message (14.4), Impact (15.3), Audience (15.1) and Task (15.4) framework. Take a short phrase for each, and weave them together into a statement. The best statements are short, memorable, and uniquely you. Feel free to try different wordings or put the phrases in different order to get something that sounds right. Several examples of statements are provided in worksheet 17.1.

A life purpose statement is something you'll want to refer back to over and over, so keep it brief and to the point. One sentence is the goal. It is better to have short and memorable phrases you can unpack than a rambling, all-inclusive statement you can never bring to mind.

Your statement should include both your call to *be* the message and to *do* a task. That's why a word like "embody," "incarnate," "live out" or "demonstrate" is included in the first line. Here are some possible formats:

To embody my **Life Message**

to my **Audience**

through a **Role** or **Task** that fits me

for a certain **Impact**.

Or change the order of the phrases:

To live out my **Life Message**

through a **Task**

for a certain **Impact**

on my **Audience**.

You can also try this:

My God-given **Passion**

Serving those God draws to me (my **Audience**)

Through my strengths, gifts and abilities (**Design**)

Also from Coach22.com

Below are a few examples of additional coaching resources from Tony Stoltzfus, available through Coach22.com or your coaching retailer.

Leadership Coaching

As a complete overview of the fundamental skills and practices of coaching, *Leadership Coaching* is a great companion to this volume. The book features an introduction to the coaching model, a look at the value system and change theory underlying this approach, and a series of "Master Class" chapters that walk you through the basics of listening, asking, building support systems and more. Widely used as a basic coaching text, this book provides the tools you need to put life purpose insights in action.

The Master Coach Series

Each of these three CDs includes an hour of input and live coaching demos on a significant coaching skill. The first disc, *Problem Solving,* covers a variety of approaches used to generate options and creative solutions without telling the client what to do. *Changing Perspective* focuses on reframing techniques that break the client out of a limited viewpoint to look at life situations in new ways. *Coaching Visionaries* focuses on techniques used to clarify, refine and test a visionary idea or calling.

Coaching Questions

This best-selling coaching reference combines dozens of practical asking tools with over 1,000 examples of powerful coaching questions. Each major area of the coaching conversation is illustrated with multiple approaches. Covering everything from options and actions to decision-making strategies and reframing techniques, this book can help everyone from experienced coaches to trainees improve their asking proficiency.

Coaching Transitions

Life goes in cycles—from seasons where the focus is outward productivity to times of inward retooling. In this two-disc set, Tony discusses how our lack of understanding of transition causes us to try to escape these seemingly dry seasons instead of being transformed by them. Interwoven into the input is a full length coaching session and two interviews with former coaching clients who discuss their own transitional experiences and how they found and embraced purpose within their transitions.

Made in the USA
Middletown, DE
06 September 2018